Praise for *Scarecrow in Gray*

"The author's elegant prose brings a poetic quality to this well-written novel."

> \- Dianne K. Salerni, author of *The Inquisitor's Mark, The Eighth Day, We Hear the Dead, The Caged Graves*

"Barry Yelton has written a book filled with loyalty and hope spread on a dark canvas."

> \- Jack Shakely, author of *Che Guevara's Marijuana & Baseball Savings & Loan, The Confederate War Bonnet, POWs at Chigger Lake*

"[O]ne of those lyrical and beautifully told stories of the Civil War."

> \- Celia Hayes, author of The Adelsverein Trilogy, *Lone Star Sons, The Quivera Trail*

"[H]eartfelt compassion ... a great treasure to read."

> \- Janet Elaine Smith, author of the Patrick and Grace Mysteries and the Keith Trilogy

"[A]n engaging read ... it was the author's evocative descriptions of the natural world, as well as the bonding of these farmers-become-soldiers, which were the strongest parts of the book."

> \- Juliet Waldron, author of *The Master Passion, Mozart's Wife, Hand Me Down Bride, Roan Rose*

"[A] vivid picture of a simple man with a powerful spirit, caught up in a complex war that made ghosts of such men."

> \- Jack Dixon, author of *The Pict, Jerusalem Falls*

SCARECROW IN GRAY

BARRY D. YELTON

Strider Nolan
MEDIA

Printed in the United States of America.

Library of Congress Catalog Card Number: 2015938115
ISBN13: 978-1-932045-36-9
ISBN10: 1-932045-36-8
Second Edition Paperback 2015
Cover Design by Michael S. Katz
Cover photo source: "Unidentified soldier in Confederate uniform with Colt Revolving rifle and D-Guard Bowie knife"; LC-DIG-ppmsca-31695; Call Number: AMB/TIN no. 2749; Library of Congress Prints and Photographs Division Washington, D.C. 20540

Strider Nolan Media, Inc.
702 Cricket Avenue
Ardsley, PA 19038
www.stridernolanmedia.com

SCARECROW IN GRAY

DEDICATION

In Memoriam

Arthur H. "Bud" Wilson, a businessman, National Funding Association Founder, photographer, musician, fisherman, firearms aficionado, backpacker, and dear friend.

1943 - 2009

ACKNOWLEDGEMENTS

I would like to thank my dear wife, Judy, for her patience and support during the long process of completing this book. It has been a work of several years and she has supported my efforts and assisted me in numerous ways. Her love and constancy provided much of the inspiration for the fictional role of Harriet Toney Yelton in the book.

I would also like to thank my good friend and fellow student of the Civil War, Lewis Spiller, for his contributions to the book, which doubtless made it a better work.

I want to offer special thanks to my wife's uncle, Dr. Edward Harrill, for his valuable suggestions, particularly regarding the role of Harriet.

Barry Yelton
February, 2012

FOREWORD

The battles still raged, but the war was over. In the gentle hills of southern Virginia, some 100,000 or more well-fed, well-equipped Federals closed in on General Robert E. Lee's starving troops from three directions. As they trudged from Petersburg, the Army of Northern Virginia numbered no more than 35,000 after massive Federal attacks forced the depleted ranks into a full scale retreat. Fewer still survived the retreat to surrender at Appomattox Courthouse on April 9, 1865.

The Confederacy had pinned its hopes on the aristocratic and brilliant Virginian, Robert Edward Lee. The South had come to look upon the man with a reverence usually reserved for the Saints of the Church. Yet he was but human and ultimately unable to forestall the inevitable end.

The great War Between the States had been fought for four long, bloody years in two primary theatres, the East and the West. A succession of ineffective Confederate theatre commanders in the West had resulted in the disastrous defeat at Atlanta in late summer of 1864, then Sherman's subsequent march to the sea, a march that defined "scorched earth" warfare. Thousands of buildings and innumerable stands of crops were deliberately and systematically burned. Farms were looted and the populace in parts of Georgia and the Carolinas was left destitute. The vestiges of that pain and trauma have lingered for generations even to this day.

During the course of the war the Southern Army had been bled white by countless battles, many of which involved frontal assaults against fortified positions and massive firepower. Generals on both sides of the conflict were enamored of the Napoleonic style of warfare, a type of combat rendered obsolete by Civil War era weapons which were both more powerful and more accurate than those of Napoleon's day.

Armies that attacked in well-ordered ranks were completely exposed to devastating fire, and men were slaughtered by the thousands. Both sides suffered inordinate casualties while being led by generals who, though professing great concern for the welfare of their men, nonetheless ordered ordinary foot soldiers into attacks which were doomed to bloody failure.

Commanders on both sides were guilty of this throughout much of the war, resulting in carnage unmatched in the history of the United States. The destruction and wreckage of human beings was unimaginable. Over 600,000 men died in a country with a population of around thirty million. Proportionally, in 2010 6,000,000 U.S. soldiers would have to die to equal the impact of the Civil War.

The North suffered, but the South was virtually destroyed. The "Lost Cause" was in fact lost from the very outset of the war. The Confederacy was simply overwhelmed by the Union's superior resources. Brilliant field commanders in the West, such as Lieutenant General Nathan Bedford Forrest and Major General Patrick Cleburne, had been continually frustrated by weak and incompetent commanders chosen for political, not military, reasons. Valor, gallantry, and brilliant tactical leadership were wasted by both overly cautious as well as overly reckless commanders.

The latter was the characteristic of the final commander of the Army of Tennessee (as the Confederate Army in the West was known), General John Bell Hood. A fearless and gallant Texan, Hood had served Lee well in the earlier battles of the War. He was an able brigade and division commander. But war wounds, including the amputation of a leg and the loss of the use of an arm, had seriously damaged his ability to lead. The injuries left him in excruciating agony. Taking laudanum and morphine for the pain, and having to be strapped onto his horse, Hood was in no condition to lead an army.

General Joseph Johnston, an able commander and close friend of Lee, had been replaced by Hood because he chose to utilize a defensive strategy against the superior forces of the advancing Sherman. This was unacceptable to the Confederate leadership in Richmond, so Johnston was relieved of command. Hood knew that he was replacing Johnston because of Johnston's cautious generalship, and he understood that Jefferson Davis expected him to be aggressive.

Indeed, he was. However, his series of attacks from the fortifications of Atlanta in late August and early September of 1864, with his 45,000 troops against Sherman's 75,000, were disastrous. After those battles, Sherman occupied Atlanta.

Hood marched north, intending to take the war onto Union soil in Ohio. An enormously costly battle at Franklin and a defeat at Nashville dismembered the Army of Tennessee, and it was no more. Sherman's occupation of Atlanta just before the elections of 1864 insured Lincoln's re-election. The anti-war forces in the North were defeated, and the pro-war factions carried the day. President Lincoln, grimly determined to hold the Union together at any cost, would continue to aggressively pursue military victory.

The War in the West was lost to the Confederacy, and so the fledging nation looked to the venerable Lee. He was named General of the Armies of the Confederacy, but it was too late to matter. After spending almost a year entrenched near Petersburg and Richmond, Lee was in full retreat, and would subsequently be trapped by the Federals.

His troops were in desperate condition. Along the path of the retreat the wounded and starving Confederate troops were often so weak, they simply lay down and awaited capture. Men were reduced to eating the basest and vilest food just to survive. Mud puddles became drinking water. Bare feet trudged wearily over rutted country roads. Draught animals collapsed with piteous cries. The once proud and virtually invincible army—through attrition, political malfeasance and mismanagement, and the relentless pursuit of Grant's army—had become but a hollow shell of its former self.

Private Francis Marion Yelton was a farmer who lived in western Rutherford County, North Carolina, and was one of many thousands of hill country Southerners who had no stake in the war, but who were nonetheless compelled to fight by duty or by force.

Taken away from their already impoverished families in the high country of the northern tier of Confederate states, these enlistees and conscripts were known to be of uneven composition.

Many were crack riflemen and most were able and fearless fighters, but because of a lack of motivation and the fear that their families were starving and in danger back home, they often resorted to desertion. Throughout the war, far more Confederate soldiers were lost to disease and desertion than were ever lost to Union fire. The men of the hill country left the fight in great numbers.

To the best of our knowledge, and according to archival and regimental records, Private Yelton enlisted in August of 1864 and remained with General Lee's Army until Lee surrendered at Appomattox Court House in April of 1865. Yelton served as a replacement with the 18th North Carolina Volunteer Infantry Regiment. He arrived just in time to experience the humiliation and defeat of the once invincible Army of Northern Virginia, of which it has been said there was never a finer fighting force in the long bloody history of warfare on earth.

Francis Yelton was wounded on the retreat somewhere near Amelia Courthouse, Virginia. Although he had a family of his own, he did not desert, as many of his fellows did. One can only conclude that he remained through a sense of loyalty and honor and possibly the certain knowledge that desertion was a frequent path to a lynch rope or a firing squad.

It is believed Francis never owned a slave, nor did any of his close relatives. He was a subsistence farmer and a grist mill worker, probably living in a small cabin in the Camp Creek or Cane Creek area of Rutherford County, with his wife and children. His gravestone can be found today at the Camp Creek Baptist Church Cemetery near Union Mills, North Carolina.

Private Yelton's great-grandson is honored to offer a fictional account roughly based on his Civil War service. No one living knows the true account. It may have been a great deal more desperate and poignant than the fictional story told herein.

The primary historical facts are as accurate as possible, though most events surrounding Francis, his family and his comrades—including battle scenes—are either fictional or speculative.

Besides Francis and Harriet Yelton, their children Jane and Susan, and Francis's ancestors, only the major military and political figures—including General Cadmus M. Wilcox, General James Henry Lane, Colonel John D. Barry, and Sergeant John Spillers—are real. General Hallman, Major Trent, Sergeant Hutchins, Whit, Lester, and the Preacher, as well as others, are fictional.

ONE

*A soldier who fights
in a war not his own,
bears the burden
of manifold tragedy.*

I am not a soldier. I have been a farmer for most of my thirty-one years. I come from the hills of western North Carolina, from a county called Rutherford, a land of hills and hollows. It is a place where the evening mist tints the ridges blue as they roll toward the far horizon, each layer of hills becoming ever lighter in hue until the sky appears to be joined to the land. The ancient mountains and lush river valleys pulse with life planted by God, and watered by the very lifeblood of my forebears. Since before the Revolution our family has lived here, farmed the land, and left our earthly remains in this good soil.

I confess that I did begin thinking about joining the Southern Army shortly after the war began, but I had a family, and there was no one else to provide for them. My brothers had their own families to look after, and some of them had already made their plans to go to war. Foolish plans they were, in a foolish time.

As strange as it may seem now, in the beginning many thought it a great adventure; lots of fun, marching and parading and shooting at Yankees. I think most learned pretty quick that fun is mighty scarce on a battlefield. I never had any illusions about that.

I am a fair hand with a musket. I hunt a little; mostly deer, rabbits and 'coons, sometimes bear. I never shot at a man before the war. That's an entirely different matter than hunting game. You shoot a deer and look in that black shining eye, and you can see there's nothing there but flesh and blood. You look into the eyes of your fellow man, no matter how debased he may be, and you know there is a soul, a being of a higher order, not just an animal.

I thought about this a lot before I went to war, and it kept me from marching off to join, I must tell you, along with the fact that I had my family to feed. I couldn't grow crops in Camp Creek from an army post in Virginia or Tennessee. And even if I went, could I really bring myself to kill my fellow man? Would I have the courage to fight? These questions burned in my mind as I watched men leave, go to war, and die. Those who did manage to come home were often maimed or scarred so badly the folks at home treated them like pariahs. They were damaged people who often could no longer work. The presumption was that somehow they did something wrong to get shot, or lose a leg or an arm or an eye. I wondered if I could deal with that if it were my lot.

Anyhow, I never owned any slaves; none of our family did. We often jested about how we worked like slaves ourselves, we just didn't have any master to feed and clothe us. All we had was what we could grow on a few acres, which were sharecropped, or bought on credit from some parsimonious banker, or maybe purchased from a hard up farmer who needed money more than land.

Where I come from, we don't take freedom lightly. Mountain folks have always been of freedom loving, independent mind. Our people fought like demons against the British and Tories in our War for Independence. My grandfather, James Yelton, was one of those who pledged his all to fight for our new country.

I suppose that hill country people's love of independence comes from having to rely on your own wit and will to survive when money is scarce and life is hard. When winter howls into the hill country, and hunger sniffs at your door like a bear out of hibernation, you have to be strong of will and body just to survive. Heeling and toeing to a tyrant was never something we cottoned to, whether it was a British or an American one. We bowed to neither foreign kings nor slave-holders from down east. We always went our own way, paying allegiance only to God Almighty. We believed that if you settled for anything other than freedom you might as well be a dumb animal.

Our folks had no quarrel with the Yankees about whether whites could own slaves or not. What reason did I have to go off to Virginia or somewhere and shoot at men with whom I had no disagreement? Recruiters sometimes came around telling me I needed to do my patriotic duty, and I told them I was, by growing crops to feed my family and others. I sold what I could to the Confederate quartermasters and the home guards, and I trusted it went to help feed the soldiers fighting in Virginia, as well as those hometown heroes whose primary combatants were colored bottles on fence posts. They paid me in Confederate script, in amounts which seemed large at the time, but when I went to buy something I found I had sold too cheap. It seemed to me it would take a wheelbarrow full of Confederate script just to buy a shoat. It also seemed to me like I was doing my duty and then some, working my body into old age, and selling my produce to the government for a song.

I served for a while as a lieutenant with the North Carolina Militia, but then folks began to accuse me of dodging the war. I pondered joining the regular army because I did not want my reputation to suffer. Fact was, the recruiters were always preaching that General Robert E. Lee needed men like me because the Yankees were coming in hordes. I usually replied that if the Yankees were coming in hordes, one more farmer with a musket wasn't going to make much difference; but I might try my hand anyway, if it upheld my good name to do so.

Things came to a head one Friday morning in late July of '64 when I was plowing weeds under and early crops. I got up about four thirty because daylight comes early in July, and I wanted to get the bottom plowed so I could move on to the west slope. I walked out to the barn to get Moses: that's what I called the old black mule I bought from Silas Freeman over by Gilbert Town.

Moses wasn't a big mule, about fourteen and a half hands, but he was well muscled and bull strong. And more than a little bit stubborn. Once you got him going he'd plow all day, as long as you stopped and gave him water once in a while. He needed to be talked to, like he was something more than a tool to be used, like he was important, which he was. He was a smart animal. I treated him well, and he knew it. Animals may be dumb, but certain things they perceive better than we of two legs. Moses liked sorghum a lot, so I dropped an armload at his feet, then I walked on down to bring him some water from the creek. Our aged hound, Samson, trotted at my heels.

As I walked I glanced up at the house and saw my sweet wife, Harriet, looking at me through the kitchen window. Her honey colored hair wreathed her face, which today wore a weary smile. She didn't have much reason to smile back then. She lost a brother in the war, and her Pa was bad sick, but most of the time when she looked at me she smiled anyway. Like she did when we were courting ten years ago.

I don't know how she kept looking so good, when I couldn't afford to buy her nice dresses and other female fixings. But somehow she always seemed to have the warmest glow about her. A few lines showed on her face, but I counted her the prettiest girl in these parts. Her penetrating hazel eyes were refreshing, like water in a mountain spring. As she looked out the window that morning, though, I saw something in her face that bothered me somehow; a shadow and a foreboding. I tried not to make much of it. I just smiled back at her, waved, and continued on down to the creek to get Moses his water.

The dawn glowed softly behind the dark bulk of the mountain, mysterious in the early morning gloom. A few high clouds streaked pink and purple across the deep blue. Samson sniffed at the creek bank. An old 'coon dipped in the creek for crawdads until he saw Samson and me, then shuffled off, flicking his ringed tail as he scurried into the brush. Samson woofed, but he was too old to give chase, and he knew it. He went back to inspecting the creek bank. The leaves on the trees along the creek rustled softly. An owl called mournfully, like it was lost in a desolate place. It was a dreadfully lonesome sound, and always made me uneasy, like I was the lost one.

I sometimes wondered about that in my darker moments. On Sunday mornings, when I didn't have to rise early to work, I would lie in my bed listening to a hoot owl off in the distance. To me his refrain was a mournful reminder of the passing of things. The Indians say that an owl calls your name when it's your time to die. I can understand why they would say that. The sad call of an owl is not quite like any sound I ever heard, maybe not like any sound on Earth.

I shook off my gloomy thoughts and dipped the bucket in the cold, rushing water, then set it down and dipped some for myself with my hands. The creek was cold and clear, and came from a gushing spring up the side of the mountain. I'd been there many times, usually hunting deer and squirrels. The water gets a thorough cleansing coming through that blue granite rock in the mountain, and the creek water has the purest, cleanest taste. It was a true blessing.

I listened to the sounds of the morning: the owl, a soft wind in the tree tops, the cheerful murmur of the rushing stream. I breathed deeply of the fragrance of summer. As I looked across the fields, and my eye traced the rustling rows of corn and traveled up the slope toward my house, I had to smile at the beauty of it all. I thanked God for giving me such a place to live and work. I thought of my ancestors who had farmed this land, fought the Indians and the British, suffered disease and want and backbreaking toil, all so we could live in this peaceful and verdant country. The thought made me humble, thankful, and very proud.

As I walked back to the barn, I looked at our little house again, sitting there at the foot of the mountain on a gentle rise, bathed in morning mist. The wood had turned dark after eight years; I couldn't afford to paint it. But that old forest pine aged well, and it would last many more years. A tendril of cooking smoke rose from the chimney, spread low across the corn crib, and mingled with the mist. The towering oak, hickory, and sweet gum trees framed the house like a picture. It was exactly how I knew it would look when I had built it eight years ago.

I had worked nights and any other spare time I had while I was a pitman at Whit Whitaker's sawmill. I stood in that pit at the lower end of the whipsaw, covered with its dust, for days on end. It wasn't bad. The sawdust that peppered my face had a sweet redolence about it. Whit paid me with lumber to build the house, much of which I helped saw myself. My brothers helped me, just as I helped them with their houses. I split the shingles for the roof myself. It took me many months because I had to work on the house whenever I wasn't farming. The house wasn't big or fancy, but it was home, and Harriet did love it so.

I stood for just a minute, savoring the hallowed morning that would soon be transformed into another commonplace day. Old Moses was stirring, getting impatient, and he let out a little "eeee-haw." He wanted his exercise, he couldn't wait to get going. But I knew that, come six, he wouldn't be able to wait to get back to the barn. Foolish old mule he was. I walked up past the field to the barn, and gave him his water. I stroked his muzzle as I put on the bridle and traces. He huffed and flicked his ears. Then I led him down to the bottom to hook up the plow. Meanwhile, Samson stood watching me. After I bent down and scratched his ears, he waddled back up to the porch to maintain his constant and somnolent vigil.

"Mule! Hup! Mule!" I shouted. I let the plow settle into the steaming brown soil. The plowshares spoke in a whisper, with an occasional clink of stone, as they cut through the soft loam. Moses lumbered along at his steady gait while I gripped the plow, and we turned the weeds under and rolled the damp soil upward. The plowed vegetation was pungent in the heavy air.

It was about as pleasant a job as any man ever had. Don't misunderstand me; it was sure enough work. A long day of plowing will make a strong man tired. You had to keep the plow straight and steady, especially when you were laying off rows; and you had to keep pace with the animal, slogging through soft soil for ten to twelve hours, sometimes more. It worked on your legs, your shoulders, and your back. But at the end of the day, you could see what you had accomplished. Making things grow from God's good earth made a man feel part of the natural order of things, something you could never get working in some manufactory or general store.

About mid-morning I saw two fellows riding up the road: one on a chestnut gelding, and the other a fine roan mare. They stopped the horses at the edge of the field, two hundred yards away, and waved down at me. I whoa'd old Moses, tied the lines to the plow handles, and walked up to see what they wanted. They were fairly well dressed fellows, and I didn't recognize them, so I figured it was official business of some kind. I hollered out, "Good mornin'," and they nodded real solemn like.

"Mr. Francis Yelton?" the taller one said like he was asking. I said I was he. He smiled a little and said, "Mr. Yelton, I'm Wallace McIntyre and this here is Joe Deck, we're recruitment officers."

They had my attention. "Mr. Deck; Mr. McIntyre," I replied with a nod.

The tall man looked even more serious, "I don't know if you heard, but things ain't goin' so well for us in Virginia. Lee's been backed almost all the way to Richmond, and the Yankees is gettin' stronger every day. They keep comin' faster than we can kill 'em. We need men like you to join the fight to stop those Yankee devils. I hate to say it, but looks like it might be now or never. We know you've served well in the state militia, but we'd like for you to join up with the volunteers. Some of the North Carolina regiments has got purty small, and they need help. What do you think?"

I furrowed my brow and studied the men. My mind was divided, and there was no getting around it. I looked from one to the other then said, "Gentlemen, I want to go but I joined the militia so I could keep on workin' the farm at least part of the time. I'm a farmer, and all I got is what you can see from your saddle. If I leave, I am afraid my family will starve. There's nobody else to take care of them, what with my brothers all dead or off to war."

They looked at each other like they had heard the tale a thousand times. Mr. Deck said, "Look, Francis, we need you in the army. The situation is desperate, and men like you are needed more on the lines than here at home."

Again I looked from one to the other of them from under the brim of my slouch hat. We were all silent.

The horses shifted and huffed, their withers glistening in the heat. One flicked his ears at a bothersome fly. There was a dull clink of metalwork, and saddle leather creaked as the horses moved. The sun beat down on the fields, the men, and me. They looked at me hard, as if expecting me to say something.

I sighed deeply, looked at the fields and back at the men. "Gentlemen, I have much work to do and I can't leave just now." I swept my arm toward the fields. "I've got crops in the ground that will need harvestin' before long, and I have a family to feed. Could I maybe join up after the harvest?"

Mr. McIntyre looked off across the fields and said, with a trace of irritation in his voice, "The need is urgent. If the Yankees reach Rutherford, your family will starve, and your farm will probably be gone anyway. They'll come into this valley burnin' and takin' everything that they can. Ask the folks up in the Shenandoah."

Mr. Deck added, in a flat, matter of fact voice, "And sometimes it's been said some of them boys ain't above takin' liberties with the women folk. Ain't that worth fightin' for? We're down to recruitin' old men and boys, and to conscriptin' those that refuse. We need you bad, and we need you now." He removed something from his pocket and handed it to me. "Here's an enlistment form. Take it to Camp Vance in Morganton within thirty days time. If you can talk any of your neighbors into coming, bring them too. We need every man."

Mr. McIntyre lowered the tone of his voice. "We know you have brothers that have served and have died in the war. We respect that. Come on to Camp Vance, and join up within the next four weeks. General Lee and his boys have fought long and hard. They's been a lot of losses in the ranks, and the army needs men real bad. Your country needs you real bad. Don't let us down." They both looked at me with hard eyes. McIntyre touched his hat, smiled slightly, and then they wheeled their horses and rode off down the road at a canter. The horses' hooves kicked up little clouds of dust. The men disappeared around the bend, the clop of the hooves fading.

I looked up at the bright sun beating down, pulled out my bandana and wiped my brow underneath my hat. My gaze turned to my house and I thought I saw Harriet's face in the window, but from where I stood I wasn't sure. My eyes turned toward the fields, the woods, and the mountains beyond. My barn, corn crib, and chicken coop. They all seemed somehow diminished. Everything suddenly seemed temporary; like it was passing away. I looked down at old Moses, patiently waiting in the shade near the creek. I looked back at the house, slowly took a deep breath, then walked on back to take up the plow again.

With my hands on the plow, the blades once again cut deep into the earth. The horse's rhythmic movements and the soft sound of the metal cutting through the dirt seemed somehow comforting. I was about half done by one o'clock, so I stopped to get a bite to eat. First I got Moses some water and tied him in the shade near the creek, then I went on up to the house. I knew Harriet would have something cooked.

When I walked in, she was standing by the stove with the most distressed look I ever saw on her face. Twisting a cloth in her hand, she said in a soft voice, "Who were those people?" I told her who they were and what they said. Her eyes dropped, and a tear ran down her cheek. "I knew this day would come," she said quietly.

I walked to her, lifted her face toward mine, and said, "I have to go, darlin'. It won't be for long; surely the war can't last much longer. And folks are sayin' I'm a dodger, and I can't have that. I've got to do my duty."

I'll never forget the look that came upon her face. It seemed to crumple, and a look of desolation took the place of her warm, loving expression. Her shoulders slumped. Her lips trembled as she said, "I am so afraid you won't come back. Mary Hollis's husband left for Virginia five months ago, and three months later she got a letter saying he was dead. Two of your own brothers are dead, and God knows what's become of the others. I can't stand the thought of living life without you."

I held her close and said, "I will come back, don't you worry. The Good Lord will watch after me." My words of comfort didn't seem to help very much. We stood in silence for some time holding each other. Our two little ones—Jane, who was nine, and our "baby", six-year-old Susan—came in from playing in the yard, and we sat down at the table to eat.

I got as much done as I could in the next few days. My girls helped more than usual. Harriet went about her work solemnly and earnestly. She read her Bible more, and she prayed a lot. We spent as much time with each other as we could. Harriet cooked my favorite foods, and sang my favorite hymns.

We sat on the porch in the evenings after the girls went to bed, and as the stars sparkled in the vast blackness above us, and the whippoorwills persisted in their plaintive refrain, she would rock and sing "Amazing Grace" and all the great hymns from church. Then we would retire, and I would lie awake for hours, it seemed, holding her in my arms, smelling her sweet, soft skin, dreading the day we would part. I kept telling myself it would not be for long, surely could not be for long, somehow.

TWO

The day dawns bright but
the prospect is grim
on the road to a land
strange and dark and violent.

Camp Vance was only about thirty-five or forty miles from my farm, so I figured I could walk it in two days' time or less. Early in the morning of August 23, 1864, I kissed my wife goodbye, hugged Jane and Susan, and started down the path to the Camp Creek Road to make my way to the post over near Morganton. As I rounded the bend in the path, my slouch hat pulled low, a bundle over my left shoulder and my musket in my right hand, I turned back and looked at my family. I felt my face get hot, and my breath got short. I didn't know if I would ever see them again. My wife stood with my two little flaxen-haired girls huddled close. She smiled bravely, but even at a distance I could see the glisten of tears on her cheeks. Little Susan turned and buried her face in her mother's dress. Jane looked at me with a doleful expression and waved. Neither of my hands was free so I gestured back with the one holding my musket, then wondered about the appropriateness of that.

I turned and walked on down the path. I left my very heart standing on that ridge above Camp Creek.

The thought of the long road to Camp Vance was oppressive to me. The things that gave me such joy, the beauty of God's nature around me, seemed superfluous and sullied somehow. My legs felt heavy before I had gone a half mile. I walked on like a man asleep on his feet, a dull ache deep down.

Life sometimes takes curious turns, and one's aspect can change from day to night and back again in the space of an hour or a minute. Such a change occurred when I had barely begun my journey. I hadn't gone much more than a mile when I saw Whit Whitaker ambling down the rutted road from his cabin on the lower slopes of Hogback Mountain. Whit hollered at me, and I stopped to wait on him. He had a bundle over his shoulder like mine. He was still a hundred feet away when his coarse voice rang out, "You goin' to sign up? I am!" I nodded.

Whit was the type of fellow who always thought he knew better than anyone else about most any subject you wanted to talk about: religion, politics, farming, or anything else. The fact was, most folks realized that half the time he was flat wrong, but everybody hereabouts knew him and made allowances. Whit was a bit older than me, about thirty-four, with brownish hair, ears rounded from too many boyhood fights, and a droopy mustache. He was two inches shorter than me and probably thirty pounds heavier, a deceptively powerful man who had worked with logs and lumber all his life. He always said that logging and lumber work would make a man out of you or kill you in the process.

Whit wore an old slouch hat like me, but with the brim turned up in front. He always had a big chaw in his mouth, and there was usually a trickle of tobacco juice running down one corner of his mouth or the other. Doc Callison in Gilbert Town said you could predict whether the weather would be sunny or rainy by which side of Whit's mouth the tobacco juice ran down that day. Doc always was one who tended to say things that were ridiculous, and try to make people believe them, but the twinkle in his eye usually gave him away.

I waited for him to catch up to me. He spat out a big stream and asked, "Did you get conscripted too?"

I shook my head. "No, I quit the militia and I'm signin' up; ain't gonna be called a dodger."

He laughed hoarsely, sounding a little like Moses when he's feelin' sick at his stomach, then drew his gaze right to left and said, "We'll most likely both end up planted on some hill in Virginia, so we'd better get a good look at this old valley now, because we ain't ever a-goin' to see it again." He grinned.

"Whit, you need to learn when to make a joke and when not to," I said, somewhat irritated. "I don't think this is jokin' business."

Whit looked a little sheepish. "I reckon it don't hurt to joke about such matters. It ain't gonna change things none." He shrugged and added, with a grin big as Texas, "At least we can go to our death with a smile."

I didn't answer him. He always did think he had to have the last word, and that what he thought was the way it was or the way it ought to be.

"Yo're lucky you didn't get conscripted," he said. "They came by Frank Scoggins's house about three weeks ago, and tole him that he had ten minutes to gather his belongin's and say his goodbyes. I heered his young'uns was a squallin', and his wife was a beggin' them not to take him. It was a regular pitiful sight, is what I heered."

I looked down at the rutted road and said, "I heard about it, too. They say they need men real bad, that sickness and Yankee bullets are destroying the army."

"Think of it as an adventure, Francis. I never seen Virginia before, and I sort'a look forward to it; though I'd as soon not have blue bellies shootin' at me whilst I'm lookin' around."

I shifted my musket. "Oh, they'll be shootin' all right, and we'll be the targets. I've had two brothers die already, and another one took to his heels. We don't know what became of him. I hear it's so bad that there's more men leavin' and comin' home than there are new ones to take their places. No, it don't sound like much of an adventure to me, Whit."

Whit grinned. "Well, Francis, we're on our way for good or ill, so let's try to act like it's an adventure 'cause it will be, one way or t'other."

He might not have been the most desirable of companions, but at least Whit was someone to talk to besides the crows and the rabbits. I tried to count my blessings. It was not easy. As I walked out of the valley, I felt like something was emptying out of me, like water from a bucket. I never felt that way before or since, but I felt it that day.

We walked for a long time without saying much. As the sun rose higher, Whit seemed to become more thoughtful than usual. I pulled out my Pa's old pocket watch and it was almost eleven o'clock, so I suggested we stop and eat a bite by a little branch of the creek that ran near the road. I had some biscuits and fried chicken, and he had some cornbread and fatback, so we sat and ate.

Whit regained his voice. "Francis, this ain't our fight. You know them politicians in Richmond is just a bunch of fools and buffoons. They gonna get us kilt." I reminded him that just a short while before he was telling me it was going to be a great adventure. He looked thoughtful for a moment, then ignored me and started in on the Confederate generals. He said, "Them generals up there is pitiful. They cain't figure out how to whup a few city-boy Yankees. They's plenty of outliers over in the high mountains, and we kin go over there and stay until the war's over. The provost marshals and the militia is afraid to go over there after them boys because they's a lot of 'em holed up in that rough country, and they don't aim to be took alive."

I looked at him and shook my head. Then he took up the theme about how it was a rich man's war but a poor man's fight. He said it was all about the coloreds, and he didn't own any, and why did they bother hard workin' folks like us anyway. I let him talk, because there ain't much else to do with Whit unless you want to slap him, because when Whit's gonna talk, he's gonna talk. I sort of faded him out, and listened to the buzz of the bees and the rustling of the wind through the white oaks instead. The day was getting hot; rolling white clouds spotted the deep blue sky. It reminded me of wash day and clothes on the line, for some reason. I missed home already.

As soon as we finished eating we got started toward Morganton again. The dusty, winding road through the mountains rose through the passes and dropped down into the valleys. Here and there we passed a farm. Most of the farmers who had not gone off to war were harvesting their crops, but it seemed their numbers were few. Most of the fields looked neglected. I felt a pang at not having completed my own work.

Between the farms, oaks, hickories, and wild cherry trees crowded the road side, and the deep forest pushed up the mountain slopes, stretching over the craggy summits. Whit kept talking, mostly complaining about being conscripted and about the "durn fool Confederate Government in Richmond that couldn't run a war well enough to whup a few sorry Yankees." It seemed to be his theme for the day. I mostly let him talk, and tried to listen to the sounds of the woods and fields and, like always, I watched the sky.

The day's monotony began to replace the anguish of leaving home. I stopped for a moment to watch a red-tailed hawk glide overhead. It flew in lazy circles, then at a point about a hundred yards away from us, suddenly hurtled downward like a bolt of dusky lightning. When the bird was about six feet off the ground its powerful wings flared wide, its talons stretched down, and it snatched up a fat field mouse and carried it away. I marveled, as I often did, at how the hawk had spotted the mouse in the tall grass from several hundred feet in the air then swooped down to the exact point to seize the little creature.

Whit asked, "Why you watchin' that hawk, Francis?"

"Well, I just find it amazing the way they hunt and catch their prey. They move so fast and right to it. God knew what he was doing when he made hawks."

Whit looked at me a bit sideways and said, "You seen hundreds of them things, Francis. What's so interestin' about 'em today?"

I smiled. "I just think it's something to be admired. Don't you?"

"Well, I s'pose so. I wonder more what a hawk would taste like."

I had to laugh. "Not too good, I think. They eat rats and snakes. I sure don't plan on finding out."

I had brought along one of my two smooth bore muskets, and a fair amount of musket balls and powder, but the weapon was old and worn. I was hoping they would provide me with a better one once we got to Richmond, or maybe even at Camp Vance. Still, I thought, better safe than sorry. When I shot a fat rabbit along the way for our supper, shouldering that old musket had felt like I was off on a long hunting trip instead of going to kill some of my fellow men.

That thought kept coming back again and again. It didn't seem to bother old Whit any, but it bothered me plenty. Truth is, I didn't know whether I could shoot another man or not. It preyed on my mind, a gnawing thought that imposed itself from time to time. Here I was, a small time farmer with forty-two acres—which I still owed the bank thirty-seven dollars for—on my way to fight for the Confederacy, and I didn't even know if I could make myself shoot a Yankee. Some soldier I was.

Along about five in the afternoon I asked Whit how much longer he wanted to walk that day. He said maybe just another hour, he was tired. I was tired too, but I said we should walk until dark so as to make as many miles the first day as possible. It took some persuading on my part to get him to agree. I told him I was going to walk until dark whether he did or not. He didn't much fancy walking alone, plus the only weapon he had was a Bowie knife, so he agreed.

The next couple of days were uneventful. It was when the sun was getting low in the sky that suddenly we heard voices, either crying or yelling, up around the next bend. It gave me a very bad feeling here in this sparse country, so I checked my musket to be sure it was ready, and we moved cautiously to see what was making all the fuss. Down the right side of the road, beyond a grassy field, there was a deep thicket. The noises were coming from there. There was a sharp scream, like a woman or a child in terrible pain. The sound made my blood chill, and Whit looked at me like he'd seen a ghost.

"We gotta find out what's goin' on," I said. Whit nodded. I checked the musket again to make sure it was loaded and capped. We ran across the field and into the thicket, me in front, Whit right behind me, his knife at the ready.

As we pushed our way into the thicket, I saw some people on the ground in some sort of struggle. There was a young girl laying there, crying hysterically, and two men cursing and laughing. One was big, with a gray hat, and he was on top of the young girl. The other man was holding her arms. He was as thin as a rail and dirty as a hog in a wallow. He laughed and grinned, toothless in front.

The girl was struggling and kicking but they had her pinned down. When I realized what was happening, my fury rose up, and my body grew taut.

Whit gasped, "Good God!" The man holding the girl looked up.

Grasping my musket by the barrel, I lunged at the man holding the girl and swung my musket. The stock caught the man square in the mouth with a loud cracking sound.

The man fell backwards with a scream, blood spurting from his nose and mouth. The other man jerked around and I saw his face was red as a beet. His eyes were wild, almost pig-like, and his fat face was smeared with dirt and grease, a scraggly beard across his ample jaw. I brought the musket back around and swung it again, hitting him a glancing blow on the side of the head. The butt plate caught his left ear and almost tore it off; blood splattered the leaves nearby.

I straightened myself as he toppled over. My heart pounded like it was going to leap out of my chest. He came up fast for a big man, pulling a long hunting knife. I yelled at him to stop as I brought my musket back into firing position, but he kept coming at me. His eyes were filled with pure hate and pure malice.

As fast as I could I cocked the musket and pulled the trigger, not even realizing that I was ready to kill my first man and it wasn't even the war. But the hammer clicked; the cap had been jarred off. The large man grinned and moved toward me, his left eye twitching. His belly bulged over his pants, and even as he came at me I wondered how he had gotten fat in these lean years. He laughed coarsely and said, "Looks like you're out of luck, mister. I'm a'gonna kill you!"

I said coldly, "You still got it to do, mister. I ain't goin' easy!" I turned the musket and grasped it by the barrel again. He came at me with his knife moving back and forth, thrusting it at me now and then, and grunting out a little laugh each time. I took a couple of steps backwards, then I leaned forward and swung the musket at his head as hard as I could. He raised his arm to ward off the blow; too late. The stock connected with his head just above his left ear with a sharp crack. He staggered to his right.

His eyes crossed, then closed, and he dropped to his knees. He stayed that way for a few seconds, then pitched face down to the ground. His skull was indented on the left side, and blood began to soak the ground around his head. Whit and I stood there for a moment. Then Whit sidled up, and said in a shaky voice, "I think you killed him, Francis."

I nodded. Then I spun quickly to look for the other man. I need not have worried; he was lying on the ground, holding his face, moaning and crying. Whit looked around and kept saying, "Oh Lord, oh my Lord." The scene was like something from a nightmare: a hysterical young girl, a dead man covered with his own blood, another rolling about in pain, and two bewildered farmers gaping and gasping for breath.

It was one of those times when something changes you, maybe forever. I had crossed a bridge I could not re-cross. As I began to catch my breath I realized that I was now a killer, something that did not wear well on me. I tried to live like the Good Book says, and treat my fellow man as I would like to be treated. I suppose coming face to face with a cold hearted animal of a man brings down the best of intentions.

The girl, crying and moaning, began to gather her torn clothes around her. She was frail, with brown hair and soft brown eyes. I went to her side but was afraid to touch her. I didn't know what to say or do. The poor girl had just been violated and beaten. So I just asked her if she was able to stand. She nodded yes, tears streaming down her reddened face, but she didn't look ready to stand. I sat down beside her, offered her some water, and asked her who the men were.

"I don't know," she said in a quiet voice.

"What's your name?" I asked.

"Janie. Janie Samuels. My Pa is Deputy Sheriff Robert Samuels. Of McDowell County."

"A deputy's daughter," Whit said. "What happened?"

Slowly she explained, "I live about two miles up the Pea Ridge road," she said. "I had been wandering around, I guess, just out picking flowers, when the men came upon me." She started sobbing again.

I said, "We'd better get you home." I gave Whit the rope off my bedroll, and told him to tie the surviving man's hands behind him.

He nodded at the dead man and said, "What about him?"

"We'll mark the place with a piece of his shirt and let someone come back for the body."

"What about animals?" Whit knew that bears and bobcats would make a feast of the corpse.

I spat out the words, "After what these two did to that girl, I don't rightly care." It wasn't the Christian thing to say, but the dead man had acted like an animal. Maybe being eaten by one would be his just reward.

I helped the girl to her feet. Whit tied up the man, jerked him to his feet, and shoved him toward the road. He took his knife, cut off a piece of the dead man's shirt, and tied it on a wild cherry limb beside the road. I tried to steady the girl as we walked. We had only gone a few hundred feet when she grew increasingly faint. There was blood running down her leg, from a private place, so I could not tell how badly she was injured. She began to stagger, and seemed about to swoon. I gave Whit my musket and bedroll and tried to steady her. Finally, I picked her up as she passed out cold.

Whit and I decided the two men must be Confederate deserters. One had an old forage cap, and the other had a military haversack.

They were probably heading for the high country, though the survivor couldn't or wouldn't talk. After Whit asked him his name two or three times, he finally mumbled that his name was Charles Shepherd. That's all he would say. He knew he was in a world of trouble whatever he did or said. Whit prodded him on with the barrel of the musket. He staggered, his head hung down, the front of his shirt covered with his own blood.

My arms and back ached from carrying the girl up the Pea Ridge road some two miles or so. It was nearing dark when we arrived at the only farm along that stretch of road. A neatly dressed lady came running out the door of the farm house with her hands up to her mouth when she saw the unconscious girl in my arms. She screamed, "Oh, dear God! What happened?"

I said, "This man and another, well, they attacked her." A big man with a pitchfork had come running out from behind the barn to see what the commotion was. We told them the story as best we could. The big man took the girl, and went inside with the lady. Whit and I stood there watching our prisoner until the big man came back a few minutes later.

He went straight for the prisoner, screaming, "What did you do to my little girl?" His voice was tight and his face was twisted with rage. The deserter was so scared he fell to his knees and begged the big man not to kill him.

The man kicked dirt at the prisoner. Shaking with fury, he turned to me and said, "I'm Robert Samuels. I'm a deputy." He stopped, like he was choking. Then he said, "I swore to uphold the law, but I'm tempted to hang this devil right now."

I looked at Whit, then back at the distraught man. "Mr. Samuels, I'm Francis Yelton and this is Whit Whitaker. We're from over near Gilbert Town. We're on our way to Camp Vance to join the army."

He reached out his hand. "Mr. Yelton; Mr. Whitaker. I am much obliged. I'm real sure that if you men hadn't come along, my daughter would be dead right now." He paused, looked down with his hand over his eyes for a long moment. Then he composed himself, and said more calmly, "I'll take care of this man. We'll tie him up in the tool shed tonight, and I'll take him into Morganton tomorrow. We'll put him in jail until the judge can hear the case." Whit and I simply nodded; it was not like we had planned on being responsible for the prisoner any more than necessary.

Samuels continued, "I would be much obliged if you fellows

would join us for supper. You can sleep in the barn tonight and start out with me to Morganton at first light. There's fresh hay, and it will be better than sleeping in the woods."

"We shore appreciate it, Mr. Samuels," said Whit.

Mrs. Samuels prepared a good meal, much better than rabbit cooked on a spit in the woods. We didn't see the girl again, though; she stayed in her room. Her mother said she wasn't hurt too bad, but I knew than an inside hurt is the worst kind. On the bright side, the girl was young and there would be time to heal. At least she would have the chance to heal.

Still, something like that will stay with her forever. In my mind I could see her as a young woman, marrying, having a family; but her mind going back to this day from time to time, reliving the nightmare all over again.

Mr. and Mrs. Samuels were so grateful they could scarcely do enough for Whit and me. We ate supper like it was our last meal on earth. We felt thankful to be alive after such an ordeal, and they were most grateful that their daughter was still with them. I guess we all shared something more than the meal that night.

Afterwards, Mr. Samuels walked us out to the barn. I told him, "We tied a piece of shirt up on a cherry tree near where the dead one is."

Mr. Samuels sighed, looked in the direction I was pointing, and said, "I'll send Luther Gates from down the road to fetch whatever is left of him tomorrow. It don't appear to be any great loss." He looked toward the tool shed and said, "I'll take that one some water … and I guess some bread." He paused, then added, "It's the Christian thing to do, though that's the only reason I'll do it." Mr. Samuels showed us to our bed for the night and walked silently back to the house.

"That poor man's hurtin' bad, Whit."

"I know. If somethin' like that happened to one of my girls...." Whit's voice trailed off.

We both lay down on the fresh straw. After a while, Whit said, "How does it feel to kill a man, Francis?"

I grimaced in the dark. "None too good. In fact, my insides are turning over."

Whit sighed. "Already killed a man, and we ain't even in the war yet. It's not a good sign, Francis."

I didn't answer. A man was dead, a girl and her family was torn to pieces inside, and you're in the middle. I stared at the rafters for a long time.

Whit rose up on his elbow and looked at me in the light of the lantern. "Thar's blood on yore sleeves." I looked at them, then at him. His eyes were intense, sorrowful. We both settled back. The barn was quiet and after a while we slept.

After that day, Whit looked at me a little differently. I guess he saw another side of a man he thought he knew. I learned that it didn't take war to bring that side out. It pains me to say, it would come out yet again.

THREE

On the long winding road
to Gehenna
I paused to look at the stars,
sparkling like the cold eye of death.

We started out early the next morning, after a delicious breakfast of eggs, ham, and some of the finest biscuits I ever ate. When we finished breakfast, Mr. Samuels saddled his horse and tied the deserter to a rope, pulling him along behind. The deserter never spoke a word the whole way to Morganton. We said goodbye to Mr. Samuels in town as he pointed us toward Camp Vance.

We arrived at the camp about seven in the evening, footsore and hungry. The camp wasn't much. Strange as it seemed, there were a couple of rows of burned out buildings and a few dozen tents to the side, like they were recovering from a bad fire. They were a few new structures and they were building a couple more, but hadn't gotten very far. The frames rose up like wooden skeletons from the muddy ground. Overall, it had a depressing look, like a place that tried hard but was still all loose ends, and shabby ones at that.

We found a group of soldiers having supper near a large tent. We asked the man in charge—he turned out to be a sergeant—where we could sleep. He said there were no tents left for recruits, but that we could bed down near the creek, and pointed to a small stream about two hundred yards to the west. He also said that we might find a biscuit or two over by the mess tent.

We walked over and asked the man there—I learned he was a

corporal—if there was any food left. He went in the tent and brought out four small biscuits and some bacon.

The two of us made our way over to the stream, which was about five feet across and maybe a foot deep as it rushed over the smooth stones. Poplars and river birches lined the banks. We found a relatively level clearing and laid out our bedrolls, then started a little fire to boil some water. After we made some coffee, we ate our biscuits and some chicken Mrs. Samuels had sent with us.

Once the food was gone we reclined against a tall poplar tree and listened to the murmur of the stream in the dark. Everything got quiet in the camp, but I stayed awake for a long time. Too much had happened already, leaving home and tangling with the deserters. I turned it all over in my mind for what seemed like several hours. Finally I went to sleep, but I kept awakening from a dream in which I was fighting off a wolf that was trying to get at my calf. I hit at it with a stick, but it kept coming back, biting at me, biting my arms and my legs. I could feel the wolf's fangs tearing at me. I would knock it down, but it kept coming back.

About five o'clock, after I had awakened from the dream for the third or fourth time, I got up and walked over to the creek. I stripped to my skivvies and sat down in the cold water to bathe as well as I could. I tried to wash the blood out of my shirt, and finally gave it up.

I didn't bother to shave. I figured that living in an army camp and maybe marching about, I wouldn't have many opportunities to shave, so I decided to let the beard grow. A lot of the men had beards, and it seemed like the thing to do. Plus, my Pa had a full beard, and I always figured I would resemble him even more if I let mine grow. It would come out brown, with some reddish tint to it.

I got out of the creek, and went back to build a fire to dry off. I patted down with my blanket and sat close to the fire until I was reasonably dry, then got dressed.

By that time old Whit was awake and I told him to hurry, that we had to report to the headquarters by six thirty according to the sergeant. He stayed wrapped in his blanket and growled, "I don't care what that old sergeant said. All my conscript orders said was that I was to be here by August 25th. That's today and we're here. That's all that counts!"

"Just the same," I said, "we ought to try to get off to a good start."

He whined, like only Whit can. "Francis, you is the durndest man I ever seen to try to go out of his way to do what somebody else thinks you ort to do, even contrary to what's fer yer own good. These fellers don't care about us bein' on time, all they want is more fodder for the Yankee cannons."

"Maybe so, but this fodder ain't gonna start out a shirker from the git go. I didn't want to come, but now that I'm here, I'm gonna do my duty if it kills me."

"Prob'ly will," Whit muttered. He rolled out of the blankets and onto his feet.

He sauntered toward the creek to do his business. I looked out over the camp as it was beginning to stir. Men started fires and put on coffee. Some were gathering at the mess tent. Daylight came, and the sky was a deep blue. It looked like a clear day, no clouds in sight. I thought about home.

As I stood there, I began to feel as if I were suffocating under a huge weight. I don't know what it was. I'm a simple man, a farmer and a worker, but I felt the weight of the world on my shoulders that morning. Our country was torn asunder; the grim reaper stalked the land cutting men down in their prime by the thousands. The death and destruction were overwhelming. I wondered if we would even have homes to come back to. I worried for my wife and my little ones. The future looked as bleak as a stony tomb in the wilderness.

My thoughts were interrupted when Whit returned from the creek. "Whooee, that crik water's cold! What say let's git some breakfast." We headed over to the mess tent, where there was a serving line and tables set up outside. The food was fine, some eggs and a little fatback, but the portions were small. There always seemed to be a shortage of some kind or another these days, never enough of anything to go around.

Talk around the camp was that things were going from bad to worse. Richmond and Petersburg, where Lee's army was entrenched, were cities under siege. Food and supplies, war materials, and anything else needful for surviving this holocaust were in dreadfully short supply.

By the time we finished our meal it was almost six thirty, so we grabbed our belongings and headed over to the headquarters building. It looked like it had just been finished. It was a little one story wooden building with a small porch and a window on either side of the door. The wood looked and smelled new, but the floor was already mud-stained. We entered and reported to a young lieutenant seated behind a little oaken desk, which was maybe two feet by three feet. The lieutenant had a real neat stack of papers on each side of the desk and he was writing on a sheet in the middle. There was a candle placed perfectly in the middle, at the front of the desk. On one side was an ink well; on the other was an ivory handled pen knife.

We handed him our papers and he studied them with a scowl on his face. Then he looked us both up and down like we were something he had just scraped off the bottom of his boot. The lieutenant looked to be no more than eighteen. He had a skimpy blond mustache which drooped to either side of his mouth, no chin whiskers. His hair was slicked to the side and curled up about his ears. Fair skinned, he did not appear to be a man who had spent much time out of doors. He was all decked out in what they call a "butternut" uniform. It didn't have a speck on it, and was resplendent with shiny boots. I wondered how much fighting he had done, and decided probably not much if any at all.

The young officer said (with a sort of sideways sneer on his face), "Report to Sergeant Washburn over at Company C," then he looked back down at the papers on his desk. I asked him how we would find Sergeant Washburn and he yelled, "Look for the flag with the big 'C' on it, or can't you sodbusters read?" I looked to Whit and he sort of raised his eyebrows, then we turned and walked out the door.

"There it is," Whit said, almost as soon as we had gotten out the door. Whit could read a little and he took every opportunity to show off his somewhat limited ability. At least he knew what a "C" looked like. Sure enough, about a hundred yards over to the left was a group of tents with a flagpole and a flag with a big "C" on it. Whit bit off a plug of tobacco and offered me some, which I gladly took, and we walked over to the tent nearest the flagpole.

"We're here to see Sergeant Washburn," Whit announced as we walked up.

A couple of soldiers looked up from a card game and said, "In there," nodding toward the big tent near the flagpole.

Inside, the sergeant behind the same kind of tiny little desk as the lieutenant had. It held an inkwell, a quill pen and knife, and a stack of papers. The floor in the tent was wooden and had been swept clean. The sergeant was writing something as we came in. He was about forty years of age. He had a shovel beard and a head full of unruly hair and just about the bushiest eyebrows I ever saw on a man. When he looked up I noticed he had a big scar which ran along his left cheek from his ear almost to his mouth, right at the line of his beard. He studied us critically for a minute, an intense scowl on his face, his hard gray eyes narrowed.

Whit seemed nervous and kept shifting from one foot to the other. I nodded at Sergeant Washburn. We handed him the papers and he looked at them like they were written in Greek. He sighed and looked up. "A conscript and a volunteer," he said to no one in particular with a tone he might have used after stepping into a cow pile. He shook his head, then he looked at us appraisingly. "Let me see you grin."

Whit looked at me, and I said, "Beg your pardon?"

He sighed. "Grin at me, show me your teeth, and then bite like your bitin' off a chaw."

"Sir?" I asked.

The sergeant closed his eyes and, speaking slowly, explained, "In order to serve in the army, you have to have two teeth that meet in the front, for bitin' open cartridges."

We did as we were told, though somewhat bemused by the whole thing. When Whit opened his mouth, his chaw fell out and splattered on the floor. Sergeant Washburn rolled his eyes and shook his head again. He growled, "Clean it up." Whit bent down and scooped up the chaw as best he could. He looked around for a place to dispose of it, and finding none he ceremoniously placed it in his pants pocket. The sergeant groaned a little. Whit grinned, pulled out another plug, and bit if off dramatically.

He looked us over and said, "I suppose you'll both do. You fellers ain't old and you ain't young; how come you ain't been in the army all along?"

Whit pursed his lips and said solemnly, "Well, Sergeant, I been busy a-takin' care of my family. I ain't rightly had time to sign up what with farmin' and loggin' and a runnin' the saw mill."

Sergeant Washburn looked at Whit disgustedly and said, "All of us has things to do. But duty comes first, which you'll soon find out." He turned to me and said, "What's your excuse?" I told him that I had served in the militia, and that I was a farmer with a family to feed, and that I had supplied corn and sorghum and felt like I was doing my duty. Besides which, I really had no quarrel with the Yanks, and I have always been happy to be an American and live in a free land, and wasn't even sure about all the whys and wherefores of this war anyway. I told him I came because I did not want to be seen as a dodger.

The sergeant got this real disgusted look and stood up. I saw that he was a stout man, about five feet eight. He took a deep breath, then began to methodically spit out his next words. "Let me tell you something, farmer." He said the word "farmer" like it tasted bad in his mouth. "If men like you don't come forward and fight, the blue-bellies will be marchin' right through the middle of this country; burnin' your crops, stealin' your women, and shootin' you down like dogs. And no hometown militia is gonna stop 'em. Hellfire, they're already doin' it! Look at Kirk." I knew he meant a certain Colonel Kirk who led a band of Yankee and turncoat cavalry on raids in western North Carolina and Tennessee. "They came stormin' through here and burned this camp not two months ago. Not to mention the gangs of deserters tearin' up jack. The Yankees and the lawbreakers will take over."

Sergeant Washburn shook his head slowly once again. "But that ain't nothin'; look at what Sherman's doin' in Georgia and what any number of Yankee vermin has done up in the Shenandoah." He paused long enough to glare at both of us some more. "I been on the front lines at Sharpsburg, Fredericksburg, Chancellorsville, and Gettysburg, not to mention a hundred dustups of one kind or another. I watched them carry Stonewall from the field after our own men opened fire on him by accident; my own outfit, the old 18th North Carolina! I saw the men fall down and cry like babies when they learned what happened."

He pointed to his scar. "I got this when a Yankee cavalryman tried to take my head off with his saber. I been shot, stabbed with the bayonet, and damn near froze to death a dozen times. I've seen men blown to pieces by Yankee artillery, and they was the lucky ones. I've seen men come back from battle missing an arm or a leg or an eye or private parts, or with holes in them you could stick your fist in, and them still walkin'. You may have no quarrel with the blue-bellies now, but that's because you ain't seen 'em up close and personal like I have."

The sergeant must have given that speech a hundred times, because he sure gave it well. Whit, of course, couldn't avoid saying say something. "You ain't exactly selling us on joining up," he said.

"I don't have to; you're already here. My job is to make soldiers out of you dirt farmers, and that I intend to do, in about two weeks' time. You just plan right now on doin' what I tell you to do, when I tell you to do it, and you might just get to go back to your little farms in the piney woods." He said this with a particular bit of disdain in his voice, wrinkling his face when he said "piney woods." He took a deep breath and said, "Now, you men go see Corporal Hamrick about some equipage, and report back here in one hour for drill." With that, he sat back down at his papers, and we knew we were dismissed.

We found our way to the quartermaster to pick up our equipage, then reported back to Company C for drill. The men gathered on the parade ground were mostly scared and depressed about the situation we found ourselves in. We had all heard the stories about the war, like the ones Sergeant Washburn told. We also all knew that more men were deserting than were being killed by Yankee bullets. While we marched to Petersburg, there would be thousands of men walking back toward the hills of North Carolina and Tennessee because they were tired of the fighting, the sickness and the starving. They were tired of getting letters from home telling of loved ones near starvation, of wives and sweethearts trying to work like men, and children dying from illness and lack of decent food.

Most of the men were not cowards in the least; they were just tired of the war. They were tired of freezing in the open when rumor had it there were blankets rotting in warehouses in Georgia. They were tired of marching on bloody bare feet when there were shoes by the thousands sitting in musty buildings near Richmond. They were tired of starving when canned food filled warehouses to overflowing in Salisbury. It is one thing to fight an enemy with the full support of your government behind you, but it's quite another thing to fight when that government is too ill-equipped or ill-managed to provide for your basic needs.

Even the most ignorant private in the ranks somehow knew that the Confederate government was woefully bad. Poor old Jeff Davis tried mightily to do his best, but he was surrounded by a lot of selfish pocket-liners and sycophants who undercut him at every turn. The Yankees had some of the same problems, but their sources of supply were far more plentiful. They had all the manufactories and the shipyards and many more able-bodied men. The South, with its little farms and plantations, had very few manufactories. So when the Confederate government messed up, it hurt plenty. The men knew this, so they were leaving faster than people like us could fill the ranks. Knowing all this made the thought of marching into what looked like a disaster all the worse. We all tried to put on a brave face, but we were scared and homesick to a man, and we wondered how we could be such fools.

Sergeant Washburn came out to the parade ground, and we drilled until almost sundown, with the sergeant yelling and waving his arms in the air most of the day. Our instruction at Camp Vance was brief but very intense and very thorough. We learned the manual of arms for using weapons in formation, to load our weapons in nine steps and four steps and at will. Over the two weeks we learned firings, direct, oblique, by file and by rank. We learned to fire and load, standing, kneeling and lying. We had bayonet exercises. We also learned how to march, a concept which amused me to no end at first because I had always thought anyone could march. I was ill-informed. We learned how to march in union of eight or twelve men, the direct march, the oblique march, and all the different steps. We learned to march by the flank, and principles of wheeling and change in direction. We learned long marches in double quick time, and the run, with arms and knapsacks, and on and on.

Whit looked confused much of the time as, I must say, did most of us. We didn't look much like soldiers, and we often felt foolish, but it slowly came to us thanks to the sergeant's persistent and rather vocal efforts.

They gave me an 1861 Springfield rifled musket, .58 caliber, probably captured from the Yankees. I told them I couldn't carry two muskets, so they said they would pay me ten Confederate dollars for my musket for the home guards to use. I might as well have given it to them. Ten Confederate dollars wouldn't buy you supper in Petersburg.

The rifle they gave me fired a large round, about the size of the last joint of a man's little finger. They called it a minie ball, named for some Frenchman. If the heavy lead round struck a bone it splintered, and the splinters tore up the muscle and flesh and the limb had to be amputated. It was not a pleasant fate. If the ball struck you in the chest or head, you would soon be saying hello to your Maker.

For two weeks we drilled and marched and practiced shooting, then we drilled some more. Sergeant Washburn said all this would be most useful when thousands of Yankees were charging your position. Most of the men could shoot, but none of us knew anything about military tactics and such. They told us we had to learn fast because the Yankees were threatening Richmond, where Lee's Army was entrenched along a line about thirty miles long from south of Petersburg to north of the capitol.

The day before we left for Petersburg, Whit and I learned that we would be joining the 18th North Carolina Volunteer Infantry Regiment in General A.P. Hill's corps, as replacements for those who had died or deserted. Sergeant Washburn reminded us that it was his old regiment—the very same regiment that he had told us had accidentally shot Stonewall Jackson in the dark at Chancellorsville. General Jackson had been riding back from the direction of the enemy with some others, including General A.P. Hill, and the North Carolina boys thought the riders were Yankee cavalry. Stonewall died a few days later from his wounds. It is said that the loss of 10,000 ordinary men would not equal the loss of Stonewall Jackson. He had been a brilliant field commander, defeating every enemy he encountered, often with odds against him of two or three to one. His name was spoken with fear and respect in the North, and with reverence and adoration in the South.

He was Lee's ablest lieutenant, and some said the best general on either side. And to think, boys from his own Army were responsible for his death. It goes to show, a battlefield can be a most confusing and heartbreaking place.

Turns out the 18th had lost its colors twice in battle. A regimental flag was a real point of honor and pride in the Confederate Army, and to lose one was almost disgraceful. But to lose two was just about too much to bear. It seemed to Whit and me that maybe we were joining up with a real hard-luck outfit, and it didn't exactly make us feel any better about things. The sergeant made it clear to us, though, that any regiment that had lost its colors in battle had clearly been in the thick of the fight. They weren't guarding the wagon trains, and they hadn't been quick to retreat.

As we walked back to our little camp for the last time before the march to Petersburg, Whit grumbled, "Well Francis, looks like you and me got ourselves into a real fine outfit. They cain't keep their battle flag, and they shoot their own generals. Do you think they know which end of a rifle is which?"

"Don't be so hard on 'em, Whit. War is rough business, which we're about to learn firsthand. I just hope that I can remember which end of a rifle is which when the time comes to use it, and the Yanks are coming at us in hordes, like the sergeant said."

Whit laughed loudly. "Well, Francis, just watch me! I'll show you how t'shoot blue-bellies, because I don't aim to be captured by no Yankee hordes. I heard the food in them prison camps is so bad the buzzards won't eat it!"

FOUR

The life of a Southern soldier
is such a life of ease;
the cold and the dark
are but a bad dream.

September 10, 1864 dawned a bit cooler than the past few days. Whit and I left Camp Vance early that morning with about seventy-five other men, to serve as replacements in various units in Petersburg. We rode in an old box car made for cattle. They herded us aboard and we sat shoulder to shoulder as the rocking train rolled toward the battlefields of Virginia. The undulating hills, woods and fields rolled by with what became a dull sameness. Decay and neglect were evident in the countryside as we passed, the steel wheels clacking rhythmically beneath us. Whit stayed close to me the whole time. He had come to look to me to take care of him. I don't know why, since I was just as scared and lonesome as he was.

During the afternoon of the 11th, it started to rain. The rain soaked us as it blew in through the slats in the car, and the wind that whipped us felt cold. It was a miserable ride toward a dreaded destination.

After riding all that day and most of the next, we got off somewhere in Virginia and marched the rest of the way to Petersburg. Sections of track in the area had been torn up by Federal cavalry, and the trains that were able to get through in Southern Virginia were needed for more important cargo I suppose. We stopped for the night about forty-five miles west of Petersburg at about seven o'clock. A light rain fell as we made camp.

I checked my Pa's pocket watch to be sure it was dry. He had left it to me when he went on to be with the Lord. He must have saved up his money for years to buy that watch. It came all the way from Switzerland and was made of silver with some fancy carving on it. He only got to use it two years before he passed on.

I remember that day well. It was a dark stain on the pages of my life. My Pa sat down in his rocking chair one night after supper, closed his eyes, and in a little while he was gone. We never knew why. He had been having some pains in his chest and arms, and some folks said it was neuralgia, but nobody really knew for sure. His passing hit me hard. I had to take care of that watch because it was what I had to remember him by. I kept it wrapped tight in a little oil cloth to keep it clean and dry.

When we stopped the officers decided on a place to camp, about a hundred yards from a sizable stream which was growing deeper by the hour because of all the rain. It had high banks, and our camp was on a rise, so we were not worried it would flood us out; though we kept an eye on it anyway. We were pitching camp when we heard a commotion over at the creek, so a couple of us walked over to see what was going on. There was a ford where an old road crossed the creek and three men were standing on the near bank yelling at someone down in the water. When we got closer I could see that there was a Negro man with an ox and a cart in the stream, and it seemed to be stuck. The stream was rising higher, and the Negro, who was almost up to his waist in water, first pulled on the ox and then pushed it. Then he slapped its flanks and yelled for all he was worth, but the old ox wouldn't pull out. We asked the white men about it, and they said the "sorry Nigger" could not get the ox and cart out of the creek and that the ox might drown if the creek got any higher.

Whit never knew when to keep quiet and he just sort of blurted out, "Well, why in the bloody hell don't you help him?"

"He's the nigger, he's 'spose to do such as this," the oldest man said.

"Well, he may be the one supposed to get the ox out," I said, "but he ain't but one man, and if you don't help him you'll lose the ox and the Negro."

The three men looked at me like I was crazy. The old man snarled, "Why don't you mind your own business!" and went back to yelling at the Negro. I suppose, being a farmer, I knew the value of a good ox and cart, and besides I couldn't stand to see a dumb animal drown because of dumber people not helping him out. I asked Whit to hold my watch and I went on into the creek to help the Negro man try to save the ox. We pulled and tugged and yelled at the old ox, then whipped it on the rump, but nothing worked. It just sort of thrashed and bellowed, churning the rushing water around us. The Negro man was so exhausted he fell and almost got swept away in the stream.

I yelled for Whit to help the man out of the water. I decided I would give one last try to get the ox out. Whit handed my watch off to a fellow name of Lester Carpenter, then came in and helped the Negro out of the stream. They sat on the bank, the Negro man panting and gasping for breath. Whit had to get between the white men and the Negro because they said they were going to lash him with a bullwhip. Whit jerked out his old Bowie knife, and told them that the first man to raise a hand was gonna lose it. I was becoming a mite concerned about then because the water was rising up almost to my waist. I could only hold my ground by bracing against the ox or the cart. I knew I was going to have to get out quick or drown. Most animals have tender ears, so I thought I knew how I might encourage the old ox to move on out. I grabbed hold of its left ear and bit down hard, actually biting out a little piece of the ear. The old ox bellowed like it was judgment day and rushed up out of that creek so fast it knocked me sideways into the water. It also knocked over the three white men who stood right in its path. Out it came, pulling the cart behind. I was swept downstream fifty or sixty feet, but managed to make it to the bank. By now most of the seventy-five men in our company were gathered on the bank watching, and they all roared with laughter and cheered for the ox.

Lieutenant Andrew Harrill and Sergeant Billy Vance came pushing their way to the front of the crowd, demanding to know what was going on. The three white men complained loudly about how we interfered with their business and stopped them from whipping their Negro, and that I had bit their ox. I was busy pulling myself out of the creek, with Whit helping me. Sergeant Vance started yelling about how he was going to have us in irons when Lieutenant Harrill stopped him and asked Whit and me what happened, since we were the ones sopping wet and muddy. I was out of breath so Whit told him everything. The lieutenant said no action was necessary, and told the white men that they owed us an apology and some thanks for saving their ox. The old one said, "That'll be a cold day in Hell," and they walked off with their Negro and their ox, grumbling all the way out of sight. The Negro man cautiously looked over his shoulder and flashed a big grin in our direction. I waved at him as they walked away.

Sergeant Vance looked at Whit and me like he had a thundercloud over his face. He barked, "Get over to a fire and get dried off! You'll catch your death and you'll be no good to the Army! Now move!"

The lieutenant chuckled all the way back to the camp and allowed as to how I should have a new nickname: "Ox." From then on to Petersburg, every time the lieutenant passed me he would say, "How you be, Ox!" and then would laugh heartily.

I am glad to report that the nickname did not stick. Back at the camp, still out of breath and dripping wet, I told Whit he did a good thing not letting the white men whip the slave, because no man should be whipped for trying his best. Whit said, "Whup the slave? I thought they was goin' to whup me!"

I looked at him, caught the wry grin on his face, and we both had a good long laugh, though I don't think Sergeant Vance ever did think it was funny.

We cooked up a little fatback and eggs for supper then soaked some hardtack in the grease for a dessert. It wasn't half bad, considering where we were and how we were living at the time.

The sergeant placed pickets at one hundred to two hundred yards out because of the possibility there was Yankee cavalry roaming about. The night was warm and the rain had stopped, so we put out the fire early. I strolled out from the camp a ways and lay down in a little clearing, and began to search the sky. The clouds had blown off, so the stars were bright pinpoints on the coal black canvas of night.

As I lay there looking up, I began to wonder if I would ever see my family again, or plow old Moses, or even see my farm again. I couldn't help it; my eyes began to grow moist. I love my wife and my children, and I knew how badly they needed me at home. I knew Harriet would try to plow the mule and keep things running, but she's a woman and was not built for that kind of work. My girls could not be of much help with the heavy work, though I was sure they would try.

I thought about the war, about why I was here, and the thoughts ran into a dead end. I lay there under the stars, looking up at God's heaven. It surely was beautiful in Virginia, a lot like home. I also thought about how good the weather was, good for working the fields, for cutting firewood for the winter, for just enjoying God's nature. A farmer always keeps a weather eye out. You have to work the fields when you can, because the times are many when the weather won't let you, when it's too wet to plow or too cold and the ground's hard. The house needs some work too. I needed to split some new shingles for the roof. Then I thought, *Lord, that roof's going to leak this winter just as sure as I'm laying here. What will Harriet do? She'll probably get a bunch of pots and buckets, and catch the water as best she can. She's like that, doesn't complain, and just does what needs to be done. Lord, I miss that woman, the light of my life.*

About the time I started thinking about Harriet, and was kind of losing myself in the thought, along came Whit with a dreadful hacking. He let go a stream of tobacco juice with well-practiced ease and said, "Better come on and get some shuteye, Francis. Long day tomorr', startin' before sunup."

"I'll be on in a bit," I said.

Of course that didn't satisfy Whit. He settled himself down on the ground beside me, and reclined with an exaggerated groan, following my gaze upward. Then he asked, "What you lookin' at, Francis?"

I replied without looking at him, "Just the sky."

He cocked his head and asked, "Why you lookin' at the sky? Worried about the weather? You don't have to plow tomorr'."

"I'm just lookin' and thinkin'."

He wrinkled his brow, "I know what you mean. I been thinkin' for some time about somethin'."

"What's that?" I asked, not really wanting to know the answer because Whit's mind is a garden of the trivial.

He said, "I was wonderin' why your maw and paw named you Francis. Ain't that a girl's name?"

I sighed and smiled to myself at the familiar question. "It is a girl's name if it's spelled with an 'e.' My name's spelled with an 'i.'"

He grunted. "You mean one little letter is the difference between yore name and a girl's?"

"That's right."

Then he asked with some agitation, "Well, why didn't they name you John, or Robert, or William or something that couldn't be confused with a girl?"

Again I smiled to myself and said, "My folks named me for the great general of the Revolution, Francis Marion. He was called the 'Swamp Fox' because he outfoxed the Brits and the Tories. He would attack them, and then fade into the swamps down in the South Carolina low country; he just disappeared in those dismal haunts like a ghost.

"My grandpa, James Yelton, fought in the Revolution. He was a diehard patriot. He lived to be ninety-three years old. My Pa was so proud of my Grandpa and his fightin' the Tories and the British in the Revolution, he wanted me to carry on a famous revolutionary hero's name. He was real impressed with the stories about the Swamp Fox, so he named me after him. That's how I came to have the name 'Francis.'"

Whit was silent for several minutes. Then he looked at me with this sort of amazed grin and said, "Well, I'll be the son of Red Coat!" He shook his head a couple of times and said, "I'll be, I'll be."

I think for once I answered one of Whit's questions without him having to follow up with fifty more. "I guess we better turn in," I said, and we headed back to camp where the other men were already sawing logs. But I lay there for a long time before I went to sleep, wondering about the future. *Will I make it home? Will I be crippled by a Yankee bullet? Will I see my family again?* It all rolled over and over in my head until I finally fell asleep.

FIVE

Loosed from their bonds
in a thousand southern corn fields
in grim and ragged array
these scarecrows looked dangerous.

The next morning we were up before dawn and started a fire to cook a bit of breakfast. Whit said he felt bad, like he was getting sick, so I cooked his breakfast for him and made sure he had plenty to eat. Whit's a strange one and has his peculiar ways, but you look after your friends, and at this point I considered him as such after these last few weeks. He seemed to feel a bit better after breakfast as we marched off toward Petersburg, shouldering our rifles and our bedrolls. They said we all needed to be alert because we were approaching the battlefield. I didn't relish the thought of shooting at Yankees, or being shot at, but I confess I was finally getting used to the thought.

The next day we left camp at 5:30 in the morning and arrived in Petersburg about eight o'clock that night. We had walked almost seventy-five miles through the Virginia countryside in three days and were very much sore of foot. Whit and I were directed to the 18th North Carolina Regiment, of General Lane's Brigade in General Wilcox's Division in General Hill's III Corps, Army of Northern Virginia. We were told it was important to remember all that. Seems now I can't forget it.

When we got to the camp, behind the entrenchments, our jaws dropped. I don't know what I expected, but it certainly wasn't what

I actually saw there. The men of the regiment, sitting around the "bombproofs" and in the trenches, were the skinniest, dirtiest men I ever saw in my life. Many were the color of dirt. Some sat back in holes dug into the trench walls to protect themselves from the shells that fell from time to time. Some lounged around the huts. Others stood posts along the earthworks that wound on and on, as far as the eye could see, north and south. Their clothes were mostly rags, and some had no shoes. They peered at us through haunted eyes, their cheeks hollow with hunger that seemed to go to the bone. Indeed, it looked like someone had pulled scarecrows out of every field in the south and put them here in Petersburg as though an army of crows had to be kept away from a sea of corn.

Whit leaned toward me, his eyes wide, and whispered, "Is this the Confederate Army?"

"I guess it is, and if this is what being a Confederate means, I expect that you and me are in for some hard times."

The fellows watched us as we came in. Whit and me had been accompanied by two other men, Lester Carpenter and Walter Gross, who were also assigned to the 18th. The veterans seemed to think we looked funny and there was a lot of jesting about the new crop of dirt farmers come to be soldiers. Some sneered at the conscripted and coerced newcomers, but there was plenty of good natured laughter and joshing about us. You could tell some of them had seen some hard fighting and hard living and needed to just keep their spirits up. One or two yelled out, "Keep yer head down, Billy's got ye in his sights." A few called out, "Hey mister, here's your mule!" I learned later it was a sort of joke based on an old farmer who lost a mule in a Confederate camp.

We got directions to regimental headquarters, and there we reported in and were sent to see Sergeant Caswell Hutchins. The sergeant was from Rutherford County, and I knew his family. They lived only a few miles from me. He was tall and angular, a huge man, maybe six four or five, with broad powerful shoulders. His hair was dark and he bore a full, thick mustache that mostly covered his mouth. The men called him Sergeant Cas and he didn't seem to mind.

He got us situated in a hut and told us about the duty routine. It was mostly spending time on watch and every third day on picket duty. Sometimes we drilled. The colonel liked to keep his men active because the army was reduced to just waiting for the

Yankees to attack. By this time in the war General Lee was not able to maneuver his army, because the Yankees had come in such numbers that he was forced back into these entrenchments around Petersburg to defend Richmond, the capital of the Confederacy. There really wasn't much he could do when he was outnumbered by three or four to one, short of supplies, and very much outgunned. Some called him the Gray Fox, and now the fox was cornered, and the hounds knew it.

The Southern politicians had counted on the North to give up the war, since so many Yankees had been killed or wounded; some said maybe three hundred thousand. And the war certainly was hard on the Yankees, but it was harder on the South. The Yankees had all the manufactories and shipyards and three or four times as many people, and Mr. Abraham Lincoln just would not give up. You had to admire him for that, whether you liked him, or agreed with him or not. Old Abe had the bit in his teeth, and he was holdin' on like grim death.

The Yankee papers said he wanted to preserve the Union. I never could argue with that idea. This is a great country, even if we were having a family quarrel.

Our problem was, the Yankees kept sending troops and guns, including huge artillery pieces and powerful mortars, a mile or so away. Like nothing the Confederate Army ever had, these were guns that would throw 120 pound shells right through the Confederate entrenchments and into the city beyond. They never seemed to run out of ammunition. The more I learned, the more amazed I was that the Yankees hadn't already won the war.

Then they told me about the character of General Lee and how he refused to give up. The men vowed that they would fight for him until hell froze over, and then fight on the ice.

In the course of evening discussions in our hut, I learned that General Lee was the son of a great revolutionary war hero named General "Lighthorse" Harry Lee, who was a trusted officer of General George Washington. Our General Lee had graduated at the top of his class at West Point, and had finished without any demerits. He was a hero in the Mexican War, and after South Carolina seceded he was offered the position of Commander-in-chief of the entire United States Army. Instead, he chose to fight with Virginia, since that was his home, and he could not raise his arm against it. He loved the United States of America, and had served it honorably and well, but to fight against his family and his home, he could not do.

He and the renowned Generals Stonewall Jackson, Jeb Stuart, James Longstreet, A.P. Hill, and others had won many victories over the Yankees. The Federals had replaced their top general of the Army of the Potomac, which was the main Union army Lee faced, five or six times. Seemed they couldn't best General Lee even with more troops, better equipment and heavier artillery. The newest general, Grant, had learned how to use his huge army to force the Confederates to maneuver backward toward Richmond. Lee had to move the army in order to cut off Grant's intended line of march, so Grant forced General Lee to entrench around Petersburg, to protect the vital supply lines to Richmond. And that was where it stood when Whit and I arrived in Petersburg, that sunny September day.

Camp routine was monotonous. The food was pitiful; we got about a pint of meal and two spoons of sugar every day. We made sloosh, a kind of soppy cornpone. Sometimes there was meat, usually spoiled bacon, and once in a while we got some cornfield peas or dried beans. And there was always hardtack.

There was a lot of sickness in the camps: typhus, measles, dysentery, and every other ailment known to mankind it seemed. We all dreaded getting sick, but the thing I learned to hate worse than anything was the lice. I had always taken pride in keeping myself clean as possible. I bathed more often than most, and my dear wife kept the few clothes I had as clean as any farmer in the county. When Whit and I settled into our hut, the lice found us. It made me feel dirtier and lower than a snake's belly. I hated the feeling of some little critter living on my skin. Whenever I could get lye soap, I scrubbed myself the very best I could. It was most distressing for anyone who was not used to living in filth. Lice were the scourge of the army, though that was only one among many. It was a hard life in Petersburg.

There were over 30 miles of entrenchments, manned by no more than 50,000 troops. The Yankees, it was said, had 100,000 around Petersburg alone. It was a wonder that they had not already overrun us. They had a huge supply port and depot on the James River at a place called City Point, just east of Petersburg. They brought in all the supplies an army could ever need: guns, ammunition, food, clothing, and other equipage. They had a hospital there. They even had a bakery which produced fresh bread every day for the troops. We would have walked five miles on our knees to get a loaf of fresh bread.

The Yankees had all the advantages, except that they were on our soil. Still, I don't know how General Lee held on. Some said Grant was just waiting to starve us out. From where I stood, it looked a lot like that just might happen.

We spent a lot of time watching the Yankees across the entrenchments. You had to keep your head down because there were sharpshooters, which we had as well; but mostly they left us alone, except for the shelling. Sometimes they came in volleys, sometimes just a single massive shell. You could hear them coming, screeching through the sky. Sometimes we heard the boom of the big guns that fired them. Out of the blue they came, ripping the air, hurtling in an arc over our entrenchments and into our camps and the city, rifled shells shrieking like hysterical birds. Death came quick if an artillery shell found you.

The day to day uncertainty wore on the nerves. Starvation and the ever present possibility of walking out of your hut and being blown to a thousand pieces kept your mind agitated and your body in distress. I often thought I would rather we just leave the entrenchments, march toward Grant's boys, and have at it. Win or lose, at least we would be doing something; not waiting to starve, or die of the typhus, or be blown apart by a random shell.

I have to say life in Petersburg was not all grimness, though. Sometimes things happened that were so funny or so strange, they made you forget that death lurked just around the corner. One day in late September, a bunch of us were watching a new detachment of Yankee troops set up camp no more than a mile away from our outermost fort. They had brand new uniforms, and were all spit and polish. Theophilus Pate had some binoculars and was watching them when he busted out laughing, threw his head back, and almost fell over backwards. It turns out he could see their latrine sinks from our position, and he said, "Look at what they're wiping theirselves with!"

We took turns peeping through the binoculars, and we could see that there was a big patch of poison ivy near the Yankees' new latrine. Maybe they had run out of paper, 'cause the men would grab up a handful of leaves as they went to the sinks. I reckon these Yankees were mostly city boys or maybe new immigrants, had never seen poison ivy, and they were using the leaves!

We all had a good laugh over that little episode. In fact we laughed so hard, men from the regiments on each side of us gathered around to learn what was going on. When they found out, half the Division was rolling around laughing. I'm sure the Yankees wondered what the Rebs were laughing so hard about. Quite a few of them found out within a day or so. In fact, for quite a few days after that, there were a lot of Yankee soldiers scratching themselves furiously about their private parts. Some of our pickets would call over to them and say, "Hey Yank, scratch where it itches!" or "How do you like that Rebel sanitary paper?" We felt pretty safe from attack from that bunch since we knew they couldn't scratch with one hand and fire with the other!

SIX

If I sing you a tune
in the star painted evening,
will you sing me one too,
when they lower my casket?

Our regiment was stationed at the army's right flank, guarding the Weldon railroad and the Boydton Plank Road from the Yankees. For the first several days we were in Petersburg, nothing much happened. I mentioned that we had got settled into a "hut," but it was mostly a hole in the ground with earth piled up and some logs thrown over the top, then covered with sticks and dirt and whatever else the fellows that built it could put together. They had pitched the roof just enough that the rain would run off. The hut had room for us because three men had died within the past month of illness.

It was hard to get good water, and getting a regular bath was out of the question. Whit and I bought a couple of used pots from a suttler, and carried water from a little stream so we could wash up when we got the chance.

Shaving was not so easy in the field, so I had let my beard grow. Whit said it made me look older. I liked it because as it filled out it kept my jaw from looking so long, a family trait.

The scarce food seemed to get worse each passing day. Any meat we got was green, and the meal was buggy. I never figured I needed to lose any weight since I always was on the lean side, but eating like this I knew I was going to be even leaner.

One morning in late September, about the 25th I believe it was, we were sent forward on picket duty. Whit and I were stationed close together. Whit seemed to think I was his keeper, and I guess I was in a way. We hadn't been out more than two hours, standing under some scrub pines watching the enemy, when we both got our first taste of fighting. Out of nowhere, all of a sudden we heard the boom of a cannon, and then another.

The fire seemed to be coming from about three quarters of a mile straight ahead, too close for comfort. Whit and I both ducked down, and three other fellows, veterans, started laughing so hard at our fright that I thought they had lost their minds. After all, here we were, just a few hundred feet from enemy pickets, with cannon just a little further and firing at us, and these fellows were laughing because Whit and I were a bit startled. It seemed they had seen so much fighting that a little cannon fire was of no great concern. I believe one of them had been with this outfit since it was formed in 1861.

The cannons fired several more times, and we could hear the shells passing overhead, a sort of ripping, humming noise. Sometimes they screamed like a woman in pain. Then, suddenly, the world came apart as one of the shells thundered down on the three men who had been laughing at Whit and me. The blast hurled them in all directions. The smoke and fire were still rolling when I heard them hitting the ground, screaming.

It was like somebody pulled the air of our lungs. Whit and I looked at each other for an instant, then we ran to the others. My heart pounded as I came upon the first fellow. Blood spurted like a fountain from a large hole in his chest. It looked like a big piece of the shell had gone right through him. I knew he was a goner and, as I bent over him, he looked at me with this sort of wild look. His mouth moved a time or two, but no sound came out. Then his eyes rolled back in his head, and he was gone.

Whit helped one fellow to his feet. He was mostly banged up, and had a few gashes from shell fragments, but it looked like he would live. The other fellow was still on the ground. I had seen him before, but hadn't really met him. This man, who had been acting like a seasoned war veteran, looked to be no more than eighteen, a skinny little fellow with a bony face and dark hair. His scant mustache made him look even younger.

His left leg was bleeding real bad, you could see bone poking out through a gash, and he was looking at it real scared with his eyes wide. I tore off a piece of my shirt and bound the wound up tight as I could. He seemed to be in a lot of pain, but he didn't pass out. It looked like he would be all right. He was a small fellow, no more than 110 pounds, so I picked him up over my shoulder, and we headed back towards the works with Whit helping the other fellow along. Another picket ran ahead for a surgeon, and we took the fellows to an ambulance which would take them to the field hospital.

The Yankees stopped the shelling as suddenly as it had started. The roar of the explosion still rang in my ears. The light carried a red tinge, and the air seemed alive around me. My hands shook.

When my ears stopped ringing, it was so quiet you could hear the wind in the pine trees. Whit and I were assigned to the detail to recover the dead man so they could bury him. We bore his bloodied body back to the works, and some fellows from a burial detail took him from there. I watched as they carried him away, the man who had found it so funny when Whit and I flinched when the shells flew over. I shook my head. The war—life itself—sometimes made no sense at all.

When it was all done, we went back out on picket for the rest of the day, until some fellows relieved us a little before dark. Whit was more silent than I had ever seen him. As we walked back, he said, very quietly, "Francis, I never saw anything like that in my life. Them fellers was a-laughin' and cuttin' up and all of a sudden one is dead, and the other two is bad hurt. I can't believe how sudden it was. What if that was you and me in that bunch that was cut up so?"

"Well, it might be some day, Whit. Only the Lord knows that. I figure all we can do is keep our eyes open and watch out for each other best we can. If it's God's time for us to go, then we'll just have to go."

"Francis, you promise me you'll watch out for me; let me know if you see somethin' comin'."

I yanked his hat down over his eyes. "I'll watch out for you the best I can, old Whit Whitaker from Hogback Mountain!" Whit rasped out another laugh. I just hoped that I could look out for the old boy, I had begun to get used to having him around.

"How 'bout a chaw, Francis?" He handed me the pouch.

"Don't mind if I do. It's been a right busy day."

When we got back to the hut we had some watery stew.

Afterwards we walked outside for a while, just looking at the sky. The night started out clear, but storm clouds rolled in from the west. We sat and listened to the distant thunder. "That's louder than the Yankee cannons!" Whit exclaimed. The sky lit up as the lightning streaked across the blackness. "The pickets is gonna git wet tonight, Francis."

"Well, I reckon most of 'em's been wet plenty of times before," I said.

The night seemed to be alive with electricity from the lightning. The points of the *chevaux-de-frise* forward of the entrenchments began to glow with St. Elmo's fire, a cold blue light that turned the rain-spattered sod an odd sort of gray. Then it began to come down in buckets. It poured, and the thunder boomed until the ground shook. I imagined an army of angels with gigantic drums marching across the Virginia hills. It seemed to me like the wrath of God was pouring out on His sinful children, Rebels and Yankees alike, for fighting and killing each other so.

"Lord, I never seen no such!" gasped Whit as we hurried back to the hut. The thunder grumbled and growled. Lightning snapped, hitting a house off to the west and setting it afire. It gave off what seemed to me an evil glow as the storm screamed on through the night, as if God had turned the Devil loose in the world. When we got to the hut, the men were all wide-eyed. One of them said, "Sounds like the end of the world."

We ducked in, shaking the water off. The other fellows had a little fire going in the fireplace. The evening was cool so the fire felt good, especially since Whit and I were both soaked.

The other men—Joe Martin, Armistead Moss, and Willie Sturgis—were all decent fellows. They welcomed Whit and me as messmates like we were all long lost brothers, something newcomers did not normally expect.

Joe Martin was a mountain man from up past Asheville. Well over six feet, he was powerfully built, but very gentle unless provoked. He had flaxen hair and a square jaw, and was about thirty-five years old. He had been with the regiment for over two years and had seen more fighting than the rest. He was a formidable man who looked like he could take on half the Yankee army all by himself. After I got to know him, he began to talk about his family. He had two children like me and he was a farmer, so we talked about children and farming, and about how much we missed our families.

Armistead Moss—who we called "Army"—was from down in Eastern North Carolina, where his Pa had made a lot of money in the tar and pitch business. He was about twenty-five, and had been in the unit for a little over two years. He was medium-sized fellow, and always concerned about his appearance. He kept a neat mustache and chin whiskers, and his brown hair was carefully combed. He always seemed to have on relatively clean clothes. He was also one of the few of us who wore anything that resembled a uniform. Some of his family sent him one, butternut in color. He was real proud of it; said it took him almost two years with this army before he got a uniform, and then he had to furnish it himself.

Army was ruddy, like he had grown up outdoors; but he never did get any darker, just redder. They said he was as brave as any in battle, but you wouldn't know it to look at him. With his Pa's money and influence he could have been an officer, but he chose to serve as a private soldier. He simply said he was no better than anyone else, and he was proud to serve as a plain infantryman. He said the Lord commanded us to be humble, and that was far more important than rank. An exceptional man he was.

Willie Sturgis was from McDowell, a county that bordered Rutherford. When he and Whit got together and started some foolishness, everybody was in stitches. Willie was about average height, a little stockier than most, with a bushy brown head of hair and a droopy mustache which he was fond of combing. He craved a chaw about as much as Whit, and between the two of them I think they used up half the tobacco crop in North Carolina.

Willie was apt to play a joke on Whit, and then Whit would get mad and they would start tussling. But before you knew it, both of them would be laughing so hard, they couldn't do anything but roll on the ground. They were like brothers, and we were glad to have them. Their antics helped lift our spirits many a time.

As for me, I never was that fond of chewing tobacco, so I took to smoking a pipe in the evenings—when we could get tobacco. I bought the pipe at a sutler's for four Confederate dollars. It was a good pipe, made of ash wood, polished real well. I enjoyed every minute of my smoke, as it was one of the few things that made a fellow feel halfway normal. In the evenings, when we were free from duty, I would light up the pipe, lean back against the wall of the hut, and listen to Whit or Willie tell some outlandish tale, or Joe talk about the crops he was going to put in when he got back home, or Army tell us about a "gallant" charge the old 18th had made and how they ran the Yankees clear into the Potomac river. In a very short time it came to be a close group. I guess that's because all we had was each other, and looking out for each other was important in this troubled time. We were better men for it.

SEVEN

I look at the enemy
in the long bristling trenches
with cannon and flags
and see myself, looking back.

One morning in late September, we got up as usual, and began to scrounge around for some breakfast. We went down to the cook tent, but all they had was some green bacon and hardtack. We choked it down with some watery coffee, and then we all assembled to get assignments for the day, if there were to be any. Turns out we were free for the day, no picket duty and no drill, which was unusual because the colonel believed in maintaining discipline in the ranks. But today we were free men for a while.

Whit and I walked down the line a ways, and then took a road that led away from the trenches, in the direction of the city of Petersburg. As we walked, I noticed that the countryside had taken on a picked-over kind of look. Trees were few, and stumps stretched in all directions almost as far as we could see. Wagons rolled by with supplies. A patchwork company headed for the front marched by us. None of them had uniforms; most likely a company of conscripts.

We stopped once in a while to exchange some camp talk with men from other units. We had not gone more than a half a mile when we came across a burial detail laying some men out in caskets. It was an all too common sight, because of the sickness and the Yankee shells falling all around. Wagons filled with the dead lined the road for a hundred yards. Carpenters nailed together crude pine caskets for each of them, and then they were carried off to the cemetery. Whit and I stood transfixed at this factory of death, this disposal system for the ever constant flow of deceased.

Two men were straining to put a rather large body into a casket. The dead man was a tall, lean fellow of about twenty-five. He had very red hair and a long red beard. In life he would have been an imposing man indeed. As we stood and watched, they struggled to get the body into the pine box. The corpse was stiffened in death, and would not fit into the standard sized casket, so the larger worker stepped up on top of the body and started stomping on it. I thought I heard bones in the dead man's legs break. I saw something like a flash, and before I realized what I was doing, I was at a dead run straight at the fellow.

Whit scrambled behind me, yelling, "Francis, don't ye do it, you'll git in trouble! Stop, Francis, fer God's sake!" But Whit couldn't catch me. I dove over the casket and caught the man in the middle, and the two of us crashed to the ground. We both lurched to our feet and I punched him. I was yelling at the man, though I don't remember what I yelled. I threw a hard left into his stomach and then a jolting blow to his chin. I was never much for fighting, but a man who works a farm on a daily basis builds up a deal of strength, believe you me. The big man staggered from the blows, but he was several inches taller and forty pounds heavier than me, and when he got his wits his left fist connected with my jaw. Then he knocked me off my feet with a big right hand to the left side of my head. He jumped on me as I lay sprawled on the ground, and jabbed at my face.

But in my fury I was much stronger than normal, and I threw the big fellow off. I scrambled to where he lay and was about to have at him again. Several men grabbed each of us and held us apart. The other fellow was spewing profanity, which I will not repeat. Suffice it to say he called me the son and close relative of all kinds of animals, and a low-life dirt farmer to boot.

I shouted back that if I saw him stomp on another dead soldier they'd be putting him in one of his caskets. Sergeant Hutchins arrived out of nowhere, and when everything had settled a bit, he asked me what happened. He was always calm and steady, and did not let the little fuss bother him too much. When I explained why I was upset, he walked over to the big man who had stomped the dead body, and asked him what happened. He admitted what he was doing. Sergeant Hutchins's expression took on the look of a thunderstorm. The sergeant put his face about two inches from that of the big man. "If I ever see you do this again, I will personally kill you. Do you understand?" The other man stood in silence and looked at his feet.

Cas told Whit and me to go back to our hut, and to stay away from that bunch. As we walked away Whit said, "Francis, you got to be the luckiest man on earth. That fellow could have killed you, or you could have been put in the stockade!"

"Well, Whit, he didn't kill me, and Cas knew what he was doing wasn't right. But you're right; I need to learn to control my temper."

Whit burst out laughing, spat a big stream and said, "Francis, the day you control yore temper will be the day pigs fly!" Whit continued to chuckle at his own joke, but I just shook my head and kept thinking, *How could a man do that to another man, especially a fellow southern soldier?* All I know for sure is that war is an evil business, and when all is said and done, there's really no glory in it. None.

EIGHT

Don't carry me back to ol' Virginny,
I've seen its cold light,
and the slaughterhouse red
of its battle scarred hills.

Two days after what came to be known in our hut as the "casket incident," as we walked out to picket duty in the evening, Whit and I ran into the fellow that had been doing the stomping. He glared at me, but didn't say a thing. I noticed he had a big bruise on his forehead, a swollen black eye, and a few cuts around his mouth. As he went by, Whit blurted out, "Francis, you shore rearranged that feller's face for him!" Then he proceeded to haw-haw so loud I'm sure the Yankees a mile away wondered what was so funny.

I suppose the fellow didn't appreciate being laughed at, for he turned around and came back toward us, walking fast. He grabbed Whit by the shoulder and spun him around. His face was red, and he looked ready to light into Whit. Instead he just stood there a minute and sputtered, then finally said, "What's so funny, farm boy?"

At that, Whit, who had been standing there wide-eyed with his mouth open, repeated, "Farm boy?" He began to laugh again, this time even harder. I stood there thinking, *This man's gonna kill Whit sure as sunrise.*

I held up my hands toward the man, and scowled at Whit. "Mister, we don't want any more trouble. I don't figure any of us needs any more than he's already got." Whit was beginning to control himself a little. The man was still shaking with anger, his mouth a thin taut line, but he backed up a step. I glared at Whit again and said, "My friend tends to get amused real easy, and sometimes when there's no call to. There's no need to get offended."

The man snarled at Whit, "You best keep your chucklin' to yourself or I'll give you a thrashin' you won't fergit." He eased up a bit, then turned and walked away. I reckon he did not want another tussle, and maybe he thought about big Sergeant Hutchins, and decided not to push things.

Whit and I continued on to our posts, with Whit still snickering under his breath. I jabbed him in the side. "Whit, if you want to start a fight, we got the whole Yankee army about a mile that way. Maybe you best save it for them."

"I guess so, Francis. But you gotta admit that feller's face looked like he'd been buttin' heads with a bull." Whit laughed again.

"Well, Whit, I don't want to fight him again. Next time I might end up looking like him." That sent Whit into another fit of laughter. I shook my head, not even sure why Whit found that funny. "Whit, so help me I think there's no hope for you."

As it turns out, about three days later the man I had tangled with was killed by a Yankee shell. He disappeared in the massive blast. Whit allowed that at least no one would have to stomp his sorry carcass into a casket. I upbraided Whit for the comment. I did not feel good about anyone dying that way, with nothing left for a Christian burial.

Meanwhile, the weather had begun to turn much cooler during the evenings, though firewood was getting harder to come by. We had to walk further to find any wood to cut, further west behind the entrenchments. The night that Whit antagonized the casket man, we had started up our little fire in our hut. The whole crew was there: Joe, Army, Willie, Whit and me. Joe had some beef jerky, and he passed each of us a piece. It was tough as shoe leather, but it was still good to chew on it, especially since none of us had any tobacco for a smoke. Whit joked about smoking rabbit tobacco, and Army allowed as how he would rather smoke dried cow patties.

Willie hadn't picked on Whit for at least two days, so you knew something was coming when he turned to Whit and casually said, "Whit, ol' feller, I understand you was about to finish what Francis started with the casket man today."

Whit said in a joking tone, "Yeah, I was about to give that feller what fer afore Francis stopped me. Lucky for that feller that Francis was there to save his bacon."

Willie looked real comical and disgusted at the same time, and said, "Well, Whit, I heered it was yore bacon what got saved!"

Whit looked sideways at Willie and said, "Well, I guess I'll just have to take it out on you!" Before you knew it, Whit grabbed Willie and they were rolling around on the floor of the hut, bumping into first this one then that. I reckon Army had had enough, and he grabbed a little piece of burning wood from the fire and stuck it up under Willie, who was on the bottom at the moment. Willie hollered like the judgment and threw Whit straight up, causing him to bump his head on the low roof. Willie went scrambling outside to find some water to put on his burning backside, although it was only a small piece of fire and it barely singed him.

Whit sat there rubbing his head and said, "I never knew Willie was that stout!"

Army was laughing so hard he couldn't talk. Joe said, in his solemn way, "You fellers ought to save some of that for the Yankees. I heard we might be seein' some action soon."

Our smiles faded and everyone turned serious. "What have you heard?" I asked.

"Well, rumor has it that the Yankees is already tryin' to move around us, extend their lines," Joe said. "And as ya'll know, we're on the right flank and if they move, Lee's gonna move us. He don't have no choice. Otherwise, they get around our flank, cut off the railroads, and the game is up."

Willie came back in, rubbing his backside. He looked like he was about to say something to Army for putting the burning stick under him, but he saw our faces and, still bent over from ducking in the door, stopped dead in his tracks. He looked around and asked, "What's happened?" Joe told him and he looked from one to the other.

Whit broke the mood when he said, "Willie, if you can throw the Yankees around like you throw'd me, we'll whup 'em shore!" The hut once again rang with laughter, but we knew that if Joe was right, some of us might not make it back to the hut tomorrow.

I walked outside to get some fresh air, and turned my gaze to the sky. The stars were out, and gave enough light to walk. There were dark shapes moving around the trenches here and there, but mostly it was quiet; the men were settling in.

A pair of fellows I didn't recognize came up to me from the north. "Howdy-do," said the smaller of the two, "We're from the 45th Georgia over thattaway and we hear tell thar's a purty good sutler's store hereabouts. Can you tell us where it is?"

I answered, "Yes, sir, I can. Go down this little road here about two hundred paces, you'll see it around the bend on the left."

"Much obliged," said the taller one. "My name's John Spillers." When he held out his hand I saw the sergeant's stripes on his sleeve.

"Francis Yelton, 18th, North Carolina."

"Pleased to meet you, Francis. This here's Sam Lanier. You been in the army long, Francis?"

"No, sir, I enlisted in August. Been in Petersburg since early September."

It seemed like the sergeant wanted to talk a bit, so I asked the same question of him. "Long enough," he said, "to get this." He pointed to a spot in his jaw where it was sunk in. "Yankee minie ball went plumb through; broke my jaw, knocked out a bunch of teeth." He talked a little like he had a chaw in, but when he held a match up to light his pipe I could see the wound better. His face below his eyes was all scars and sunken flesh. I was amazed the man was alive. "We're sharpshooters with the 45th; we've seen quite a bit of action. We hear tell they's gonna be some more."

"I heard the same thing, Sergeant, sir."

"John, call me John. Your North Carolina boys have sure done your share of the fightin' and the dyin'. I suppose we Georgia boys have as well. It always seemed to me that it made us kin of a sort. Listen, Francis, you're new and all, but you look like a stout feller. Keep your head about you and you'll be all right. We better get on down and see if'n the sutler has any coffee or tobacco, before it gets any later. Might be an early mornin' tomorr'."

I nodded. "Good night, John, Sam." Then they were gone.

The Georgia boys were tough veterans. You could see it in their faces. I tried to imagine the battles they'd fought and how many men they may have killed, but I realized it was useless. Unless you've been in a soldier's shoes, you can't know; you can't even imagine.

NINE

Now in the gloomy shadows
before the sunlight falls
we step to the beat of the drummer
the reaper waiting in darkness.

At about 4:00 AM the next morning the orderly came by yelling, "Fall in!" We grabbed our gear and piled out of the hut. We were told to cook three days' rations, and assemble for the march. The sergeant said we'd better bring anything we wanted to keep. We didn't know it at the time, but it would be the last we ever saw the hut. An hour later we stood in ranks in the cool damp air waiting for orders. I felt a little weak, and my stomach rolled as I stood with my rifle on my shoulder. At that time the regiment only numbered about 300 men, one third its original strength.

Company H could only muster about 50 men. They called us "The Columbus Guards" since the unit was originally formed in Columbus County. I sort of liked that, taking the name of the man who discovered America. I sometimes thought that if the Lord blessed me with a son, I could name him Columbus. Sometimes the irony of the name struck me, though. We were named for the man who discovered America, but we were fighting with other Americans. It was one of the absurd things about this war—one of many.

Our regimental commander, Colonel Robert H. Cowan, walked smartly out in front of the regiment and spoke loudly enough for everyone to hear. "Men, we're moving out. Be sure you've got your gear and see that you have ammunition and three days' rations. We may be in the field for a while, and we may see some action soon. I know I can count on you men as I always have." With that, the company commanders passed the order to march and we were on our way.

As we moved out it appeared that the whole division was on the march, maybe other divisions as well. You could feel the mass of men moving out. Whatever this was, it was important. Of course the men didn't actually know what was going on, they hardly ever did until they were in line firing at the Yankees. I tried not to think about it. I hadn't seen much action, other than cannon fire and once in a while shooting at Yankee pickets if they moved too close. This looked like the real thing, like we were moving to the attack.

Whit was right behind me, and of course he wanted to talk. I didn't feel like talking, but Whit rattled on anyhow. His voice became like a "tinkling cymbal," and seemed far away. I looked around as we marched, my head in some sort of fog. The whole thing became a sort of dream to me. Camp fires flared here and there to our left, toward the entrenchments; they kept them burning between us and the enemy to disguise our movement. You could see shadows moving around, thousands of men marching south. It looked like an army of ghosts, or of ragged skeletons which had been raised from the depths the earth, streaming grimly down the road, tattered clothes blowing in the cold breeze.

The fierce firelight from scores of campfires cast weird shadows and glows among the gaunt spirits as they moved. An army from hell, grim demons bent on killing, backed into a corner and dangerous. The wind picked up and carried a warning chill; it moaned just a bit, like something in pain. I shook my head, and tried to clear the fog that seemed to hang over me. These weren't spirits or demons; they were flesh and blood, and many would fly to paradise or sink into hell this very day. I thought I might be one of them, one of the ones whose family might never know what happened to him. I also thought that this army looked tired, all used up and worn out, weary to the bone, and more desperate than anyone could imagine.

The grim-faced troops continued their march southward in the early morning darkness. We walked for about an hour and a half until daylight came and transformed the collection of demons into just a ragged group of men who had seen too much death, and had been in a far country too long. The rising sun made the world seemed more real, but I wasn't so sure that reality was any better.

A sharp pain stabbed at my stomach, drawing me almost double. Whit called out from behind me, "What's the matter, Francis?"

"I'm fine. I guess this army food's not settin' too well on my stomach." The meat we had been eating was mostly spoiled, but we ate it anyway because it was all we had. The quartermaster said all it would do was give you the old soldier's disease. I can testify that it often did that and much more. It seemed we spent half our time at the sinks. But when a man is starving, green meat is better than no meat. I took a swig of water from a beat up old canteen. Whit gave me a slap on the back and told me I was too tough to get sick. Somehow I didn't feel too tough today.

After a few more hours of marching the colonel yelled to his officers, "Tell the men to fall out and form for battle!" I couldn't see any Yankees, but we readied ourselves and checked our rifles. The regiment was faced to the left. Whit and I were assigned to be skirmishers, along with Army and Joe. Willie was lined up among the files, with the bulk of the regiment. As we began to advance across a rolling wheat field, we could see bluecoats along a tree line no more than three hundred yards away; thousands of men, at least a division. The regimental battle flag was raised, and Colonel Cowan led the men toward the Yankees, in step with the other regiments in our brigade. Two more brigades joined us, and soon several thousand men were on the march toward the Yankees who were forming up just inside the tree line.

They seemed surprised at first, but recovered very quickly, and began firing as soon as we were within range. There was the ragged tearing sound of hundreds of muskets in the stirring air. The first volley tore through dozens of our soldiers. I could hear minie balls humming past my head like a swarm of angry bees, felt the ripples in the air as they passed my face. The tail of my jacket jerked as a round passed through it. Being under fire like that can make a man want to crawl in a hole, but we moved forward, stopped and fired, re-loaded, and moved forward again.

The air was humming, buzzing. I began to wonder if it was the minie balls, or if it was in my head.

Men fell like wheat before a scythe. The field was covered with the smoke from black powder. There were vivid colors, too: the red, white and blue of the battle flag, the blue of the sky, the white of the smoke, the red of the blood.

Colonel Cowan screamed at the top of his lungs, "Follow me, boys!" He drew his saber, and he and the battle flag moved forward at the double-quick. I fixed my eyes on the regimental colors. They drew me along toward the enemy.

We took up the Rebel yell, thousands of men shrieking like the hounds of hell. It was a sound that struck fear into the enemy, that caused many a Yankee to turn and run like he was being chased by the devil himself. The sound grew above the roar of the rifles, like a rushing gale. I wondered if the angels could make a sound like that, or maybe the demons.

The Yankees reloaded and fired as fast as they could. We were close enough to the Federals now that I could see the expressions on some of their faces. I saw fear in some eyes, fury in others. The same emotions could be found in the eyes of my comrades. Men fell by the score. Lives wasted or ruined in a painful instant, impassive lead shattering God's precious creations like the fist of Satan.

Whit shouted to no one in particular, "Give it to 'em, boys!" As we stopped to fire, the rest of the regiment closed up on us. A man beside me was hit badly in the head, and his blood splattered my face. Someone fired over my shoulder; the musket's roar rung in my ear. The world seemed to spin around and I thought I was going to fall. I don't know how many times I re-loaded and fired, moved forward, stopped, re-loaded and fired.

The taste of gunpowder was sharp in my mouth as I bit open the cartridges. Rammed home the powder and the ball. Flipped off the old cap, stuck another one on. The routine was fixed in my mind, each of the nine steps to load the rifle. I did it just like the old sergeant taught us back in Morganton. "Load in nine times." Load, raise the rifle, full cock, and fire. I sighted the Yankee color bearer, hesitated, then fired. The round struck his right shoulder and he pirouetted to the ground. A man beside him dropped his rifle and picked up the colors. An instant later he fell with a wound in the leg. The Yankees began to break backward. It was a stumbling, fumbling sort of retreat. They looked uncertain, like they did not want to leave but surely did not want to stay.

We grimly advanced, our ranks thinner than before. Sergeant Hutchins roared, "Close it up! Close it up!" The screaming was incessant. Men with painful wounds rolled about on the ground, writhing in agony, their faces masks of pain and terror. I heard men call for their mothers. I heard men pray, begging God to let them live or let them die. I tried to understand what they were saying, even as I loaded my rifle with shaking hands.

I moved forward again, stumbled over something, and pitched forward to the ground. As I started to get up I was looking straight into the face—or what was left of the face—of a dead Yankee. About a third of his head was gone. His mouth formed the letter "O." I thought he seemed surprised, like maybe he thought he wasn't supposed to die, but all of a sudden God told him today was his day. His brain was exposed and the top of his uniform was more red than blue. I thought, *He can't be more than eighteen, just a boy.*

Someone tried to help me up, but I jumped to my feet and moved forward, stopped again with the rest of the line, and fired.

Off on our left flank, artillery roared. Gouts of fire, dirt, and smoke erupted from the ground around us. Men were flung in all directions. There was an explosion about twenty feet to my front. Something struck my chest hard and staggered me backward. It fell to the ground in front of me—the severed head of a soldier named Walter Gross. His face bore a look of dull surprise. My stomach knotted, and I gagged painfully. My knees seemed to buckle for a moment. I took a breath, shook my head, and looked away. With my left hand I absently rubbed at my chest.

The barrel of my rifle was getting too hot to touch, and I was afraid the powder would flash in my face as I loaded. Whit came up beside me, raised his rifle, fired, and said almost casually, "Well, Francis, I guess we done seen what a real battle is." I looked at him vacantly, and nodded.

Then the movement of the men around us slowed, and the din of the battle changed. The moaning in the wind ebbed and flowed like an ocean current. The buzzing, ripping, clanking, and roaring filled my senses. The yells and the screams all mingled into one ghastly reverberation, a clamor across the Lake of Fire; Hell itself come to Earth.

The trees were only maybe fifty feet away by then, but suddenly the men were no longer moving forward. We were all just milling around, confused, for a time. I staggered and looked around, wondering what was next.

Some of us started to think we might have even taken the day, when what looked to me like a Yankee corps of maybe 15,000 men appeared on our left flank, a quarter of a mile away. They began to advance on us, giving out their own yell, a low pitched "Hurrah!" The Yankees we had been pursing had stopped their retreat, and began to reform their lines.

A messenger from General Lane, our brigade commander, rode up at full speed, his poor horse lathered and winded. I heard him tell Colonel Cowan to retreat; we were in danger of being flanked and overrun. It was clear to anyone but a blind man that we were outnumbered on the field by five or six to one, and retreat was the only thing to do.

Not one man ran, though; no one dropped his rifle, except the dead and the wounded. We pulled back about a mile and a half into some woods at the edge of a farm; I believe it was called the Jones Farm. We began to pile up logs and rocks, whatever we could find, for breastworks. The Yankees halted some distance away, and did not pursue us any further. They brought forward their artillery and began a desultory fire, but that shortly subsided. We could see large numbers of Federals on the move. We knew we hadn't stopped them, only slowed them up a little. They kept getting stronger, and we kept getting weaker.

I was out of breath and my head kept swimming, even as I tried to help pile up logs and fence posts. I was feeling very sick, and vomited a number of times. I stumbled and fell once and Whit told me to sit down, but I knew the regiment couldn't spare a man.

We carried the wounded to makeshift hospitals at our rear. A litter carrying a badly wounded fellow passed by. It was our friend Army, his left arm drenched with blood and his face pale. He was unconscious. He looked like he was already dead, but they told us he was still alive, and that they would try to save him. I remembered having seen him well out front, yelling and firing for all he was worth, his face an expression of grim calmness. He seemed to have had no fear, to have gloried in the battle. I don't think I ever knew a braver man, and I knew without any doubt that he was going to die.

They told us later that he passed on while they were amputating his arm. He bled to death. I got on my knees that night and prayed for his family, and I thanked the Lord for allowing me to know a good and brave man like Army. A passage from the Good Book came to my mind: "No greater love hath any man than this that he lay down his life for his friends." I think Army died the way he would have preferred, with his face to the enemy, fighting alongside his friends.

The fall breeze that night seemed cool to me, even cold. The air had a rank, bitter smell; the mix of black powder smoke, blood, vomit, and sour sweat. Camp fires flared fitfully. Men moved in the darkness, talking softly. Each of them was alone with his own private sorrow: a friend cut down, a painful wound, the biting pain of hunger. The stars were out, so I looked up for a long time. It was too painful to look anywhere else.

That night the stomach pains kept me awake, and I vomited several more times. Then the dry heaves took over. Whit got me some corn bread. I don't know where he found it, but when I ate it I felt a little better, though my head kept spinning all night.

Sergeant Hutchins told me the next day that he was going to write Army's family and tell them that Army died a valiant death. I hope it was of some small comfort to them, but he was gone just the same. I could picture his young wife opening a letter from a stranger, reading the words and sinking to her knees in anguish; her little ones watching her, wondering what was wrong. Then her having to tell them that their Pa would not be coming home, facing a cruel, hard world without her husband. Once again, I got so choked up I could not speak. I imagined my Harriet getting the same letter. *Best not dwell on that too long, Francis.*

A lot of brave men died that day—on both sides. But the Confederates had more reason to dread battle. Always outnumbered, and always outgunned. A war of attrition favors the side with the greater numbers. It is but a mathematical formula; the odds grow longer as both sides are reduced in similar numbers. Even if the side with more numbers loses in greater proportion, the odds may still favor them. And the North could replace its losses; the South could not. I saw enough of the Union troops to know that they were well equipped and well clothed. I didn't see any of them barefoot, like many of our men were. Barefoot Rebels marched and fought right alongside the rest, although I don't know how. At least my old brogans held up fairly well, and I thanked the Lord for that. Our scarecrow rags did look pitiful, though, beside the blue wool blouses worn by the Yankees. I wonder if our grandchildren and great-grandchildren will realize what sort of men these Southern soldiers were and what they endured for the love of their country.

The day after the battle we tried to keep ourselves as busy as we could, and tried not to think about the dead and the wounded. Poor Willie had got shot in the knee. The round almost tore his whole leg off, shattering the bones, and they had to amputate it. The sergeant gave Whit, Joe, and me permission to visit the field hospital for a few minutes to see him. The surgeons had set up in a barn and were amputating arms and legs left and right.

At the side of the barn we saw something strange, some sort of pile, like bloody wood. As we got closer we realized it was a pile of arms and legs, about five feet high and eight feet around. It did not look real. The blood drained from our faces. We gave it a wide berth.

The surgeons didn't have anything to kill the pain except a little corn whiskey, so the screaming was bad as you can imagine—or maybe worse. I have been in a slaughterhouse, and the blood and screams of the pigs were not much different than those of the men in this so-called hospital. The bone saws made a singing sound as the surgeons efficiently performed their grim but needful work. The faces of the injured soldiers were twisted in pain, pale, and scared.

We found Willie lying on a blanket to the side, and he seemed to be in reasonably good spirits. He flashed his crooked smile when he saw us, which was all the more odd because his mouth was still black from biting open powder cartridges. He said weakly he guessed he was finished as a soldier. Whit cackled and replied, "I don't figure you'll be dancin' too many airs neither!" We started to laugh, but then we glanced at the den of misery around us.

"I reckon not," Willie said.

Whit asked, "Does it hurt much?"

"What do you think?"

"Looks like it would hurt a mite," Whit said.

"If'n it had been yore leg, Whit, you'd be passed out cold right now!" Willie said. Whit smiled at his friend.

Willie got to go home after that. We never heard from him again. That's the way it was. You made friends, some got killed, and some got wounded and went home. Some just walked away. The war wounded a man's spirit in more ways than one.

We went on back to our place at the breastworks, and got back at it. As we swung our axes and piled the logs, I prayed for Army's family and for Willie. Willie was going home to the mountains, and would plant a flower garden for his young bride. Army had gone home to be with the Lord. That was a lot to take in when just a few hours before we had all been laughing, and Willie had been tussling with Whit in our little hut a few miles north.

The Yanks stayed away that night, but we knew they were

shifting to the right, moving around us, threatening the Weldon railroad that brought supplies from North Carolina to Petersburg and Richmond. If they cut off the railroad, things would get quite a bit rougher.

TEN

I saw a ghost on watch last night,
the kind that don't speak
just standing, looking
wondering if you're afraid.

From October on through the winter, we skirmished some with the Yankees, but mostly we settled in to our new quarters on the Jones Farm. We cut down trees and built huts and lean-tos. We dug deep into the Virginia soil and threw up breastworks that stretched for miles, six or eight feet high. We worked on the enemy side of the entrenchments, so as we dug out the dirt for the ramparts, at the same time we were creating deep trenches in front of the works. One more barrier to keep the Yankees from breaching our fortifications.

We constructed gabion revetments, big wooden baskets of dirt to hold the earthen ramparts in place and protect us from enemy fire. Before long we had entrenchments as good as the ones we had left, maybe better. In addition to all the rifle positions, there were gun emplacements in *redans* for artillery spaced about every one hundred yards, and traverses which ran perpendicular to the breastworks so we could get there under fire without being exposed from the flanks. It turned into quite an engineering project. The officers and the men knew how important the fortifications were, because we all knew we were trying to defend against far superior forces.

Camp routine was dull and monotonous. We had little to occupy our time off duty, so I always looked forward to our Sunday services. There were a number of good preachers who "rightly divided the word of truth" to saint and sinner alike. I hung on the words from the pulpit for hope and for inspiration to get me through this time away from everything I held dear.

As the fall turned into winter, there were more and more desertions. One evening, while we were on picket, Whit told me quietly that some of the boys were trying to get him to leave with them. They said they had some outlier friends in the high mountains, near Asheville, where they could stay until the war was over. They figured the North was going to win, so when the war was over, there would be no punishment for deserting. I asked Whit if he planned to go. He just grinned and said, "Now, Francis, I cain't go and leave you here. Somebody has got to watch yore back." I smiled and shook my head. Whatever else Whit was, he was a loyal friend.

I have to admit, the temptation was strong. I had received a letter from Harriet two nights before, telling me how she was afraid sometimes that something was going to happen to the girls and her, because there was very little law, with deserters and outlaws roaming the countryside. My stomach turned over when I read her words. She said she had faith that the Good Lord would look after them, and she wanted me to do my duty. She said they would be all right. I was much more afraid for her and the girls than I ever was for myself. It was a strong pull, families hurting; with dismal conditions here and weather getting colder and more unbearable. I could understand why some men would desert. But I felt I owed it to my friends to stay as long as they did. I had to put Harriet and the girls into God's hands. It was my duty to see this through.

I wasn't concerned about "The Cause." All I knew was that I signed on for the war, and, like my Pa, I believe you should stick with what you started. Whit had decided to stay as well, though his wife had written begging him to come home. She said that his little ones barely had enough to eat, that the crops in the county were being sent to the Confederate Army or were burned by Federal raiders. Harriet never asked me to come home, scared as she was. She was a strong woman, stronger than a lot of men. My heart ached to see her and the girls, but I knew I must stay.

I was real proud of my Harriet. She always put on a brave face in her letters. She said that they had enough food to last the winter. She had harvested all the crop of Irish and sweet potatoes I had put in, and she had dried a fair amount of beans. She had traded some of the vegetables for enough flour to make bread all winter. I asked her in a letter to share some food with Whit's family, that they were having it hard. I knew she would, because it was the Christian thing to do.

She told me that Moses missed me. That made me laugh—that old mule! He probably did miss going out into the fields every day. Harriet and the girls were trying to plow with him, so maybe he wouldn't get too lonesome. I hoped I would be home for the spring planting. Dear Lord, I hoped I would be home.

Harriet said that she and the girls had been cutting firewood. I had cut a couple of cords, and she said they had doubled the stacks I left, so the family would be warm at least. I felt a wave of pride and admiration when I read that, a nine year old and a six year old cutting and splitting wood! I wrote telling her to please keep reminding them to be careful with the ax and the maul. There again, I had to leave them in the Lord's hands.

That little house in the valley had a powerful pull for me, the thought of those two sweet little girls who looked up to me like I was something special, that beautiful wife who dedicated her life to the girls and to me. I must confess I ached in an almost physical way many a night thinking of them. The thought of getting back home to them kept me going.

Christmas of 1864 was hard. It was hard on us soldiers because we were always cold and hungry, but harder still because we were away from our loved ones at this sacred time of year. Still, we worshiped as best we could, remembering the coming of our Dear Lord. On Christmas Eve we gathered around a big campfire and sang hymns, especially those of the season: "Silent Night," "Joy to the World," "Oh Come All Ye Faithful," and others.

Somebody had foraged up a scrawny chicken. We cooked it over the open fire and divided it up, about a mouthful for each man in the group. We drank some coffee made with burnt corn husks. Sergeant Stephen Waters—who we just called "Preacher" because he was one—read the Christmas story from the Gospel of Luke. As I listened my eyes got moist, and I longed even more for my precious wife and two little ones. I wondered how they would remember Christmas this year. They would probably get together with some neighbors and kin, and maybe have some hot cider and a bit of roasted pork. I knew for sure that Harriet would lift her golden voice in song, and angels would hover near. The thought almost brought me to tears, but I dared not. I had to be strong, and I could not show too much sadness or despair to my companions. They too missed their homes, their wives, children, and sweethearts.

As we sang in the cold dark, around the blazing fire, I saw many watery eyes. Our stomachs knotted with ever-present hunger, our minds wandered homeward to the warmth of family. Each man was lost in his private thoughts, trying to escape in his mind to a better place. Missing home was the hard part. The killing and the dying were just the backdrop to our lonely lives. We struggled through each day with the hope in our hearts that we would soon be headed home.

After our little Christmas service broke up, men headed to their makeshift shelters, rough log huts, to try to keep the cold wind at bay. As I often did, I walked out a ways from camp a bit, toward the west, away from the enemy. That particular night the sky was a vast obsidian dome infused with sparkling points of light. I looked around for the brightest star, and found it to the southwest in the direction of home, low in the sky. It radiated a steady brilliant light, so soft and beautiful. To me, it was the star of Bethlehem, hanging directly over my home hundreds of miles away. As I stood shivering in the cold, I gazed at it and prayed for my family; I prayed for my comrades; and yes, I prayed for myself. Dear Lord, I wanted to see home again.

Our ranks continued to thin out. The typhus and pneumonia took many. The flux took others. Some just gave up and died from weariness and hunger. Some froze to death standing watch and others just walked away.

When the Yanks threatened and we went up to the breastworks, the spacing between us became farther and farther apart. One day the men were three feet apart, then five, then ten. If the Yankees had been a bunch of old women armed with rakes and hoes, I doubt we could have stopped them. There just weren't enough of us.

We were mostly skin and bones, but somehow Whit and I, as well as Joe and Sergeant Cas, managed to get enough food to get by from one day to the next. We would also scrounge up an old blanket here, a coat there (sometimes off of a dead Federal), enough to keep our bodies from freezing as winter howled through the Virginia hills.

It would be hard to imagine the suffering that winter if you weren't there. Some of the men who were barefoot still had to stand watch, so they would dig holes in the ground, put their feet in them and cover them up. They said it worked tolerably well. I often thought it was a lot like dying and being buried a little at a time. It was a fitting metaphor for the lives of Southern soldiers in the winter of 1864. The ones that got pneumonia were lucky. They passed away quiet and peaceful, like those that froze to death. It was how I hoped I'd go—quiet and peaceful right into the presence of the Good Lord.

When I looked out across the lines, I could see the Yanks trying to stay warm like we were, except they had good clothes. I didn't see a one in rags. Sometimes we wished they would attack, so we could get some of those warm coats off the ones that were killed. That's what war and cold and starvation does to a man. It makes him think only of survival. When you're cold, all you can think of is getting warm. When you're starving, all you can think of is getting something to eat. I confess, we took quite a bit off of dead Yankees when there was a picket skirmish and some were killed. I didn't feel bad about it, because they didn't need it anymore and we did. "Food and clothes from the corpses of our foes." It was a little rhyme that stuck in my head as we took coats, blankets, and hardtack from dead Federals on the rare occasions that we had the opportunity.

The doleful winter days stretched on. January and February came and went. Whit and I were sick about half the time, cold and hungry almost all the time. Joe got a bad case of pneumonia, but got better after a couple of weeks. Sergeant Cas never seemed to get sick. He was tougher than a pine knot. The Yankees would shell us once in a while, but mostly they were quiet. Their General Grant seemed to be content to let the cold and the hunger and disease do his work for him.

ELEVEN

Cross frozen field
I see the hue of winter,
rimed and clear,
polar sag of a tired year.

One cold February morning, I was just finishing up some hardtack and a piece of green bacon for breakfast when I heard a commotion on our left flank. There was cheering as a group of riders approached. The word got passed down the line. It was General Lee and General Hill! They were inspecting the fortifications. General Cadmus Wilcox joined them and pointed out our breastworks and the trenches and traverses we had dug. They reined up near where I was standing and I studied their faces as the men crowded around.

General Lee looked tired but his face was filled with determination. He never smiled, but nodded and gestured from time to time. His face was as kind as it was tough. It was the face I always thought Jesus probably had, manly and strong, but benevolent and full of love for his fellow man.

Everyone knew he was an expert at fortifications, and when he spoke, all his subordinates listened carefully. His voice was calm, deep, and strong. The troops stood a respectful distance off, but no one could take their eyes off him. He was a magnificent fellow, a true warrior and leader of men. No doubt, he could have eventually been elected President of the United States if had chosen to go with the Union at the beginning of the war. But instead he chose his beloved Virginia and the South.

General Hill, our Corps Commander, was very different. He had red hair and a full red beard. He looked like he had been sick and was in some pain. It was rumored that he was often sick and not able to lead his corps. Whatever his illness was, it looked to me like it was killing him. Still, he was a man you didn't trifle with. His reputation for hard fighting was known throughout the army. He had won many battles for General Lee.

The generals rode on down the line, Lee's fine gray horse prancing a bit as they moved on. I always felt proud to be in General Lee's army. I just wished there was a little more of it.

TWELVE

You can ask for a miracle
in the dead of the night
but the answer's not coming
so you best march on.

By early March of 1865, we got to know some other fellows very well. Preacher Waters came from the high mountains west of Rutherford, about forty miles from where Whit and I lived. Most men thought he was too kindly to be a soldier, but I had seen him in battle and he took on another personality when confronted with the enemy. He saw the Yankees as an invading horde which had to be driven out, and he fought like he was fighting for his home.

Preacher knew about history, particularly the history of the South. He admired General Stonewall Jackson and said that had Stonewall lived, we wouldn't be in the predicament we found ourselves. He told me Stonewall was a Godly man who believed his army was the army of God, and that he was doing His work.

Preacher also told me that before the war, Stonewall taught a Sunday school class composed of Negro slaves. He was very proud of that class and kept in touch with some of its members while he lived. His faith was his shield. He went into every battle with no fear whatsoever, because he felt his life, his very soul, was in the hands of God and he had no reason to be afraid. If he lived it was because of Divine protection. If he died, it was God's time for him to come home.

It was said that there never was a calmer, more composed man on the battlefield than Stonewall Jackson. Though excited by battle and his leadership in it, he rode back and forth, giving instructions to his subordinates, as if he hadn't a care in the world, completely unafraid of the thousands of deadly missiles which filled the air. He succumbed to pneumonia after he was severely wounded at Chancellorsville. I'm told that shortly before he died, he uttered these words: "Let us cross over the river and rest beneath the trees." He knew he was going home to be with the Lord. Preacher said that he wanted to be like that, totally assured he was going to be with the Savior, and totally unafraid all the while.

But Preacher was a realist, and he once told me, "It's a whole lot easier to be a fearless hero in front of a cabin fire, with no danger about. It's a whole different thing indeed to be brave when the minie balls are humming about your head, and the concussion of the exploding cannon shells is tearing at your clothes. I only aspire to be like Stonewall; I doubt I ever shall be quite that brave."

Preacher was a bit broader than me, though about the same height at six feet, with piercing blue eyes and flaxen hair growing thin at the front. At 41 years old, he was one of the older fellows in our ranks and we all looked up to him. He was a self-educated man, and spent most of his off duty time reading his Bible and a few other books he had with him. He read books like *The Odyssey* and *The Iliad.* He read Plato and Plutarch, the works of Shakespeare. He could speak "with the tongues of angels" though he was unfailingly humble.

When I confided in him the problems I had controlling my anger, he smiled knowingly and said it came from my Celtic heritage. Then he proceeded to explain to me that my Scots ancestors were known for being people of strong emotion and strong will. They were a fierce, independent people who fought the British against overwhelming odds. The Romans, before the British, were so afraid of the barbaric Scots that they built Hadrian's Wall to keep them out of their empire. He said I got the hot blood honestly, and said I should be proud of such a heritage. It did make me feel a bit better—though I knew it would be a lifelong struggle to control it. I suppose he taught me something about who I am.

I remember one particular Sunday service when Preacher delivered the message to our regiment. He talked about how all things and all people are passing away. No matter how rich or powerful a person is, his life is but a vapor. He drew his message from Psalm 103: "For He knoweth our frame; he remembereth that we are dust. As for man, his days are as grass; as a flower of the field, so he flourisheth. For the wind passeth over it, and it is gone; and the place thereof shall know it no more." That passage and Preacher's sermon stuck with me. We are passing away, slowly though it may seem to us. We are but a breath or a vapor in the air. Everything we are on this earth will soon be gone and mostly forgotten. The good as well as the bad are temporal, soon to fade like shadows. I thought of my father and grandfather. They were so real and so strong, and now they are gone. I thought of Army and other friends who just days before had been laughing with us at our little jests; now they were gone for all eternity. The fleeting nature of this life came to be very clear to me in those bleak and fearsome days.

The Preacher was up to date on the latest philosophies and sciences of the day. He spoke of the foolishness of a certain fellow named Darwin, who proposed that we were descended from apes and held other curious notions. Preacher was also well informed about the various religious movements that were taking hold around the country. He spoke to me once about those who believe that they have God within them based on the way they act or don't act. He laughed to think of the arrogance of lowly mankind to presume that they could do anything good apart from the very presence of the Holy Spirit of God within them through our Lord Jesus Christ.

Preacher also spoke with us like a father. He spoke with the wisdom of years and of much study. I admired him greatly. He once said to me, "We can believe whatever we want. It doesn't matter one little bit unless it is the truth as expounded in the Holy Scriptures. Mankind is forever making his own rules, his own god, based on what he feels is right or the way he thinks God ought to be. We had best be finding out how God really is, and there is no source but the Scriptures. All else is 'sound and fury, signifying nothing.' If there were another source of truth, surely the angels would trumpet it from the rooftops; but nay, only the Scriptures contain the very word of God."

One evening I found Preacher sitting outside by a small fire, sipping some coffee made from burnt cornhusks. He smiled weakly as I sat down across the fire from him and said, "Good evening, Francis." I nodded and pulled out my old pipe, filled it with some tobacco I had taken off a dead Federal picket who had been at the wrong place at the wrong time, and lit it. Preacher stared at the fire for a long time and I sat, puffing my pipe, looking at him, then at the fire, then back at him.

There were just the two of us, and I spoke first. "Preacher, you look like you got something on your mind." As soon as I said it, I thought, *That was foolish; we all have many things on our minds.*

There was a silence, and then he said, "Francis, I know you miss your family." I sighed deeply and said, "Yes, sir, I most certainly do. I think about my wife and girls all the time. I worry. I know it's a sin, but I worry about them. They're females trying to work a farm, and Jane and Susan are so small."

He looked at me with a mixture of sadness and something else, I didn't quite know what. Another silence, then he said, "I miss my wife Catherine. I just got a letter from her." He fell silent for a long time. He looked up toward the sky and with watery eyes said, "She's sick. Doc Wells in Asheville says she's not going to get better, some female problem."

"Preacher," I said, "surely she will get better. I do pray she does."

He sighed deeply, the lament of a very tired and resigned man, and looked at me with inexpressible sadness. "I wish it were so, Francis, but I am afraid it is not." His voice broke. "Doc Wells has been her physician since she was a child. He knows her very well, and he's very good. He says this is something that no one can cure, and I believe him. She won't see another winter, maybe not another fall. Doc says she will probably be with the Lord within a few months."

I did not say anything, just listened to him. He continued, "Francis, we've been together for twenty-three years. She is my everything on this earth. We never were blessed with children. My folks are gone. She is truly my only family. Her kin, well, we never were that close. They never thought I was good enough for her, so they don't come around much, and they surely won't be around at all after she is gone." I looked at him like I was seeing him for the first time. I was honored that he was telling me things I am sure he must have kept to himself up until now.

His pale blue eyes grew even more watery in the light of the flickering fire. "I have to go, Francis."

My eyes widened, and I looked around to see if anyone was near. No one was. I spoke softly. "You mean ... desert?"

He nodded solemnly. "You know they won't let me go on furlough. Not now. The war is lost, it's almost over, it doesn't really matter anyhow, but they won't let me go and I can't stay. I just can't. You understand, don't you, Francis?"

I did not know what to say. I was so stunned—not because a man was going to desert; that happened all the time. But this was Preacher. His idol was Stonewall, the bravest, manliest general in Lee's army. How could he do this? But I knew that if my Harriet was going to die, I would leave tonight, no question about it. When I did not answer for a space, Preacher looked up. "You think I'm all wrong, don't you, Francis?"

I replied hesitantly, "Preacher, I don't know. A farmer with only a few years of schooling is not in a position to judge a man like you."

He sighed again. "It doesn't have anything to do with schooling, Francis. It is a question of loyalties. After all, that's what this war is all about: loyalties. Lee had to make the hardest decision of his life when he chose to fight for the Confederacy."

I thought for a moment, and then it all became clear to me. I said, "Preacher, you know what General Lee chose? He chose family and home over his own government. I can't advise you on what to do. For each man, it's a matter of conscience. But I know what I would do. I hope to see my family soon, that this bloody business will be over forever, and we can go home where we belong. A gun doesn't feel right in my hands. Plow handles, now they feel right. I want to go home. Lord knows how I want to go home, but I'll stay as long as I think my family's all right. But if, may the Lord forbid it, something like this happened, I would be headed toward Rutherford County within the hour."

"I don't know, Francis. I have to go, but it hurts me greatly to think of abandoning the fellows; you especially. You're a good man, Francis. We have only been acquainted a few weeks, but I know a good man when I see one. You try so hard to do the right thing. I do as well. I just don't quite know what it is now. I used to be sure, very sure, but this is different. I can't save my wife, but maybe I can see her. I know I will see her in the Resurrection, but I am human, I need to see her before she goes. You understand?" I nodded. He continued, "But if I go, someone may die because I wasn't there to save him, or to die in his place."

We again fell silent for several minutes. The Preacher wore an expression of the most extreme distress.

"I hope you will pardon me for being so bold, but it's not your job to die in someone else's place, Preacher. That job was the

Savior's. Now, it is a noble thing to die saving someone, but I think it might just be more than a little bit high-minded to think you're ordained to do so." Preacher smiled wanly and looked at me with those piercing blue eyes. "You're also a wise man, Francis, in your own way." He took another sip of the so-called coffee, grimaced and dashed the rest of it out. "I'll be seeing you, Francis. I covet your prayers."

I looked at him sadly and said, "And I yours, Preacher. Godspeed." I rose and left him sitting by the fire.

Three days later, after we rose from another fitful night of sleeping on the hard makeshift bunks, Whit and I stood in front of our hut. We watched from a distance as some riders approached, a wagon following behind them. As they drew closer we could see some bodies in the bed of the wagon. I thought, *Lord, will it never end. Will the earth not be filled with the dead?* As the wagon grew closer, I got a very uneasy feeling. I realized the wagon was not coming from the front lines or the encampment, but from well behind the lines, down the road that led into the countryside. I thought for a moment, then turned to Whit. "Something bad, Whit, something very bad."

I walked toward the wagon, Whit behind me. I called to the riders, who were provost marshals, "What happened?"

They didn't even bother to look at us. One of them said, "Deserters, shot 'em last night six miles behind the line. This is what happens to cowards." My chest tightened, and I ran up to the wagon. There were five bodies in it, including one big man with sandy hair who lay on his side, a large crimson stain on his chest. Preacher. I felt weak and sick.

"It's Preacher, Whit, it's Preacher!" I cried out. I walked alongside the wagon for a time, resting my hand on Preacher's arm. "Oh my Lord, you'll see her soon, Preacher. You'll see her soon." As I looked at the chest wound, I felt anger boiling up. I turned to the nearest marshal. "This man was shot in the chest. Was he surrendering?"

No answer. The marshals just looked ahead and rode on, their horses at a casual walk. I ran up beside another one. "Was he giving up?" Again, no answer.

"You miserable vermin murdered him, didn't you?" I screamed. "Answer me, you devils!" They just looked at me with twisted grins. One let loose a stream of tobacco juice that barely missed me. I started for the leader's horse at a run when I was hit from behind and taken to the ground. I twisted and squirmed around to try to get at my attacker, and saw that it was Whit.

He shouted, "Francis, now you just cool down! No need to get in trouble." I struggled to throw Whit off. "There's nothing you can do. Calm down, Francis, you hear?"

The captain of the provosts turned his horse and walked it back toward us. He was a big man with flowing blonde hair and a full beard. An ostrich plume adorned his beaver hat. "What in hell do you think you're doin', Private?" he asked, his face full of fury and dark light in his narrowed eyes.

Whit answered quickly. "Nothing, sir, we just know one of these fellows, and Francis here is purty tore up about it. We wants no trouble."

The captain glared at me. "You got sympathies for deserters, Private?"

Before I could respond, Whit again spoke up. "Sir, I think I speak for both of us when I tell you that we don't cotton to no deserters, no sir. We are true blue—er, gray—and we're here for the rest of the fight, yes, sir."

The captain's horse stood no more than three feet from me. He glowered down at me and said, "Soldier, if I even think you might consider desertin' or helpin' a deserter, I will buck and gag you myself until you've had time to think it over. You understand me?"

"Yes, sir," Whit answered. "We learned our lesson, you can believe that."

The captain put the spurs to his horse. Mud from its hooves splattered us. My fury rose up and I started to shout at the captain, "You son of—" Whit grabbed me around the neck and yanked me back down, cutting off my air so I couldn't speak. The captain rode on, ignoring us.

Whit released his hold.

I shook my head. "He was a good man, Whit, a saint. God in Heaven, he didn't deserve this!"

"I know, Francis, but you're just gonna get put in the stockade if you go after an officer, maybe even shot!"

Two of the marshals looked back at us and smirked as we sat on the cold Virginia earth. "They killed him, the butchers. They killed him, Whit!"

"I know they did, Francis. But it's done, and he *was* a deserter, God rest his soul. They woulda hung him anyhow."

I sat with my head in my hands, beside the little muddy road that led from the breastworks back into the country. Dark clouds heavy with rain lumbered across the dismal sky. A cold tear ran down my cheek.

Whit looked at me sadly. "We have to get back, Francis. I think they want us for pickets." He helped me up and we walked slowly back toward the huts.

Sergeant Cas Hutchins was standing by the road. His face showed that he knew. "I know how you feel, Francis," he said, "but you can't help him now. He was a brave man and a fine soldier, but he made a bad choice."

There was silence for a long moment.

"Loyalties," I said softly.

"What?" asked Sergeant Cas.

"Loyalties. We talked about it the other night. His wife is dying. He said he had to go. He put his loyalties with family, hearth and kin. Just like General Lee. Except they killed him for it."

Cas frowned. "Look, Francis, don't speak to anyone about this. You could get in trouble too. I understand the choice he made, but the army has to have regulations, rules of conduct, and Preacher broke one of the most important."

"Well, so have about a million others, Sergeant," said Whit.

"That doesn't make it right, now does it?" Cas replied.

I thought for a moment. "Cas, you're a good man and a smart man. You probably should be an officer. No, there's no probably about it, you *should* be an officer. We all know that General Lee could be hanged by the Yankees when this is all over for helping lead a rebellion. But Preacher didn't lead a rebellion; he just wanted to see his dying wife, his only family. Now why should he die for that?"

Cas hung his head. "I don't think he should have died, Francis," he said quietly, "but I don't run the army." He sighed. "Now, we best get back to business. You two have picket duty, you'll be out on the right flank of the regiment about three hundred yards. Corporal Allen will show you where."

I couldn't let it go. "He shouldn't have died, Cas. He was a good man, maybe too good for this earth."

"Francis, there's a lot of men who shouldn't have died, a lot of them just boys. We have to keep our heads about us, we have to keep strong. We have to stay and fight. The Yankees will be coming soon, as soon as old Grant thinks he can finish us without losing half his army. They'll come, and we'll need every rifle." He looked grim. "We don't have the right to decide who should stay and who should go, certainly not who should die or who should live. We're soldiers, for now. We have to fight, because it's the only thing to do. The alternative is too bad to consider."

I looked in the direction the marshals and the wagon had taken, though they were long gone. "I'll stay, Cas, don't worry. And I'll fight. I want to see my family. Maybe the best chance is to see this through, then go home when the rest do."

"Well, pshaw," Whit said, "I guess I'll just stay too." He started to laugh, but it trailed off in a big sigh. We had lost a good friend, the likes of which we were not likely to see again.

As we walked toward our picket post, I said, "I know one thing, Whit. Heaven's a better place now."

THIRTEEN

*Off in the distance
the grumbling of cannon
orders the foot soldiers
on to their deaths.*

The following day we woke before dawn to the thunder of cannon in the distance. "Those boys over there sure do like to play with those big guns," said Whit, "and before a man has had his breakfast, too. They got no consideration whatsoever."

I rubbed my eyes, rose, put on my old slouch hat, and walked out the door of the hut. The thump, thump, thump of the cannon was followed by booming explosions off to our left, toward Petersburg.

Joe Martin and Sergeant Cas Hutchins walked up, looking in the direction of the cannon fire. "That sounds like more than just normal shelling," I said.

"Sure does," Cas replied. "Wonder what they're up to."

Joe Martin, who seldom spoke in a group, said, "They're testin' us and tryin' to soften us up a bit. They'll be comin' soon. But I won't see 'em come."

Cas studied him. "Joe, don't even joke about that. Desertion is a hanging offense."

"Yes, if they bring you back alive," I said bitterly. Then I turned to him. "You planning something, Joe?"

He paused, and kept looking in the direction of the cannon fire. "I don't know. I just don't see being here when they come."

Cas and I looked at each other. Joe Martin was different. He was a quiet man, a family man with a little farm, a lot like mine. Steady in battle, he always stayed calm, even in the heat of it. Minie balls would be flying, and Joe would just stand his ground, load his rifle, raise and aim and fire again and again, like a machine. I would try to be steady, but sometimes when the balls were flying thick, I had a hard time just making myself stay and fight. Not Joe, or so it seemed. I think he would have fought a whole Yankee corps all by himself. I never saw him so much as flinch, though I have seen him come back with holes in his coat where minie balls passed through. A half a dozen times he was grazed by rounds, but he paid them no more attention than a mosquito bite. He just kept raising his musket and firing, over and over, steady. An army of men like that could conquer the world.

When I first met Joe he had been a big, muscular man, even in a world of want, where there never was enough food. Now he, like Sergeant Hutchins, was lean and gaunt. Their eyes were beginning to take on a hollow look. When I saw these powerful men begin to look frail, I knew the army was starving. We would soon be gone, even if the Yanks never came. The men—like the very army itself—seemed to be wasting away. The Yankees' work would be easy. When they came there wouldn't be much to stop them, unless grim determination alone would do it; because that's about all we had left.

"Joe," I said, "you'll be here when we're all gone."

He looked at me vacantly. "No, Francis. I am afraid I won't. It's just something I know."

Two days later, Joe was dead. When we arose at sunup, Joe didn't awaken. He had died in his sleep. He had never uttered one word of complaint, but he must have been sick. Maybe his big heart just gave out.

We never did know, and never will.

Another good man died.

Seemed it happened all the time now.

I wondered when my time would come.

FOURTEEN

At the hearth in the hills
a tired woman rocks,
two little ones at her feet,
praying for her soldier husband.

Letters from home were the greatest things a man could receive in that sad and desperate time. I learned that things had been rough that winter in Rutherford County. The weather had been bitter cold and snowfall had been the heaviest in many years. By early February, when Harriet wrote the last letter, food was getting low. They had to butcher both our hogs. Old Jack Parker let her hang the meat in his smokehouse and helped her prepare it—salt it down and such. Jack was a good man; too old to fight at sixty-seven, he did what he could to help the womenfolk whose men were off to war.

But lack of food wasn't the worst of it, as I learned after I returned home. A few days after I got back from the war, we sat on the porch and she related a story to me that made my blood run cold.

It was early January and Harriet was just about to put the girls to bed, then retire herself, when she heard our hound barking at something. She knew Samson didn't bark for no reason at all, so she got my Pa's old flintlock down off the hearth and loaded it.

As she charged the musket, there was a sharp knock at the door. She called out, "Who's there?"

A man's voice said, "Just a couple of soldiers, ma'am, traveling home from the war. Can you spare us some food and maybe let us sleep in the barn?" When she didn't answer right away the voice continued, "We're friends of your neighbor, Silas Henson, up the road. He said you wouldn't mind if we stayed in your barn."

"Why didn't you stay there tonight, if you're friends with Mr. Henson?" she replied. "He has a barn twice as big as ours."

"We wanted to cover a few more miles before we stopped, that's all. We were so hungry, we ate what little Silas could spare and we're still hungry."

Now Harriet is as good a Christian as I ever knew and she was always one to help, but she wasn't foolish in the least. She told the man, "I am sorry, but I can't let you in. You'll have to go somewhere else for food and lodging."

There was silence on the other side of the door, and another voice spoke. This man sounded older, and his voice was more sinister in tone. "Now, ma'am, you ain't gonna turn away two brave Confederate soldiers just back from fighting to protect you and your family, now are you?"

Harriet said, "How do I know you're not a couple of deserters out for no good?"

Apparently the men realized she wasn't going to let them in voluntarily so they began to threaten. "Lady, if you don't let us in, we will burn this house down and you and yours with it. Do you understand?"

Harriet was now in a state of real alarm. She looked up at the loft where the girls slept, then back at the door. "Please leave us alone. We don't want trouble."

"Oh, lady, you got trouble. Only question is how much do you want?" With that she could hear the men laughing their raspy, coarse laughter.

The other one chimed in again, "I bet you're real purty, now ain't you? Why don't you come out, and let us get a look? We promise no harm will come to you."

Harriet was now angry as well as scared, and she shouted, "Go away! Go or I'll shoot."

The men laughed again. "Lady, we been fightin' Yankees for two years. Do you think we're afraid of one little old country girl with a shootin' iron? Now open the door or we're gonna light your house!"

Harriet walked to the back of the house and shouted to the loft for the girls to get up. They did, and she quickly told them there were some deserters at the door and for them to get dressed. Being the bright farm girls they were, they knew immediately to obey without question. Harriet thought about running out the back, but she knew if they did they would surely be caught. She checked all the doors and windows to make sure they were shuttered and bolted.

As she was checking the back window, there was a pounding on the front door, like it was being kicked. The door shook, again and again, more and more violently. A dish tumbled off a shelf and shattered on the floor. Harriet raised the musket and prepared herself.

Finally the door came crashing inward. There stood two of the dirtiest, vilest looking men Harriet could imagine. The oldest held a Bowie knife in begrimed fingers, his thin lips spread in a lopsided grin. He leered at her beneath shaggy black brows. Behind him was the younger man, who wore a tattered slouch hat, his yellow hair matted and dirty.

Jane and Susan scrambled behind their mother. Harriet shouted, "Get out or I'll shoot!" She leveled the musket at the first man's chest.

Both men laughed, showing their blackened and missing teeth through scraggly beards. The older one spoke, "No missy, I think we're gonna have us some fun first. Now you put that there musket down so's nobody gets hurt."

Harriet hissed through her clinched teeth, "So help me, if you move a step further I will kill you!"

"Boy, she is a feisty one now ain't she?" said the younger with a laugh.

"Purty too," the older said. Then his smile faded. "Now you lay that gun down real soft, little lady, and we promise we won't hurt them little ones."

The younger man stood just behind the older. With only one round in the gun, Harriet did what she had to.

As the older man moved toward her, she fired. The musket belched smoke and flame. The deserter was thrown backward into the younger man. He fell to the floor and didn't move. The younger man stepped over him and charged at Harriet, spewing the vilest of oaths. She tried to swing the musket like a club, but he caught it and shoved her to the floor. The girls started screaming, and he yelled at them to get away. He climbed on top of Harriet, and started tearing at her clothes.

She fought him as best she could, but he grasped the musket and pressed it down on her throat. As he pressed harder and harder, she struggled to breathe. She began to lose consciousness. Somewhere there was a scream. Stars raced through her field of vision. A black cloak enveloped them all.

"Mama, Mama! Oh Jesus, please help us, Mama!"

Harriet slowly regained consciousness.

"Mama, are you all right?" Jane cried.

"I'm.... I think I will be all right," she rasped as she struggled to breathe in ragged little gasps. To her left, the young deserter was lying on his stomach. The handle of my Pa's razor sharp hunting knife was hilt-deep between his shoulder blades. Blood oozed from a mortal wound.

"I had to, Mama, I had too," Jane wailed.

Little Susan's eyes were round with fear. She trembled violently. Harriet held both girls close and comforted them. "I know, my dearest, I know," she said.

Jane. My nine-year-old daughter. This cursed war had done this to her. I often later thought, with bitter self-recrimination, *To the devil with the provost marshals. I could have hidden from them, they couldn't have caught me. I could have made it home. Why didn't I just come on home? My wife, my precious little ones; dear Lord, I should have gone home.*

FIFTEEN

In the spring of life
the willow sways in leafy abandon
the blue bird's melody is sweet,
sweeter still the kiss of a lover.

Harriet Toney became the love of my life in the spring of 1854. We met at a church social after worship service, one breezy May afternoon at the Camp Creek Meeting House. She came to visit our church with her aunt, Mrs. Florence Toney, and they stayed for our little celebration. There was no special reason for the celebration, other than that it was spring, and church folks in the mountains didn't need much of an excuse for a social.

She gained my attention the moment she walked into the church before the sermon began. Her honey colored hair flowed across her shoulders. Her gingham dress was so white it seemed to glow. Her smile contained a portion of sunlight, and her hazel eyes sparkled with the sweet joy of her youth. I could not take my eyes off her lovely countenance. When she glanced in my direction, my heart was held more surely than if she had grasped it in her delicate fingers.

I knew the minute I saw her that I had to meet this lovely stranger. I didn't know that I was in love, but for certain my interest was as high as a Carolina pine. She and Mrs. Florence Toney sat across the aisle from me, on the same row. I could not help looking at her during the sermon. My Ma noticed my distraction and jabbed me in the side several times, her lips tight, but I was powerless to keep my eyes off of this vision from afar.

After the sermon, which seemed to be the longest one our preacher ever delivered before or since, we all went out where tables had been set up under a grove of pin oak trees. The air seemed to be alive with excitement as I strode outside, with the intention of getting myself introduced to Mrs. Toney's niece. My excitement faded when I spotted her happily talking with Jacob Bowen. His father ran a general store in Gilbert Town, and his family owned a lot of land and a fine house. My heart sank when I saw them talking. I watched them for a moment, then inspected my shoes. One had a small hole in the toe. I doubted that a poor farm boy with holes in his shoes could compete with a well-to-do fellow with great prospects like Jacob.

I reluctantly gave up on introducing myself to the fair and now distant maiden. Instead I went over to help Mrs. Lattimore and Mrs. Crowder carry food from the wagons and set it on the tables. The smell of fried chicken and sweet potato pie, which usually so entranced me, somehow held little interest today.

The grove rang with the happy murmur of church people who had heard a good sermon (at least the ones not distracted by proximate and captivating beauty), and who were now ready to enjoy a good meal on a pleasant afternoon. It was the sound of people who enjoyed socializing with their friends and kin even more than consuming a delicious meal in a shady grove on a sunny spring day. The joy of the occasion was now totally lost on me. It may as well have been gray, rainy November.

I had carried Mrs. Crowder's ponderous basket from her wagon to the serving table, and was setting out the food when someone tapped me on the shoulder. Mrs. Sally Henson, a proper lady of the church with graying hair and a stout build—a woman who seemed to think it was her mission on this earth to find me a wife—stood there with a smile as broad as Green River. She said, "Francis, I would like for you to meet someone. Say hello to *Miss*"—she put heavy emphasis on the word—"Harriet Toney from the Westminster Community." Mrs. Henson had Harriet by the arm, and pulled her toward me slightly. Harriet smiled shyly, and looked at her feet, then looked at me with her head still slightly bowed, the smile widening just a bit.

I started to speak, but my mouth fell open and I froze and stared, as would a frightened deer, into those beautiful eyes. I tried again. "I, uh, I, uh ... I am pleased to, uh, meet you Miss Toney. I, uh, I am ... am Francis Toney." Harriet giggled and my face flushed. "I mean, uh, Yelton." Harriet smiled widely and the sun shined brighter. I was having a hard time catching my breath.

"I'm pleased to meet you, Francis. Do you attend church here regularly?" Her voice was pure music to me.

Mrs. Henson chirped in reply, "Francis is here every time the church doors open. His Ma sees to that!"

I nodded. "I try to come regular. Our preacher is very good, and he preaches the Word, and I do love to hear him, and I love to be here. Do you go to church regular? Where do you go to church? I find that there's no better place for a fellow to be than at church." Now that I had started talking I could not stop. All of a sudden I felt foolish, and once again my face flushed.

About that time Preacher Bailey walked up, and he and Mrs. Henson began a dialogue about some arcane church matter of which I now have absolutely no remembrance. Harriet looked at me and smiled, and I am afraid I had about as foolish a grin on my face as a young man could have; but I couldn't help it, and at the time I didn't know or care how foolish it might have been.

The preacher got the crowd's attention and said grace. Then everyone lined up to fill their plates from the feast set before them. I asked Harriet if I could join her, and to my astonishment she said yes. We sat and ate our fried chicken and biscuits, and talked as if we had known each other our whole lives. I hesitantly asked her if she and Jacob were friends. She smiled and said yes, but they were also first cousins. The sun got still brighter.

When we parted, I asked if I could call on her. Again she surprised me and said yes. Thus began our courtship. I was so blindly in love that I could barely concentrate on my work. When we were apart, I could only think of her. We were married less than a year after we met. Our folks helped us as they were able, but we still had next to nothing in those early days of our marriage. She only complained when she thought I worked too hard and too long.

We moved into an old abandoned cabin on Pearly Walker's land. He allowed us to live there for free, and in return I helped him around his farm when I wasn't working with my Pa. We moved in with my Ma for a while after my Pa passed away. Then I began to build our own house to Harriet's great excitement.

Harriet was as diligent in her work as she was generous and humble as a person. She made that little cabin a home to which I dearly loved to return each day. Her affection and constancy have been a continual wonder to me. Now it is impossible for me to imagine life without her. She is my anchor as well as my best friend and my one true love. Life without her would be colder and lonelier than a Union prisoner of war camp. That is why getting home was the most important thing in the world to me.

SIXTEEN

It's springtime in Virginia
the flowers begin their blooming,
so why does the world
seem to be dying?

As spring grew near, there was a growing sense of foreboding. We knew the Yanks were approaching, maybe for the final blow; we just didn't know when. Whit and I had lost some of our best friends. The hunger and privation continued, and we were beginning to get so weary, we just sort of stumbled through our days, numbed by what we had seen. I knew I had to be brave whether I felt like it or not. The big fight was coming.

On April 1, 1865 we heard the echoes of a battle to the south of us. The ragged sound of musketry was punctuated by the boom of big guns. It made us all uneasy to think that we might have the Yanks coming up our right flank. But the sounds faded as the day wore on.

The following morning we rose early. The stars were bright and the air was crisp, promising good weather for plowing, for those fortunate enough to be back on their farms. Whit and I were up around 4 a.m., although we had early watch the night before and did not get into our bedrolls until around midnight.

The air was full of expectation. Something was brewing, and we thought we knew what it might be. Whit and I had just stepped out the door of our hut when the world seemed to come apart. Two large blasts threw Whit backwards into me, and we both went sprawling. The air was full of dirt and smoke and heat.

Whit landed on his side, and I on my back. For a moment I couldn't breathe. I could hear men yelling and running. As I struggled for air, I looked over at Whit. He was covered with dirt from head to toe and laughing hysterically. A trickle of blood flowed from his forehead, but otherwise he seemed to be all right. "Looks like some Yank artillery man decided to serve up a couple of twelve pounders for breakfast," he said. "I'm all right. You in one piece, Francis?"

"Yes, I think." We picked ourselves up and gathered our rifles. "I think we'll be needed on the line," I said.

About that time, Sergeant Cas came running from the direction of regimental headquarters. "I think this is it, boys. Take your positions."

"We're on our way, Sergeant," Whit said with a laugh. "We goin' to greet the Yankees."

We quickly moved up to the forward breastworks, running down traverses that led toward our rifle positions. By now, all hell was breaking loose. The boom of Yankee cannons was being answered by the roar of the Confederate guns. "Well, well, well," said Whit, "What a fine day for a fight."

"Glad you think so," I said as we ran. "I never saw a fine day for a fight, and this don't appear to be it either."

The roar of the artillery from our side, and the explosions from the incoming Yankee shells, was deafening. Smoke swirled around us. Then the Yankee guns across the way went quiet. The fire from our cannons slowed. There was a cease fire for a few minutes.

We peered across the ground beyond the breastworks; dawn colored the fields gray. A noise began to rise on the wind as it blew across the battlefield. It was a sound that you might hear from a choir of thousands, beginning some great aria; the first note: *A-a-a-h-h*. The Yanks were yelling their "Hurrah!" Deep and resounding it came, over the tattered ground through the swirling smoke. I peered through the gloom, and the hair stood up on the back of my neck. There was just enough light to see an ocean of blue, a roaring sea, come pouring over the battlefield straight toward our position. It was an irresistible mass of men, roaring their deep Yankee battle cry.

Whit tucked in a chaw. "Well, it looks like they mean business this time. Too bad we ain't got them fancy repeater rifles. We shore do have plenty of targets."

I looked at him. "Whit, you have a way of looking on the bright side in bad times and the dark side in good times. You ever think you might be confused?"

Whit brayed his sick mule laugh. "Francis, what I am is ready for some fun. We been waitin' on them Yankee boys for months, now here they come."

"Yeah, Whit, here they come. More of them than three times our number could handle. Looks like a whole Yankee corps, coming right at us."

All around us men with grim faces took positions on the works, the officers trying to space them to have the greatest effect. We were spread out as much as ten feet between each man, and no reserves behind us.

I said softly, "You know we ain't got a prayer, don't you Whit."

"Oh yeah, I know, Francis, but what the hell; it's a fine day to die."

Sergeant Cas strode up beside us. "Hold your fire, boys; wait till they're closer." He said to me, "This is the big fight. No skirmish here. They're comin' at us with all they got."

"We'll do our best," I said.

"I know you will, Francis; Whit. Keep your heads down."

The blue sea moved on. Out front, their pioneers hacked away at the *abatis* and *chevaux-de-frise* obstructions, shoving them aside to make a way through. When they were about a hundred and fifty yards away, we heard "Fire!" all up and down the line. So we fired, and then reloaded and fired again.

The blue sea kept rolling toward us. I put the Springfield to my shoulder, sighted in a Yankee trooper a hundred yards out, and pulled the trigger. The Springfield bellowed, and an instant later the blue trooper fell. I watched as he went down, through the smoke of battle. He swayed backward with the impact of the heavy minie ball, his cap tossed to the side as his head snapped forward. His rifle flew out of his hands and he sank to his knees. I couldn't tell how old he was, probably just a kid. He had coal black hair. Then he crumpled to the ground like a rag doll dropped on the floor by a little girl.

I paused and stared for a second. I had shot him through the heart. *We're killing our friends, our brothers and our cousins.* Troops stepped over his body, which was soon obscured by the moving mass of blue coats.

We fired again at a hundred yards; the blue sea wavered just a little in front of us. I heard the colonel say, "My God, they're coming in a wedge; looks like General Wright's whole corps!" To our right, the wedge moved on, their pioneers hacking at our barriers, slowing only a little.

The Yanks kept coming. Fifty yards.

"There are too many. We have to pull back," said the sergeant.

Twenty-five yards, and I was loading and firing faster than I ever had before. Yet my hands would not move fast enough. I tried to shoot them all, tried to stop them. The rest of the men did too. We fired and loaded and fired.

It didn't seem to make any difference. There were just too many.

All of a sudden, it seemed, they were on top of us, scrambling over the breastworks. We rose to meet them, but there were ten Yankees to every Confederate. To that point I never thought I could bring myself to stab a man with a bayonet. I used my rifle like a club, thrusting this way and that. I hit one Yankee in the mouth, a little fellow, and he hit the ground moaning. I completely missed the next man and he tried to get me with his bayonet, but I managed to sidestep him and he ran by me. He swung back around toward me and, gritting my teeth, I stabbed him with my bayonet. It sank into his chest like it was a rotten log. He let out a cry, then he sank to the ground, holding onto my coat with his free hand. He was saying something; I think he was praying.

Our faces were only inches apart. The noise of the fighting seemed miles away. We looked at each other for just a moment and I said, "I'm, I'm sorry." His eyes fluttered and he stared at me sadly. His blue blouse was covered in blood, but his face was calm, resolved.

His mouth was moving but all I heard him say was, "Forgive." Then he fell to the ground face first.

I felt a minie ball pass by my head. I swung around; another blue trooper was charging at me. Whit stepped in front and ran his bayonet through the Yank's neck. Blood gushed like a fountain and the trooper made a gurgling sound as he fell.

Then to my left two more blue coats came at us. I sidestepped another bayonet thrust and ran my blade through one Federal's chest. He cursed and tried to pull my bayonet out, but then his eyes rolled back and he dropped to the ground. The second trooper went for Whit. I threw my leg out and tripped him. He pitched forward to the ground, and when he went down I brought the butt of my rifle down on his head as hard as I could. The butt plate crushed his skull.

I felt sick.

To my left Lester Carpenter quickly loaded his rifle, but before he could ram in the minie ball, blue troops were upon him. He raised his rifle at the nearest Yankee, the ramrod still in it. The rifle fired, there was a strange sound, and the blue trooper was impaled by the flying ramrod. He stood in shock for a moment, looking down at the thin shaft protruding from his chest. Then he dropped where he stood. Lester grimaced, and joined Whit and me in the hand to hand struggle.

More blue coats poured over the earthworks. Sergeant Cas was hard put. Out of the corner of my eye I saw him pick up one Yankee trooper, raise him over his head, and slam him into five or six Federals who collapsed in a heap. He grabbed the Yankee trooper's rifle and fired it into the mass of men, then began clubbing Union soldiers with powerful, vicious swings of the musket. He was crowded by more Yankees, and he moved backward, fighting furiously. More blue-clad men crumpled to the earth under his powerful blows.

"Whit, we gotta git!" I screamed. "Lester! Cas!"

Whit was thrusting his bayonet at anything blue and trying not to get stabbed back. He looked like he was dancing to fiddle music, moving this way then that, spinning around, his arms pumping with the thrusts of his weapon. I never knew he could move that fast or be that deadly.

Two blue troopers came at me yelling. I swung the rifle again; one went down and the other stumbled over a body, his bayonet just missing me. As he fell, he reached out and pulled me to the ground.

We both lost our rifles as we fell side by side. He grabbed me by the throat and both of his thumbs closed on my windpipe. A large, powerful man, his hands were like a vise; I couldn't breathe, and I couldn't break free from his grip. I felt my life ebbing, my lungs screaming for air as we rolled on the ground. The sky looked like amber glass, slowly darkening. Desperately, I jammed my right thumb in his left eye and gouged as hard as I could until I felt it give. Blood and fluid poured out. He screamed and rolled to the side away from me. I left him on the ground, and started to race back toward the trenches.

Out of nowhere, shells exploded with a roar around us. The Yankees were confused for a moment, and Whit and I and rest of our regiment headed toward the rear. I grabbed up a rifle and we bolted from the entrenchments. We weren't retreating; we were running. I wasn't so afraid of dying, but I did not want to spend a year in a Yankee stockade. I had heard enough about the awful conditions, and how they treated the Rebs like dogs. Besides, I could not stand the thought of being penned up like an animal. I would rather die.

We had done what we could do. One man can't whip ten, and dead or captured, we would be of no use to anyone. The drummer tapped retreat, almost an afterthought, but after a few beats, the drum went silent. I turned and saw the young drummer falling, a trickling red spot in his forehead.

Some of the artillery men had managed to limber up their pieces and they were riding furiously toward the rear. The others just ran with the rest of us, their guns in the hands of the enemy. The Army of Northern Virginia crumpled backward, pressed on all sides by an enemy it could no longer defeat, nor even slow down very much. Our line was broken right in the middle, our brigade and our division split completely in two. We turned and fired as fast as we could, then moved back again. Some artillery to our rear had found new positions, unlimbered, and was pounding away at the center of the attack. The blue sea wavered, pulled back slightly, then flowed into our old fortifications. Some of the Federals to our right turned southward. Our troops continued the retreat, more like a "skeedaddle" as some like to say. The Federals then began firing at us from our old positions.

We sprinted across the Boydton Plank Road and through the fields beyond. The officers tried to form the men up in a battle line, but there was mass confusion. Units were mixed together. I didn't see any of our regiment's officers. Lucky for us the Yankees were content with taking our entrenchments, at least for today. Their confusion was almost as great as ours. If they had pressed the battle, they could have destroyed most of our Army within hours.

We continued to run headlong across the fields. Minie balls filled the air with that strange, singing sound. Dirt flew up where they struck the ground. Every now and again I could feel the air whip my neck as one flew close by. One of the balls ripped a chunk out of my left ear. It felt like somebody hit me with a club.

Men dropped everywhere, many of them dead. A fellow we knew, Abraham Perry, was felled with a bullet to the leg. Whit and I threw his arms around our shoulders and drug him along. He kept saying, "Thank ye, boys, thank ye!" We must have drug him a quarter of a mile, when Whit stumbled and went down. As Abraham's weight shifted, I was pulled to the side and the two of us I went down as well. Whit and I got back on our feet, picked Abraham up again, and went on. Rifles in one hand, holding Abraham's arms across our shoulders, we ran—or, I should say stumbled—forward. All of a sudden, I felt Abraham's body jerk, then go limp. We lowered him to the ground; a minie ball had caught him in the back. He was gone.

Just at that moment, I sensed something behind us that made me turn and scream to Whit, "Get down!" A ten pound solid shot was bouncing along the ground. It struck the earth thirty feet away, hopped about six feet in the air and went flying over us as we dove to the dirt, then struck a man about twenty feet beyond us. He never heard it coming as it hit him at the base of the neck, and tore his head clean off as it continued on its way. His body dropped to the earth.

I said, "Let's get goin', Whit!" I started ahead, but Whit didn't move. "What's wrong, Whit?"

He was staring at the headless man before us. "Lord, I don't want to die like that. Not like that."

"Whit, we don't know how we're going to die, but I do know that if we don't get moving the odds are goin' up that we will, and soon."

Whit stumbled forward, looking at the headless corpse as we went by. He had seen a lot of death, but this one seemed to bother him more than most.

We were once again running, now trying to catch up with the main body of the army that was ahead of us. We reached them a few minutes later.

The day ended with the Yanks in control of what were once our lines. We threw up hasty works about two miles back of where we had started the day. Word came down that we would be retreating even further, leaving Richmond and Petersburg to the Yankees. The end was nigh upon us.

SEVENTEEN

In the fading light of day
the bitter taste of defeat
mingles with the grim satisfaction
of just being alive.

After we threw up some fence poles and small trees for a makeshift fortification, the officers ordered some men out on picket. There was a great deal of balking since men were taking orders from officers from other companies and regiments, something Confederate soldiers disliked intensely.

It seemed that most of the 18th was scattered all over creation. Whit and me were left alone for the time being, and we sat down with some boys from another regiment and settled around a small fire. There was nothing to eat, but Whit and I shared a little water from my canteen. I did have a little tobacco, so I pulled out my pipe and tried to get comfortable.

My blood covered hands shook as I lit the pipe. The random boom of artillery and the occasional rattle of musketry in the distance meant there was still some contested ground, though it seemed the battle was moving west of the Petersburg/Richmond line. The plank road was now a mile or more to our front and the Yankees had taken Petersburg and Richmond as well.

The capitol of the Confederacy was in Yankee hands for the first time in the war. It looked like the city of Richmond was on fire, as to the north we could see thick black smoke rising thousands of feet in the sky. It seemed to be the Confederacy's funeral pyre.

We hadn't been settled down for more than an hour, when one of the strangest things I have ever seen happened. Whit was propped against a rotten stump, just sitting and staring at the fire, when a young rabbit scrambled around the fire and scurried up under his knees. I guess it was confused and scared from the battle noises, and Whit's propped up legs looked like a place to hide. Whit cocked his head in that quizzical way of his then slowly looked down at the rabbit.

A fellow in the group around our fire, Jubal Nance, whooped, "Here's our supper, boys!"

Whit slowly reached under his legs, took hold of the rabbit and put it in his lap. The little critter was trembling. "I never seen no rabbit do this afore," Whit said, his mouth agape.

"Give him here, Whit, and I'll skin him," Jubal exclaimed. "There'll be a few bites for each of us."

"Hold your horses," Whit growled. "Ain't nobody gonna hurt this here little critter. Why, he wouldn't even make a bite for each of us."

Jubal gaped. "Whit, are you out of yore mind? Here's food come runnin' right up to us and you say we can't eat it?"

Whit looked at him fiercely. "That's what I said, Jubal. And if'n you don't like it you can find another camp."

"Well, I say you're tetched in the head," Jubal grumbled as he stood and shuffled off.

No one else spoke for a while. This was an amazing thing; another strange occurrence in a strange war. The rabbit sat still as stone while Whit stroked its back.

"Whit, do you plan on keeping that rabbit? They ain't good for much."

"I don't know, Francis. Maybe."

I said, "Well, if you keep it, you'll have to clean up after it. You know they ain't particular about where, or when, they do their business."

Whit grinned. "Won't be the worst thing I ever had on me."

Bobby Callahan said, "He won't stay around. Who ever heard of havin' a rabbit as a pet? You might as well keep a chicken."

Whit just grinned and said, "I think I'll name him Cadmus, after General Wilcox."

Everyone around the fire either rolled their eyes or chuckled. "Well, Whit," I said, "you better watch Cadmus close or somebody will eat the little general for supper!"

"Don't you worry, Francis, me and old Cadmus here will stick close." There were groans and shaking heads around the campfire.

The balance of the day was uneventful, and as darkness fell, the men tried to get comfortable for the night. Tomorrow would certainly bring more hot work. Nobody expected the Yankees to be content with holding Richmond and Petersburg. They would be after us as soon as they got organized.

I stood and walked away from the camp. There were fires strewn across the hills, like a reverse image of the stars flung down to earth. The wind was restless. I could hear the murmurs of a hundred conversations, quiet, composed on this side. I could also hear laughter and some fiddle music from the Yankee side. I stood for a long time, looking at the constellations as they glided in their slow, glittering parade across the night sky.

As always, my thoughts went back to the cabin in those Carolina hills and my sweet wife and two little ones. In her last letter, which I received about three weeks before, she had told me that she was soon going to plow the ground and put in some early crops. She planned to put in some pole beans and some corn by late March, hoping the frost wouldn't kill the young plants. Early crops are not as likely to be eaten by the insects. Of course she couldn't put in what I normally would. But she did the best she could with the farm and still took care of the girls.

They were beginning to get some schooling, and they had learned at school that many of their friends' fathers were not coming home, killed by Yankee bullets or dead because of sickness. She told me she was worried that they had already given me up for dead. She said they did not smile much these days, and when she mentioned me, Jane got a far off look. Little Susan just stared at her feet. It was like they did not want to hope that their Pa was coming back when so many fathers had not. They were afraid and sad all the time. No Yankee bullet could hurt as much as the thought of my little ones hurting. I guess that letter as much as any almost set my feet to walking towards home.

As I stood there with these thoughts, I once again felt that glow of love and admiration for Harriet and the girls at how they were handling the farm. It is a good thing I did not know about the deserters that broke into our home, because I was worried enough as it was. Harriet later told me that the situation with the deserters had frightened her but she carried on bravely. After the attack she gathered the girls' things together and they went over to stay with Pearly Walker's wife for a day or two. Mr. Walker notified Sheriff Coffey, and he and his men carried away the bodies and tried to put our cabin back in order. The sheriff came by the Walker's home the next day and spoke with Harriet about what had happened. He was amazed that none of them was seriously hurt and that a slight woman and two children had dispatched two desperate deserters.

Turns out they were a couple of men from over in the high mountains who had left Lee's army two months before. They had already raped and killed a woman in Salisbury, and the home guards and the sheriffs in the western part of the state were out looking for them when they showed up at our cabin. Sheriff Coffey allowed as to how Harriet saved the law the trouble of finding and hanging the men. Harriet told the sheriff that she would respectfully decline his thanks and that she would grieve for the rest of her days that she had taken a life, even though she knew she had to. She told the sheriff, and she later said to me, "Our Lord forbids killing another person. I know I had to protect my children and myself. All the same, I took lives, and my children had a part in it. We will have to remember that for as long as we live."

Clouds rolled in from the west, covering the stars. A faint breeze ruffled the leaves in the post oak and hickory trees. I tried to tune out the hum of voices, the distant thunder of the field pieces, the fiddle tune coming from the Yankee lines. I tried to listen to the voice of God.

I only heard silence.

I had killed men, I don't know how many. I am a soldier and I had to do my duty. I wondered why killing was a duty. I wondered especially why killing Americans was a duty. What sort of power brought all this to pass? What could be so important that we and the Yanks slaughtered each other by the thousands and had for four long, sad years?

My reason for coming here was because my government needed me and would not take no for an answer. What I wanted made no difference; I either came or they would have brought me at gunpoint eventually. I had no quarrel with anyone. The Lord commands us to live in peace with everyone as far as we can.

I thought, *The whole time I have been here I have not felt right about things. It's like a leaf floating down a river. The leaf doesn't have a say in where it's going. It just goes because the water takes it. I guess I am like that leaf; just floating along with the current, getting swept first this way then that. Rushing through the rapids to ... what?*

My mind went blank for a few minutes. I sunk to the ground right where I was and prayed for my family. I prayed I would get to go home and see them. They seemed so very far away.

EIGHTEEN

The dew falls soft
on the brow of the dead
though the hot winds of war
blow in the land.

I went back to camp and lay down beside Whit. He was snoring, with Cadmus the rabbit on his chest, staring, dark eyed, and flicking its ears. I lay awake for a long time looking at the stars until the clouds covered them all. The blood on my wounded ear was crusted and hard and it burned a little. I wet my bandana and dabbed at it.

I fell asleep but woke when drops of rain began to pelt the camp. The fire steamed and sputtered, then soon went out as a spring downpour rolled over us. The men muttered and groaned, trying to at least shelter their faces as the rain streamed down. But I sat up and just looked into the rain, letting it wash over my face, hoping it would wash away whatever guilt I had.

The young soldier I shot a hundred yards away; the Yankee praying as I killed him. Lord, what have I done? What have we done? These people are the same as us, exactly the same. They worship the same God. They have mothers and fathers, wives and children. They hurt and they hope. How many have I killed? God help us all.

Whit turned to his side and put Cadmus under his beat up old jacket. The rain lasted for maybe fifteen minutes and then stopped, just a spring shower. I dozed off again, but was wakened by a lieutenant I did not know, shaking me and telling me I was needed for picket duty. Some of the boys had been shot in the night, and a couple had run away, toward the Yankee lines. They had had enough of the war and thought they would eat better in Yankee prisoner of war camps than with the Army of Northern Virginia; and they were probably right.

I roused myself the best I could and shouldered my rifle, gathered up my bedroll and haversack. A lot of the boys left their sacks and bedrolls at the huts and bomb-proofs there in the trenches. I sometimes did, but yesterday morning I thought it might be best to have it with me when we went out to the line. Whit had done the same. My stomach was knotted, so I sipped a few drops from my canteen. My water was almost gone, maybe three or four swallows left.

The lieutenant looked tired. He also looked very sad. He paired me up with a corporal from another unit, and told us to move out toward the right flank. When I asked him where it was, he pointed southeast and said, "Go that way until you see Yankees. Try not to get killed. We'll send out some relief in a few hours."

The corporal's name was Jeremiah Brooks, from somewhere east of Raleigh. He said his family owned a sizable farm there and grew tobacco. He was a tall fellow, thin like the rest of us. He had a heavy beard, and dark eyes that made him look like a tough character.

We talked quietly as we walked. I found out he had been in the army for over two years. He had been in the middle of Pickett's charge at Gettysburg. He told me he had never seen such mass murder as happened that day. The Yankees had the high ground and they fired from behind a stone wall, while Pickett's men had almost a mile of open field to cross and marched, en echelon, toward the Yankee lines. The Yankee cannon opened up first, blowing holes in the ranks. When three or four men were blown out of the ranks, the rest would dress the line and march on, just like a parade. As they got closer the Yankee artillerymen switched from shell to canister and grape shot. Their field pieces became giant shotguns hurling out dozens of lead balls the size of large grapes or small hen eggs. The effect was to completely destroy a man's body. In many cases, there was not much left to bury, the grape shot literally tore the soldiers into pieces. The living would dress the lines and march on.

Then the Yankee infantry opened up with all they had, joining in the slaughter. Lane's brigade moved up the flank and fought like demons even as other brigades retreated. The corporal said he was almost to the stone wall when most of the men of the brigade finally began to retreat. Jeremiah raised his rifle and fired point blank at a Yankee officer standing just beyond the wall, waving his saber to rally his troops. The officer fell backwards, mortally wounded.

The corporal then began to walk backward towards his own lines. Minie balls whizzing by, cannons thundering a few yards away, and he walked backward. You see, he did not want to be found dead from a wound in the back. He felt, as many did, that it would be dishonorable. If he died, he wanted everyone to know that he died with his face to the enemy. So he slowly walked backward until he reached the relative safety of his own lines.

I had heard stories like this from other veterans so I did not doubt it. That day saw courage the likes of which is rare on this earth. When the corporal had finished his story, he fell silent, and we stopped. I realized we were as far out as we were going. We could see the Yankee fires as close as about three hundred yards away. We might only be a few feet from Yankee pickets. We decided to pull back a ways, and we quietly moved about fifty yards towards our men.

The cannon were silent for now. There was no noise coming from the Union side. To the north I could still see the hellish red glow of Richmond burning. The corporal turned to me, a smile animating his face as he said, "I cannot wait to get back to Smith's Field and see my wife and boys. I think this war's about over and maybe soon we'll see our families. I do so look forward to my wife's apple pie and to teaching my boys how to play the fid—" The corporal's face exploded, spattering my face with his blood. I heard the distant boom of a musket as he slumped to the ground. Another boom, and a round struck the tree behind us. Blood roared in my ears; I knew I would be next.

I dropped to the ground and scrambled behind the tree. Yankee sharpshooters were hidden in the woods maybe fifty yards away. I listened for a moment, then I eased around the trunk of the tree. *Whap-boom!* A minie ball struck the tree just above my head. The Yankees knew my position. I dropped to the earth again. I couldn't see exactly where the gunfire was coming from. I could hear the wind rushing through the trees overhead. I could see the clouds rolling across the face of the moon; they seemed in a rush to get away.

Whang! Another ball ripped across a rock just beside me. Where were they? I moved a little further to my right and tried to make myself invisible. There had to be two of them. The fire was coming too quick for one. I breathed a prayer to the Good Lord, because I was sure I would be seeing Him in person very soon.

It seemed the air was vibrating. My heart pounded. *Whoomp!* Another round ripped into the tree. I waited for the bullet that would blow my head apart. There was silence, except for a tree frog chirping nearby like nothing had happened. Then I heard the boom of a Springfield from about seventy five yards to the north, from our side. I heard "Aagh!" from the position of one of the Yankee shooters. I stayed as still as stone; then I heard movement from the direction of the shooters.

I stayed right where I was because I wasn't sure who was where, and I didn't want to get shot by the Yankees on purpose, or by a Confederate by mistake. Just to the left of my position, from the general direction of where the Confederate shot had come from, someone shuffled through the woods. I heard a familiar sound, "Haaak, ptoo." Whit. He came strolling up, grinning, and said, "I think I ruined that Yankee's day, Francis."

"There's two of 'em, Whit! Get down!"

Whit shook his head. "They're gone, Francis. One's down; the other left. I saw his back as he skedaddled."

"Corporal Brooks!" I exclaimed. I ran to where he had fallen. He was face down on the ground, not moving. I gently turned him over. Most of his face was gone. The Yankee minie ball had struck him in the right cheek bone and had torn it away.

Whit said, "Whew, I'm glad that ain't you, Francis."

We were silent for a space. I sighed. "This was a good man, Whit, a brave man. He was at Gettysburg and most of the other big battles. He retreated backwards."

"He did what?"

I said, "When they retreated, he walked backwards so he wouldn't be shot in the back. He wanted people to know that he had courage, and honor."

Whit looked at the remains of the corporal's face and said, "Well, courage and honor don't help him much now, does it?"

"We'll take him back, Whit," I said in a shaky voice. "A brave man deserves a decent burial, not to be left out here for the buzzards to pick at."

We carried the corporal's body back to camp. I found the young lieutenant and told him about it. The lieutenant's face was a mask of grief. Corporal Brooks had been a friend, and he said he would write the man's family. He sent two other men out on picket so we could bury him. Whit and Frederick Solomon helped me dig a grave and, as dawn dressed the Virginia hills in golden light, we laid him to rest under a tall pine tree.

Whit asked me to say a few words. I looked at the fresh grave. I looked at the lightening sky, the dark shapes of rain clouds scudding through the ether like they had somewhere to go. I thought for a moment before I spoke. "Lord, You know this good man didn't have to die, and I sure don't know why he had to. I hope someday You'll tell me because I am sure beginning to wonder about what You have in mind with all this." Whit looked at me. "Anyhow, as far as we know, he was a good man and a brave one. We pray You will give his soul rest and look after his family at home. Amen."

The lieutenant yelled at us, "Get in line, boys, they're coming!" About six in the morning of April 3, the Yanks came again.

It wasn't a forceful attack; just enough to set us back on our heels. We fought a rear guard action for a while, then we pulled back as the army retreated south and west. Whit and I were beginning to get very hungry, having had very little to eat for weeks and nothing for the past day and a half.

"You know a man can only go so long without vittles, Francis," Whit said.

"Don't complain, Whit. I'm sure we'll get something today."

"Well, if them Yankees would just charge again, maybe we could get some vittles off'n them!"

After we had walked about an hour, up rode Lieutenant Walters from our regiment. He stopped beside us. "You men are a little ahead of the rest of the regiment. Wait here and they'll be along shortly."

"I thought we were the rear guard," I said.

"You might have been, for a while," he replied. "Things are changing fast. All I know is we had better organize this retreat or the Yanks will be all over us." Then he rode on, no doubt looking for other strays to round up.

Whit yelled after him, "Have a lovely day, Lieutenant." The lieutenant either didn't hear him, or just ignored him.

"Why did you say that, Whit? Are you looking to get in trouble?"

"I don't rightly care, Francis. Trouble is my middle name." With that he let loose with his famous horse laugh, which ended in a fit of coughing, and out came a huge wad of tobacco.

"You're going to strangle on that someday," I told him.

He said, "Well I would rather strangle on my 'baccer than take a Yankee bullet!"

"What's one got to do with the other?"

He grinned. "Nothin'. I was just statin' a fact."

"Whit, you are one character," I said ruefully.

"And proud of it."

After a confused day like yesterday, with lines being broken and battles raging, units often get mixed up. Then people like Lieutenant Walters have to ride around and gather up all the stray sheep. They also have to deal with people like Whit, and worse. My Pa used to say it's like trying to herd squirrels. Discipline and control in a major battle are almost impossible to maintain, especially when formations are broken up.

I looked around. "Well, let's just settle ourselves here. Our boys will be along shortly and we can take a little rest while we wait for 'em."

Whit said, "Sounds good, Francis."

We were not unusual, sitting beside the road as the ragged army marched by. Many men sat or lay by the road, wounded or exhausted, or, like us, waiting for their unit. While we were there we saw men trying to walk who should have been in an ambulance. Men with stumps for arms, men with heads wrapped so that they could barely see out of one eye, men leaving a trail of blood in the dirt. Every single one looked worn out, starved, done in.

As I watched the parade of wretches I noted, "We never had a chance."

Whit shook his head sadly. "You know what, Francis, yo're right."

NINETEEN

I've been to Gehenna
to the Valley of Death
if I march long enough
will I find home?

We waited for about an hour beside the road, and then along came what was left of the 18th. The colonel and several other officers rode grimly by on horseback, the men trailing behind. We waited until we saw Sergeant Cas Hutchins. He had a nasty gash on his check which was oozing through a bandage someone had tied on him. "Sergeant," said Whit as we fell in beside him, "you all right?"

"Never better," said Cas. "It will take quite a bit more than a Yankee minie ball to take me out of this world."

I asked, "Sergeant, how many are left?"

Cas looked around. "It looks like about one hundred and fifty are still with us. We started the day with three hundred." He shrugged. "Some could still be mixed in with other units. Anyhow, we are not much of a regiment anymore; maybe a respectable company."

Whit asked, "Where are we going?"

"Well, said Cas, "word is, General Lee wants to try to move southwest and link up with Joe Johnston in North Carolina. One little problem he's got is maybe a hundred thousand Yankees behind and to the south. They say he is going to try to get away and save what's left of the army. We hope to make Amelia Courthouse before nightfall. That's about fifteen miles from here." Whit and I looked at each other. Normally a fifteen mile walk wouldn't be a problem, but in our condition, with no food and water, it was like climbing the Blue Ridge Mountains in lead boots.

"Sergeant," Whit said, "a lot of these fellers ain't goin' to make it, and I might be one of 'em."

The sergeant smiled slightly as he walked with his eyes on the road ahead. "Whit, we just do the best we can, ask the Good Lord for strength, and keep on marching."

"Well," Whit said, "I hope the Good Lord has got a plate of fried chicken around the next bend. My stomach is about to say howdy to my backbone, I'm so empty."

We were quiet after that, even Whit. Hunger and thirst were now more formidable enemies than the Yankees. We shambled down the rutted road. Some stopped to drink out of muddy puddles. We saw some fellows kneeling on the road, and as we walked by we realized they were picking through horse droppings for kernels of undigested corn. They washed the corn off in the mud puddles, and then later fried it up over a campfire. As I watched them I could only shake my head in amazement.

Whit's face wrinkled up. "I shore ain't that hungry yet!"

"Neither am I."

A major rode past us from the rear and barked, "Move faster men, the Yanks are just down the road." As we approached Amelia Courthouse, they threw us out in battle lines. We struggled to pile up fence posts, rocks, small trees, whatever we could find to make some fortifications.

The tree line was only a couple of hundred yards in front of us. We heard rifle fire to our right, then more just in front. Yankee cannon began to open up. They found the range quickly, and shells began to thunder down on us.

We crouched behind the little breastworks we had thrown up. The shells landed within thirty or forty feet of where Whit and I huddled, and dirt and rocks fell on us like rain. Canister shells exploded over us and balls shrieked downward, smoking as they struck the ground. We could hear men screaming when the balls and shell fragments found them.

The cannon fire slowed, then stopped. There wasn't a sound for several minutes; even the musketry fell off.

Then we heard it, the low roar of the blue ocean, coming out of the woods in our front, then the pounding of thousands of horses' hooves. The Federal cavalry came riding hard, roaring their deep-throated yell.

Whit said, "I'm about to get tired of these boys. They're about to make me mad."

I said, "Well, let's make them pay for troublin' us like this."

The Yankees charged out of the woods and our boys let them have a withering volley of rifle fire, the roar of muskets ripping the still air. A hundred saddles were emptied in an instant. The rest of the cavalrymen fired their carbines and kept coming.

Behind us Caleb Marsh cried out. He had been hit in the leg near his groin and blood was gushing out. He gasped, "I'm bleedin' to death!"

He was exposed to enemy fire ten yards back of our makeshift breastworks. Rounds struck the ground like leaden raindrops, throwing up dirt around us, but I ran to where he lay despite the galling fire. I grabbed him around the middle, stood and lifted him to my shoulder.

A stab of searing heat ran through my thigh and I dropped down. The two of us hit the ground hard. There was a bright flash. Then there was quiet darkness.

TWENTY

The bluebells are blooming
in the rolling fields
they toss their heads
above the bloodied ground.

"Doc, you got to save him. He's my friend. Don't you let him die!"

I heard Whit imploring someone to save somebody. I heard myself say from far off, "Whit, don't be bothering the doctor. I'm sure he is doing the best he can. Who's there to save?"

"Francis! Yo're alive!"

"Am I?" I could see Whit and the doctor as they looked down at me, but their faces were hazy and I was confused. The upper part of my right leg was infused with a liquid fire.

"You lost a fair amount of blood, soldier," the regimental surgeon explained. "That's probably going to hurt some," he said with practiced understatement. He put a bottle to my lips and I felt the unfamiliar sting of rye whiskey. I took it, even though I am not a drinking man. The doctor disappeared and all I saw was Whit's face, grinning from ear to ear.

He had an odd tone to his voice as he said, "Francis, you scared the very devil out of me."

"Well, that's … sayin' something, Whit. Where … where are we?"

"Oh, about three hundred yards from where you got shot. I carried you here myself."

I asked, "Where's … Caleb Marsh?"

"He didn't make it, Francis. After you two hit the ground, another round hit him square in the chest. You were right behind him. If he hadn't been there, that one would have got you!"

I shook my head and mumbled, "I tried to save him … tried to get him away; but I got hit."

"I know what happened, Francis. You could have got yoreself kilt."

My thoughts were becoming a bit clearer. "Is … is my leg … is it still there?"

Whit barked his hoarse laugh and said, "Why, a certain it's still there. You got yoreself a nice hole in it, though, courtesy of a .56 Spencer. A Yank cavalryman got lucky. It didn't hit the bone, if that's what yore wonderin'. Doc says if it don't get too infected, you'll be walkin' normal in about two months. Here, I found a little Union salt pork, courtesy of a dead Yankee horseman. I washed the blood off. It's purty good."

He put it in my mouth and I took it. I chewed and swallowed. Whit gave me some water he said he had fetched from a small stream nearby.

He looked grim as he told me, "They don't have anything to give you for the pain, Francis. Next few days will be purty rough. I'm goin' to see if I can get you a ride in an ambulance. Don't go anywhere, now." He laughed loudly at his little joke and disappeared.

The sun was going down. The sky looked surprisingly normal, high purple clouds edged with yellow and gold. I could hear men around me moaning in pain. I turned my head shakily and took it all in. I was in a makeshift hospital under some willow trees. Some of the men had bloody bandages; mine looked like Whit's shirt.

Every now and then a man would scream. One fellow, just a boy of about sixteen, shrieked loudly, then it turned into wailing. He cried for his mother.

I was sort of numb all over, though my leg let me know I was still alive. It throbbed in a painful, burning way. The lower part of my leg felt a bit numb, though I could still move it. It hurt considerably to do so. I tried to pray, but the pain kept demanding my attention. My head pounded.

The sound of artillery was off in the distance, some dull rattling of muskets. To our front the woods looked like they were on fire. I could hear men screaming in there, like they were burning;

probably men who were wounded and could not get out of the way of the spreading flames. At first I was confused, and then it came to me: *It didn't rain here when the shower came the other night. Woods must be dry. The cannon shells probably lit the underbrush. God help those poor devils.*

I think I passed out again, because the next thing I knew, I heard Whit saying, "Isaiah, you get his feet, I'll get his arms. Easy now." I felt myself being lifted and set down, then lifted again as they raised me up on a litter.

I heard Isaiah Tate say, "Whit, I don't think we can carry him all the way. It's a half a mile to the trains."

Whit growled, "We'll carry him, blast it! And don't you drop your end, even a little. Easy now, this is my friend."

"Your friend?" I said weakly. "I thought I was the fool that was going to get us both killed in Virginia."

"Back with the livin', are we," said Whit.

"I suppose I am, though only about half way."

"Well, a couple of days rest and you'll be back to shootin' Yankees by day and starin' at the stars by night, just like the olden times." Once again, Whit found his own words very amusing and took to laughing the sick mule laugh, hocking and spitting. Cadmus the rabbit peered out from the open collar of Whit's shirt. I wanted to laugh, but didn't quite feel like it.

Whit and Isaiah Tate carried me to the converted freight wagons now used as ambulances. They gently lifted me into a covered wagon which held four other fellows. Then Whit said, "I'll be right nearby, Francis. If you need anything just holler."

I gasped in pain and said, "I don't know, Whit. The way this leg hurts, I might holler a whole lot." Once again, I heard raspy laughter as Whit walked away.

Two of the boys in the ambulance had wounds so bad that they died within a few hours. The teamsters took them out of the wagon and drove on. I don't know what they did with the bodies, I was in too much pain to ask.

The dirt road was rutted and the wagon had no springs, so we bounced roughly with every turn of the wheels. Every time the wagon wheels hit a hole there was a jolt, and the dried blood on my bandage rubbed the wound. It became increasingly raw as the journey went on. Each bump was painful, and the stiffened bandage rubbed the wound over and over like a rasping file.

The pain screamed at me. I began to cringe at each bump, and my breath grew rapid. I tried not to cry out, but a couple of times I couldn't help myself. The other men in the wagon moaned and cried out, too. I found I was sweating even in the cool night air. We must have gone three to four miles before it was too dark to see.

The teamster stopped the wagon, then came back and looked in. "Anybody else dead in dere?"

One fellow I didn't know, who was also wounded in the leg, said, "Well, nigger, I don't suppose they'd be tellin' you if they was dead, now would they?" It was sort of funny, though I thought it was very unkind of him. I felt too bad to say anything.

"I was just askin'," said the colored man, humbly. Then he left.

The pain came on me in waves, like the ocean. It would subside, then I could almost see it coming, rolling red across my vision, an angry heat that took the breath away. I gasped. I had to think of something else. I looked up at the wagon's dirty white canopy. I counted the ribs in the top at least a hundred times before it got too dark to see. Little lights swam in the darkness. They floated gently, then the angry hot pain came and they exploded.

I rose up on my elbows to look out the back of the wagon. I could see fires spread over the battered countryside. To the south artillery flashes lit the night sky. The boom of the big guns was punctuated by the ragged tearing sound of muskets. Then I saw Whit's face as the cannon flashes lit the night. He looked in and grinned. "Settin' up, are we? I brought ye some hard tack and some coffee!"

I was astonished. "Where did you get that?"

"Oh, I got my ways."

I shook my head. "Dead Yankee, I suppose?"

He grinned. "Yep, a cavalry officer *and* his aide. I got food, water, and a purty nice pair of boots."

"You're wearin' an officer's boots?"

"Yep. They feel real good, too. My brogans was wore plumb out and the soles of my feet was kissin' the hard Virginny ground. Cadmus, say howdy to Francis, maybe it will cheer him up." Whit held his little rabbit out toward me. Without thinking I reached and took it. "Francis, would you mind if Cadmus rode with you? He ain't no trouble, and I thought he might like to ride with you instead of jostlin' around inside my shirt."

I looked at the rabbit, then at Whit, then back at the rabbit. How could I say no? "All right, Cadmus, I hope you don't mind a bunch of groanin' men. I suspect you'll hear a couple of strong words and some hollerin' too."

"Oh, he don't mind," said Whit. "If he can stand me, he can shore stand you! Haw, haw, haw," he said with another cough and a loud hock.

I said, "Whit, I'm much obliged for the food. Could you maybe get some more for the boys here?"

He rummaged in his haversack. "Why, shore, Francis. Here, I got several pieces of hard tack in my sack." Whit reached in and pulled out the cracker bread. He handed it into the wagon and the other two men took it eagerly. Then he passed his canteen around.

"Whit, you know the Lord's gonna reward you for this."

Whit laughed. "Well, maybe he'll mark off some of the bad things I done, too. I got to go out on picket, Francis. I'll see you in the mornin'. Try to get some sleep."

"I am much obliged, Whit," I said. With that, he was gone.

About an hour passed and Sergeant Hutchins came by. He looked in at me and said, "How do you feel, Francis?"

"Like there's a hot poker in my leg. How's your neck?"

He shrugged. "It's nothing. We'll be moving early in the morning, soon as it's light. The Yankee cavalry is nearby, and their infantry is only a couple of miles down the road. They're tryin' to cut us off and destroy the whole army in detail."

I was quiet for a moment, then said, "It looks from here like they've purty well done that already."

The sergeant laughed. "Not quite; this army's still got some fight, and they know we're dangerous. That's why they are movin' cautiously, tryin' to surround us." He patted the knee of my good leg. "Well, I had better get back. I need to send out some pickets. Rest well, my friend."

I nodded. "Thank you, Sergeant." He looked at me a brief moment then disappeared.

The man next to me spoke for the first time. "You friends with the sergeant?" he asked.

I said, "Yes, we serve together in the 18th."

He took a deep breath and said, "My name's Arthur Bloome, from Charleston."

I turned in his direction and for the first time realized he was a lieutenant. I said, "I'm sorry, sir, I did not realize you were an officer. My mind is a bit feeble here lately. I never thought they would put an officer in with privates."

He smiled and said, "It's all right. I supposed we are just making do right now. We're all in the same boat here."

I asked, "Where are you injured, Lieutenant?"

"Left leg, just above the knee, right arm and right hand. No bones broken, thank God. I got caught in a fierce crossfire, just west of Amelia Courthouse. Yankee cavalry tried to make me Swiss cheese."

I furrowed my brow. "I don't understand, sir."

He said, "Swiss cheese; you know, full of holes."

"Oh," I said, though I had never heard of Swiss cheese.

The lieutenant laughed softly, then said, "The doc says I will be okay, if a bad infection does not set in."

"That's just what he told me," I said.

The lieutenant smiled. "I'll bet it's part of a well-rehearsed speech. It's nothing, though. Before this I was wounded a total of seven times in four different battles, starting with Fredericksburg, then Chancellorsville, then Spotsylvania, and then Cold Harbor. These make ten wounds in all."

His voice took on a wistful tone as he continued, "You would think that's enough, that they would let me go home. But that never seems to happen. Of course, they have promoted me. I enlisted as a private in October of '62. I've served the better part of three years, and I've seen so much fighting, so much death, that I don't think I will ever be able to go back home and be a normal man again." His voice grew thick with emotion. "I was a deacon in my church; I was an attorney with a good practice in Charleston. Now, I am a worn out old soldier, at thirty-nine, with enough holes in me that I'll whistle like a pipe organ in a strong wind." He shook his head and laughed wryly.

"Well, Lieutenant," I said weakly, "I am afraid I cannot compare to you in my service. I enlisted in August of last year. By the time I joined the army, it was in the Petersburg trenches, and the Yankees had us pretty well nailed down. I've only seen a few fights, but that's been quite enough for me." My voice seemed distant, hollow. The pain came, then receded. Where did it go?

"And only one wound, the one I have in my leg. That is quite enough, too...." My words trailed off. The canopy above looked hazy.

The lieutenant said, "Well, Private, we're all soldiers, baptized by fire. We all want to go home."

"Yes sir, that we do," I said as my eyes went out of focus, "that we do." Unconsciousness closed over me like the lid of a coffin.

TWENTY-ONE

*From my front porch
in the star painted evening
the whippoorwill calls
and the night wind sings.*

"Francis, wake up." I heard Whit's familiar voice.

"I'm awake," I rasped.

"No, yore not, yore eyes is closed."

"I'm awake," I said as I opened my eyes.

Whit looked somber. "You don't look too good, Francis."

"Why, thank you, my good friend," I said, raising my hand shakily to my forehead. "You sure know how to make a feller's day brighter."

He said, "No, I mean yore pale, and yore eyes look weak."

"Well, I guess they feel weak, Whit."

"I brought you some bacon and some fresh water," he said.

"From the dead Yankee general store, I suppose."

Whit spoke with mock peevishness. "Well, no, as a matter of fact, Mr. Francis, I got it at a supply wagon. They had a few vittles there. I fried it up real quick and here it is." He handed me three thick pieces of bacon. I started eating. Then he handed me a canteen and I drank deeply. My throat was bone dry.

Then I said, "Where are my manners?" I turned to Lieutenant Bloome. His eyes were closed and I hated to wake him, but this food was a special occasion. "Lieutenant Bloome, would you like some bacon?" I asked.

Whit spoke softly, "I don't think the lieutenant will be needin' any bacon, Francis."

I realized that the lieutenant's wounds had bled him white during the night. The ground under the wagon was soaked with his blood. Despite my overwhelming hunger, I couldn't stomach the rest of my bacon and stuffed the two uneaten pieces in my shirt pocket.

Whit called to the regimental surgeon, who came and looked in. His face was lined and haggard as he climbed into the wagon and grasped the lieutenant's wrist. Then he slowly shook his head.

He asked me how I was doing and I said I was still breathing, though the leg hurt a mite. He showed me a rueful smile and said, "Soldier, I don't have a thing to give you. If it hurts badly enough, maybe you will pass out for a while. That's the best you can hope for."

The surgeon examined the other wounded soldier riding with us; he had also died during the night. That left only me in the wagon. The teamster and another Negro man came and took the dead men away. They would pick up more wounded. It was just a matter of time.

Suddenly I wanted out of this place of death. I couldn't breathe. "Get me out of here, Whit," I gasped. Whit helped me out of the wagon and steadied me as I stepped, trembling, onto the ground. My wounded leg throbbed as I set it gingerly on the ground.

Whit watched me carefully and said, "You don't look too good, Francis."

"You told me that already, Whit. I think I understand what you're tellin' me."

He said, "Eat yore bacon. I'll see if'n I can round us up some coffee."

"I don't even want to wish for that." I said. I sat down on a fallen log to the side of the road. Whit looked around and then walked off toward a group of wagons. If anyone could sniff out foodstuffs of any kind, it was Whit.

Around me was a tableau of death and suffering. The walking wounded, as well as the "able-bodied" among the ragged, starving army, were trying to gather themselves to march on.

The scene was nightmarish. Here and there a gaunt, trembling mule or horse would drop in its tracks, jerking the lines and panicking the other animals. The lucky ones got a bullet in the brain. Some just lay there and suffered, nobody even taking the time to put them out of their misery. Their plaintive cries filled the oppressive early morning air.

Those poor dumb creatures had no reason to die here. All they did was to haul their burdens day after day, and then this was their reward. Now that the army had no provender, they slowly starved to death. Sometimes they were butchered for meat. It was truly a wrenching sight to see a once powerful draught horse or mule stagger and fall, never to rise again. The animal deaths were almost as sad as men dying.

I would never have believed that sorrow could be piled on sorrow such as it was now in this time and place.

The teamster on our wagon walked over to me and said with a kindly smile, "Um, suh, I believe I heered the man say yo' name is Francis."

"Yes, sir, that's what it is," I said. He called me *sir,* so out of politeness I called him *sir* right back. That seemed to surprise him, as his head rocked back slightly. He looked to be about thirty years old, though it was hard for me to tell the age of colored folks. He was a big man, over six feet, with broad shoulders and skin the color of dark mahogany wood.

"I just wanted to tell you we gwine to be pullin' out here d'rectly, maybe in about fifteen minutes time," he said.

"My friend was goin' to try to find us some coffee," I said.

The teamster looked somber. "They ain't no coffee, no food. I ain't et in two days," he said without any trace of anger or reprobation.

I pulled the two uneaten pieces of bacon from my pocket and handed them to him. "Here, have some of this. I don't want this much."

His eyes lit up and he smiled broadly. "Why, thank you, suh! You is a saint." He ate the bacon, seeming to relish the salty taste.

I said, "Well, I wish I was a saint, but I must admit that I am very much the sinner, Lord only knows." He responded with a sad smile. I asked, "What is your name?"

He seemed surprised I cared enough to ask. "My name? My name is Cyrus Holland. Named after my master, Major Holland.

He got kilt about a year back, and they put me on a wagon. I told them I could fight, but they said that niggers wasn't goin' to do white man's fightin'. They said we could not be trusted with guns."

His face was kindly, and so far seemed to have a perpetual smile etched upon it. I asked, "Where are you from, Cyrus?"

"I come from down Charleston way, down on the rice plantations."

"I've never been there, but have heard it is very fine town. I was named for the Swamp Fox, Francis Marion, who was born in Charleston, South Carolina."

He cocked his head and said, "Well, I'll be! You don't live in the low country, do you?"

I laughed. "No, I live up in Rutherford County. That's in North Carolina, in the mountains."

Cyrus chuckled and said, "Shoulda known. You sho don't talk like them low country folks. Don't act like 'em neither. They wouldn't waste three words on me, and they sho wouldn't give me bacon, when they didn't have much theirself."

"Well, there are quite a few of us from Rutherford County serving in this here army, and I like to think they would all treat you decent."

"Can't say as I know anything about North Carolina, but Rutherford County at least sounds like a fine place. I am much obliged, Mr. Francis."

"You're welcome, Cyrus."

Whit returned with a tin cup of steaming liquid in his hand. He looked back and forth between Cyrus and me; a quizzical expression played across his grimy face. "I hope I ain't interruptin' nothin' important."

"No, I was just telling Cyrus, here, about home."

"What, Rutherford County? A fine a place as a man ever seed," Whit said. "I always used to say 'Fer I druther be in Rutherford than anyplace I know.' I come up with that all by my lonesome." He grinned. "Anyway," he handed me the tin cup, "I could only find one cup of this stuff, and all they had was coffee made from burnt corn."

I said, "I hope the corn hasn't already been consumed by a mule."

Whit threw back his head and laughed. "Well, since I been sippin' at it, I hope it ain't neither!" He handed me the cup. The hot liquid tasted pretty good. I took a couple of swallows.

I noticed Cyrus was looking at the cup. "Here, Cyrus, take some." I handed the battered cup to the teamster. Whit looked at me with that odd, quizzical look he can get.

Cyrus stared at the cup, then glanced at Whit. "No suh, I can't do that," he said.

Whit spoke up. "Why, shore you can, my good man. It's okay by me. Have some. It could be worse, and I'm purty shore it didn't come from the south end of a north bound mule." Whit wore a big grin.

Cyrus put the cup to his mouth and took a couple of sips. "Thank you, Mr. Francis, sir...," he said to Whit, not having learned his name. "I best be seein' to the livestock. Mr. Francis, you best be gettin' back in the wagon now. You'll surely have some company shortly. Good mornin' to you both, and ... may the Good Lawd bless you both." He nodded awkwardly, turned and went around the wagon.

Whit watched Cyrus as he left. "He seems like a regular feller."

"Yeah. You know, you and me have been fightin' to keep fellows like that in slavery."

"Not me," Whit said. "Not you, neither. That ain't why you and me been fightin', at least." He looked at me and added, "As for any of them what's been fightin' with us, Francis, I don't want to think about that too much. It could get on a feller's conscience."

I heaved a big sigh and gently rubbed my wounded leg. "It does, Whit. It surely does."

TWENTY-TWO

The sky is rusty iron
I can taste it
the hot wind rattles the trees
the earth swallows us whole.

We continued to retreat westward. The few days since I was wounded seemed like an eternity. The leg hurt every time I tried to walk, but I walked anyway. I didn't want to take up ambulance space when there were many who were wounded much worse.

Whit found me another rifle, and about forty cartridges and balls. It was a '63 Springfield, so it was probably off a dead Federal. It looked too new and shiny to have been used much. Whit had come to think of dead Yankees as general merchandise stores, where everything is free.

Some of the fellows took more than shoes, clothes, and food off of the dead soldiers they found. They would take purses, watches, and money. I refused to take anything but what was needful to survive or to fight. Beyond that, it was robbery.

Somewhere west of Amelia Courthouse, a big Yankee unit with heavy artillery batteries caught up with us. Somebody said it was General Sheridan. Their artillery was unlimbered and began to fire on us from a grassy hilltop about a mile away. The cannon fire seemed strangely ominous as it thundered with sonorous booms, foretelling some unspeakable disaster. Cannon fire had a power that overwhelmed foot soldiers. Like some vengeful monster in a dream, it thundered down on you as you cringed helplessly in the trenches. Men were known to lose control of their bowels and their bladders in the midst of a massive cannonade.

The remainder of the 18th and a couple of other skeletal regiments were thrown out into defensive positions on either side of the road. Whit and I and some others were placed in a ravine just south of the road. It was about ten to twelve feet deep running roughly east to west, and we positioned ourselves inside it, using its banks as fortifications. The ground in front was mostly open, stretching up the slopes of the grassy hill to our south, with stands of trees scattered about what had once been a pasture.

We didn't have the time or the strength to build breastworks. Everyone was hungry and thirsty and worn out, and the artillery signaled an imminent attack. We looked like an army of invalids, some men so weak that they staggered to their positions like drunkards, clambering up the slippery banks of the gully and digging out foot holds on the slopes of the bank.

The explosions from the artillery rounds slowly walked across the field toward us, each blast a little closer. The thunderous explosions made us flinch. This was well directed and accurate fire. We hadn't seen any cavalry in front of us yet, though we knew they were there. A shell exploded directly in front of us with a roar. Dirt and rocks flew by our heads. A second shell hit even closer.

This time I was lifted from my position like someone picked up a rag doll and tossed it. Whit was likewise thrown backward into the ravine. He sat up and looked at me, blood trickling from a cut on his lip. He said, "Lord have mercy; that was close! Whar's my rifle?"

He jumped up and looked around the bottom of the gully where men were sprawled, some lifeless. One fellow had an arm and part of his side blown off; another had a gaping wound in his stomach and his intestines spilled out onto the blood-soaked ground in a blue-gray heap.

The left side of my face was wet with blood from a small cut and I wiped at it with my filthy hand, succeeding only in mixing dirt in with the blood. I still held my rifle in my right hand. I struggled to my feet, using the rifle as a crutch. Pain shot up the wounded leg in a red wave. I fought to get up to the rim of the slippery gully. My leg trembled like it had palsy as I tried to climb the muddy bank. My mouth was parched.

Whit found his rifle. He had tied a turkey feather on it, so it was easy to pick out. He clambered easily to the top of the gully, propped his rifle on the edge, and peered through the smoke for what we were certain would be a cavalry charge, a fiery look in his eyes. Whit said, "Come on up, Francis. This here would be a fine place to die." This time he didn't laugh. His face was grim.

I struggled up, and looked out through the woods. The artillery seemed to have found its range, and the range was us. Plumes of dirt, rocks and smoke roared up out of the ground around and within the ravine. Men were thrown screaming into the gully. An explosion to our left killed three men and blood and fragments of flesh splattered us. Whit exclaimed, "Great God in Heaven, Francis. The whole Yankee army is trying to kill the two of us!"

I wiped at my face again, turned my head, and retched violently. I gasped, "Probably just a battery from a cavalry brigade, Whit. But that's quite a bit more than we can handle."

The cannon grumbled in the distance. More pounding explosions shook the ground. As if an order had been given, the remaining men of our regiment peeled away from the embankment and ran up the opposite bank, away from the brutally accurate cannonade. A few officers tried in vain to hold the men on the line, waving their sabers and shouting oaths, all to no avail.

Whit turned to me. "Let's git, Francis! If'n we don't go, we'll be facin' that brigade all by ourselves." We rose and ran down the bank, with me struggling to keep up, and then we started up the other side. My leg was on fire and kept giving way underneath me. It was stiff and weak; the pain took my breath. The leg just would not do what I told it to do.

Whit was at the top of the gully when he turned and saw that I was just beginning to struggle up the side. I lost my footing and went down hard at the bottom. I stood and tried to start back up, but the slippery dirt kept giving way, and it was hard to climb with my bad leg. Whit slid back down into the gully. "Come on, Francis. I'll give ye a boost." His strong hand grasped my arm.

I weakly tried to shrug out of his grip. "Go on, Whit. I'm holdin' you back."

He threw his head back and gave a long raspy laugh. "Now, Francis, I ain't goin' nowhere without you! Why, you and me is like peas...."

The world exploded with a colossal roar that jarred me to the bone. The wind roared around us with the heat of a furnace. Rocks and dirt tore at my face. Something wet. My lungs burned. The bank seemed to dissolve under us. Whit's strong hand was pulling downward now, dragging me down the bank to the bottom of the gully.

We crashed in a heap. The concussion rang in my ears; my thoughts were confused. I somehow struggled to my feet, staggered crazily, and looked around. Whit was on his back in the gully. "Whit. Whit, you hurt?" He uttered a long slow moan. I wiped at the dirt on his face. Blood flowed from his left eye.

He gasped. "Francis! Is it night? Did I get knocked cold? Is it night?"

I said uneasily, "No, Whit, it's still daylight."

He gasped again; his hands trembled as he raised them to his eyes and shouted, "I can't see! I can't see! My eyes is on fire! A blind man can't foller a plow!"

The cannonade slackened for a space. Smoke drifted through the gully. Men were moaning, writhing on the ground, some screaming in pain.

I reached down to Whit and said, "It's all right. It's gonna be all right. We just got to get you out of this ditch. Come on."

Whit brushed my hand away and shouted, "Cadmus! Where's Cadmus?!"

The little rabbit had been safely tucked inside Whit's shirt, and had fallen out during the last blast. But it was creeping around near our feet. I picked it up, tucked it inside my shirt, and told Whit, "I got him. We gotta move, Whit, or we're gonna die!"

"Is he okay? Are you sure he's okay, Francis?"

"He's fine, Whit!" I said. "Let's go!" This time I was the one trying to pull Whit up the bank. He was thin now, I noticed, not the beefy Whit who came with me to Camp Vance eight months ago. He was just a scarecrow, like the rest of us.

A few other soldiers struggled out of the ravine. I slung one of Whit's arms across my shoulders and said, "We gotta go now, Whit. Come on, help me." My bad leg moved jerkily and I tried to will it to move faster. It seemed like a bad dream, a dream where you want to move and you can't.

The artillery fire resumed with a vengeance; it pounded incessantly, explosions rocking the ground around us like the fists of an angry god. The roar and concussion of the explosions consumed my senses and confused my thoughts. Shell fragments flew by with a whipping sound; I don't know how we kept from being cut in half.

Whit turned this way and that, gasping and moaning, though he seemed to be all right except for his eyes. He was dazed and in terrible pain but we scrambled and fumbled our way up the bank and out of the ravine, my bad leg giving way again and again. More Federal shells were falling, and I knew in my heart it was just a matter of time before one found us. It seemed like the whole battery had opened up on the two of us. We moved as fast as we could, the lame leading the blind. We struggled through the falling shells and the smoke, until Whit gasped, "I gotta stop, Francis. I gotta pray. I gotta rest."

We had staggered for about three quarters of a mile across a grassy field and then through a broken copse. Panting from exertion, I said, "Okay, Whit, we'll stop now." The artillery fire had slackened, a cavalry charge never came. Men of our regiment sprawled nearby, some looking around in confusion, others with their eyes closed either in prayer or in pain. Whit sagged to the ground with a long agonizing groan.

I found Lester Carpenter and asked him to stay with Whit until I figured out where the regimental surgeon was. Lester looked at Whit, then at me, then back at Whit. He nodded slowly. He got out his canteen, gave Whit some water, and wiped at the blood which streamed down Whit's face.

Whit kept mumbling through his pain. "The mule don't know where to go, a blind man cain't foller a plow, cain't saw lumber." I knew what was on his mind. A blind man can't farm, can't do much of anything in the unforgiving hills of home.

TWENTY-THREE

The eyes of faith
will light the path,
when darkness is deep
and the way unclear.

I found the regimental surgeon … lying face down in some tall grass, a gaping hole in his back where an exploding canister shell had found its mark. He had apparently been hit just a minute or two before, because two of his aides came running as I stood over him. They turned him over and checked him quickly. He was gone.

I shook my head sorrowfully and said, "I am truly sorry. He seemed to be a very fine man." I looked at the two young aides. "Do you know where I can get some help for my friend? He is blinded."

The two aides looked at me with a confused look. They were just boys, and looked as though they were weary beyond words. Their clothes were so covered in blood that they looked like they served in an army of scarlet. Flies buzzed around them, attracted by the fetid smell of the blood.

One of them said, "The field hospital is that way." He pointed to a grove of trees about a half a mile away.

I looked in that direction and said, "In that grove?" He nodded, then looked back down at the dead surgeon.

I ran as fast as I could on my bad leg, in a crazy, rocking sort of gait, back to where I had left Whit with Lester Carpenter. Whit sat still as stone. He moaned in a low voice. His eyes and cheeks were a mass of blood. Lester was trying to tie a piece of his shirt around Whit's head to cover his eyes.

Whit said, "Francis, is that you?"

"Yeah, Whit, it's me. We're gonna get you to the field hospital."

Whit grimaced. "Well, I cain't hardly wait for that!" Field hospitals were places of dread. They were scenes of death, dismemberment, and extreme pain. Whit knew what lay in store.

I said, "Well, I don't think they will amputate your eyes, so don't worry about it."

Doctor R.L. LeMaster from the 54th North Carolina was tending to the wounded at the field hospital. He looked at Whit and his face went grim. He looked at me. "You his friend?"

I said, "Yes, sir. What can I do?"

"Well, Private," he said, shaking his head as he looked at Whit, "you can pray." After examining Whit, he took me by the arm and walked me about twenty feet away, then said quietly, "The right eye is damaged, but not badly; he could be able to see out of that eye after a while, though the Lord only knows when that might be. But his left eyeball is ruptured."

"Ruptured?"

"Yes. The fluid in the eyeball has leaked out. He is blinded for life in that eye. Our immediate problem is we have to remove what's left of the eyeball."

I was taken aback at the thought of them taking out Whit's eye. "You do?" I asked.

The surgeon explained, "I need to clean out the socket as best I can. We must do this or gangrene will set in and he will die." He yelled to an aide, "Cummings!"

I gasped. "What, now?"

He spoke hurriedly. "Yes, right now." As he walked me back to Whit he yelled again, "Cummings!" When the aide hurried up, Doctor LeMaster explained what needed to be done. Cummings took Whit by the arm and walked him over to a table.

The surgeon told me, "We have no painkillers, and he will have to be kept still. You and your friend will have to hold him. Cummings will strap his head down so it won't move."

Even though I was standing next to Lester, I repeated what the surgeon had said. "We have to hold him down."

Lester's eyes had grown wide. "I guess we'll do what we have to do," he said quietly.

The aide, Cummings, had placed Whit on an old oaken table. They looped straps across his forehead and tied them tightly through the boards of the table.

"Francis, what are they doin'?" Whit asked, his voice tinged with anxiety.

"It's all right, Whit. They have to work on your eyes. They have to do it to save your life."

Whit was breathing rapidly. "Francis, don't let 'em do it! A blind man cain't foller a plow. What will I do?"

I said, "Whit, the doctor says ... maybe you will see from one eye later on ...," words started to fail me, "but they need to ... clean things up ... the other one damaged ... they have to."

"Oh, Lord, Francis," he screamed at me. "Please don't let 'em do this. Yore my friend, don't let 'em!"

The surgeon said, "Hold him tight. Don't let him move."

I will go to my grave remembering that day. I did not watch what the doctor did. I tried not to hear Whit's suppressed screams.

In thirty minutes, it was all over. Whit's eyes were bandaged tightly; at least that was a blessing. He shook with sobs and moaned in pain. I sat for a while, giving him water, listening to him groan. It grieved me to see my friend in such distress. I resolved that I had to do something for him.

I looked around at what passed for a hospital in what passed for an army. Desperation rose in my chest. Something tightened up deep inside. I said, "Whit, I will find you something for the pain. I'll be back as soon as I can."

I found Sergeant Hutchins. "Sergeant Cas, they had to take Whit's eye out," I said, breathing hard.

The sergeant's expression became grim. "Take his eye out?"

"Yes, it was ruptured bad and the doc said it had to come out. He is in terrible pain. I have to find him something for the pain. Do you know where I could find something?"

The sergeant looked away from me and shook his head. "There's nothing with this army; everything's been all used up." He sighed. "Maybe if we pass by a farmhouse or an inn they'll have something; although the odds of finding anything are slim."

"He needs something now, Cas."

"I understand, but I can't give you permission to go looking, Francis."

"Just point me in the right direction and I'll do what I have to do."

"I can't do that, Francis. You can't go on your own. You could be shot by the enemy, or caught as a deserter and hanged by your own army. You know the risk you'd be taking."

"Yes, Cas, I know the risk." We both thought of our friend, Preacher.

The sergeant looked at me solemnly, weary eyed. "There used to be a tavern and a small settlement about two miles north of here. If you cut through those woods, go due north, you should come to the Old Lynchburg Road. It was somewhere along there. That's all I remember. And there's Yankees all about, so if you go, be careful."

"Thank you, Sergeant. Say a prayer for me." With that, I grabbed my rifle and started off to the north, not knowing what I would find, or whether I would find anything.

As I walked—hobbled I should say—I tried to examine the situation. *Even if I find the tavern, it will probably be burned down or cleaned out. It most certainly won't have any whiskey. What am I doing?* I knew the answer to my own question: my friend needed something and I had to try to find it. Maybe I would run into some dead Yankees with something Whit could use.

I crossed the field and went into the woods, my leg throbbing with a burning sort of pain. As I went past the pickets, Hezekiah Smith, a man of our company asked, "Whar you a'goin', Francis?"

I said, "I'm not sure. I'll tell you when I get back." I was out of sight within a couple of minutes. I began to feel an increasing sense of danger, as I knew what I was doing was probably suicide. The enemy was all about, in hot pursuit of Lee's floundering army, and Federal pickets would be quick to pull the trigger if they caught sight of me. Cavalry units roamed the countryside, and they, too, would not think twice about shooting down a stray Rebel.

I moved like an Indian, staying in the shadows, using the undergrowth for cover where I could, measuring my steps, careful not to step on a twig that would snap and give me away. I could hear the rattle of muskets off to the east, and noted the sharper pop of Union cavalry carbines down toward the south. Now and then I caught the dull grumble of distant artillery.

I crept through a large stand of Virginia pines, the green boughs slapping my face as I struggled through the undergrowth. The cat briars grabbed at my pants legs, scratching like their namesake.

I had gone about two miles and, as I eased through the last of some thickets before a clearing ahead, I heard voices. A commanding voice was saying, "If we push in this direction now, we can get in front of the Rebels and they will be snared. We may even be able to cut Lee's army in half and destroy it in detail. Take this information to Division Command."

I heard a horse whinny and then hoof beats faded away toward the east. I eased on through the pines, very, very slowly, expecting to feel the impact of a picket's bullet at any time. As I came to the edge of the trees and peered through a thick pine bough, the scene before me made me freeze.

There were four Federal officers sitting on fallen logs, talking quietly among themselves. Their horses were hitched nearby. A wagon stood off to the side, where a teamster bent over a small fire. Suddenly, a covey of quail flushed near me, fluttering away noisily. I saw the men look in my direction. If I ran they might give chase and I could be caught. So I did what I thought General Lee would do; I made a bold move.

I took a deep breath and stepped into the open with my rifle raised. "Don't ya'll move a muscle or you'll be dead men." The officers jumped to their feet. "I said don't move!" I bellowed.

One man began to speak. From his uniform it appeared he was a brigadier general of the Union Army. He said, "Soldier, you best put that rifle down and surrender. We know you only have one round to use, and there are four of us."

I swallowed hard and tried to speak in as commanding a voice as possible. "Well, sir, begging the general's pardon, but if I have to use that one round it will be upon you, sir." I aimed the musket directly at the general's head and tried to keep my hands from trembling. The general's expression became very solemn, and I thought I saw the first evidence of fear in him as his eyes widened a little and his face began to flush. He had probably only seen us Rebs at a distance and had never had a rifle pointed directly at him. "I mean it, sir. I will kill you even though it means I die, too."

The general was a large man, with a reddish brown beard and an immaculate blue uniform. I could tell he was pondering the situation, calculating odds, considering and disposing of options.

He recovered his composure, licked his lower lip slightly and said, "Do you mean to take us captive?"

I said evenly, "No sir, but I do need something from you."

The officers looked at each other. One man with icy blue eyes and a hard expression spoke up. "I can't believe we're standing here talking with this piece of Rebel trash. I know one thing: if they are all in this condition, we'll finish them off soon. I still think we can get him before he gets us."

I said, "Let me remind you that if you move, your general dies, just like that. Rebel trash or not, I can still pull a trigger, and .58 caliber's worth of bad news will be coming at your general's head before you can blink. You understand that, sir?"

The general barked, "Keep quiet men!" Then, turning back to me, he snapped, "You said you need something?"

"I have a friend who is bad wounded, thanks to your artillery, and they had to take his eye out. He needs something for pain, and our surgeon has nothing to give him. That is what I am searching for. Do you have any whiskey in that wagon?"

He replied, "I expect we do."

I thought a moment. "Might you have anything else, like laudanum or morphine?"

"Maybe…," said the general in a too casual sort of way. I moved closer, the barrel of the rifle pointed precisely at his forehead. His eyes widened further.

"Sir, do not make light of this situation if you ever want to see your home and hearth again," I said. Out of the corner of my eye, I saw the Negro teamster moving around the wagon away from us. I shouted, "You—teamster—get back around here or your general will be killed." The Negro hurried back around the wagon. "All of you," I yelled at the officers, "drop your weapons on the ground and move back five paces."

"Sir," the blue-eyed officer yelled, "we can take him now!" His hand seemed to vibrate, as if he was itching to go for his pistol to fire it at me, not drop it on the ground.

The general bellowed, "Trent, do what he says, blast you! It's my head that rifle's pointed at!"

No one moved. Time was not my friend. The pain in my leg screamed at me; the red wave rolled in; my hands trembled, and I struggled to get them under control. I thought to myself, *This is insane; you'll never get out of here alive.*

The Federals glared at me. I knew they were trying to think of ways they could take me without the general being killed. I could almost hear the wheels turning in their heads. My heart pounded, my breathing was quick and shallow. I tried to swallow but my mouth was powder dry. The officers watched me carefully. I tried harder not to let them see my own fear. I steeled myself to do what I had to.

I said in a low steady voice, "Teamster, get down on the ground with your arms stretched out where I can see them." The Negro, used to taking orders from white men, complied. "Now, gentlemen, unbuckle your belts and drop the pistols and sabers, very slowly." The officers did as they were ordered, though showing as much possible disdain for me as they did so. I breathed deeply and said, "Now move backward five paces, very slowly." The general and the other officers complied, each moving exactly five paces. I retrieved the nearest revolver, checked to see it was loaded, raised it at the general, and placed the heavier Springfield on the ground.

I spoke to the youngest officer. "You, sir, please take the cinches off those saddles, cut them if you have to, and tie these men up. I suggest you do it in a way in which they cannot get loose for some time. I'll be checking." I pointed to the general's horse. "Leave that one alone, I'll be borrowing it." The young officer retrieved the cinches and began tying the officers' hands behind their backs. They allowed him to tie them up; they were suddenly getting used to taking orders from a mere private. I thought, *Now there is something to sit and ponder over sometime.*

When he was finished I told him, "Help them all sit down." They all sat. I called to the teamster and pointed at the young officer. "Now, you come and tie this man up." The teamster's eyes grew large. I barked, "Do it, man. I have six rounds, I can kill them all." He quickly grabbed a cinch strap and tied up the young officer.

I walked around the men, testing the cinches, all the while keeping the revolver pointed in the general's direction. They all appeared to be tied securely. I spoke again to the teamster, "Now, pull off their boots." The teamster complied. "Throw them as far as you can in all directions. Do it now!" It was probably a greater precaution than necessary, but I was in a state of mind to be very careful.

The teamster flung the boots what appeared to be at least a hundred feet in all directions. Then I looked at the general and asked, "All right, sir, you said you might have morphine?"

The general looked at me glumly and growled, "In the wagon, there is a medical satchel."

I spoke to the teamster. "Get it. And if you are not back in one minute, they will all die." The teamster scrambled to the wagon and practically dove inside. While he was gone, I untied all the horses, except the general's, aimed them toward the Rebel army, and slapped their flanks.

They galloped off. It seemed funny at the time, so I smiled at the officers and said, "Looks like your horses are deserting to the Confederates. I suppose they are not diehard Unionists!"

The teamster came back with a medical satchel. When he was a couple yards away from me I said, "Stop where you are and toss it over here." He did as he was told. I caught it in the crook of my left arm, then opened it and looked inside. It contained small, clearly marked bottles, including morphine and laudanum. There were also syringes, bandages and other medical items. The general was a man who believed in being prepared.

"Now, teamster, have a seat." He looked around for a place to sit, but before he could do so I stopped him. "No, wait. I suggest you start walking down that road toward the Yankee lines. And if you so much as turn your head to look back, so help me, I will kill all these men. Do you understand me?"

His eyes were wide as he answered, "Yassuh!" The man was as terrified as any human I ever saw. He knew he would have a lot of explaining to do if these officers were killed.

"All right then, go!" He turned and ran as fast as ever I saw a man run.

I watched him until he rounded a bend in the road and was out of sight. Then I turned to the officers, who had not taken their eyes off me. I waggled the barrel of the revolver I was holding in a jaunty salute, then said, "Gentlemen, I am much obliged for the medicine."

The barefoot officers scowled at me. The blue-eyed one was the only man who spoke up. "Rebel, just who do you think you are? Do you think a lowly, starved out vermin like you is going to get away with tying four U.S. Army officers up like dogs? You are not. I will kill you, Rebel. It is now a matter of honor!"

Though he was clearly dead serious, at first it struck me as humorous. Then I am afraid I lost control just a little. Thrusting the pistol in the steely-eyed officer's face, through gritted teeth I said, "You fellows might feel a little ashamed that one pitiful Rebel got the drop on you, but at least you'll leave here breathing. I can't say as much for many of my friends. And let's not forget, Lord knows how many of your own poor boys that you've sent out to be slaughtered! You order them to make senseless charges against fortified positions, knowing they would be killed by the thousands. Men with homes; wives and children. You were so determined to beat the Rebels that you sacrificed thousands of good men, and for what? So you could get promoted to the next rank?"

The officer made a noise as if he intended to respond, but I cut him off by tapping the revolver on the tip of his nose. I could feel myself getting flushed, both from the pain in my leg and the rising anger in my heart. "Let me also remind you that you are in the Southland, and you most certainly did not have to come here. Nobody invited you. You came to kill and destroy. No, sir, this is not all the fault of the South or Lee or Davis. If your President had just been a little more patient; if you fellows had just stayed home; there would not be this kind of death and destruction."

At this point I was almost shouting. "Therefore, sir, if you see me again and want to kill me, just have at it, because I have a better home waitin' and, after all, I will just be another poor farmer you butchered."

By this time the Colt was pressed hard against his nose. His thin face was taut. He glared back, his eyes wide. I was breathing hard and my grip was tight on the pistol. I was afraid I might pull the trigger.

I let out a deep breath, pulled the gun away from his face, and turned to the others. More calmly, but with a trace of cynicism, I said, "I regret that ya'll have been inconvenienced and, although I would like to stay and talk over the issues of the war," I looked down at the satchel, "I must get back to my friend. He needs this medicine. Goodbye."

I hung the officers' gunbelts on the pommel of the general's saddle and stuffed any extra ammunition I could find into the saddle bags. I picked up my rifle and mounted the general's horse, then started it back towards our army. I am not a thief, but I thought I had a better chance of getting back riding than walking on my bad leg.

The cold-eyed officer screamed after me, "You will die, Rebel! You will die!" I rode on.

As I neared our pickets, I draped my rifle across the saddle in front of me and raised my arms in the air. I identified myself to them, and fortunately I had returned to a handful of pickets who knew me. With looks of amazement the four men took in the big, brown Yankee horse, topped with a blue Union saddle blanket trimmed in gold, and ridden by a ragged Southern private. It was almost too much for them to believe.

As they waved me on, one of them called out, a quizzical expression on his face, "Francis, what the...?"

I smiled. "You fellows don't have to salute." As I rode on by, I looked back at them. They stood with their mouths hanging open and gave each other questioning looks. I think some of them thought they were seeing things.

After a brief search, I found the surgeon who had operated on Whit. I dismounted, satchel in hand. "Doc, I have something for you."

TWENTY-FOUR

Raw are the wounds
of the battered warriors,
in the fading light of a ragged day,
rawer still, the edge of the soul.

Doctor LeMaster looked through the medical satchel with his lips pursed in thought. "I haven't seen these items in some time."

"I give you these on one condition, Doc," I said. He looked at me in surprise, probably not used to being given conditions by someone of my lowly stature. "You must save enough to keep my friend free from pain for at least the next few days. That is my only condition."

The doctor looked at me, looked down at the medical satchel, then said, "Private, I believe you have earned that much."

"Thank you, sir. Now, will you please give some of this medicine to my friend; he is in great pain."

"Yes, indeed I shall, Private."

With that we headed over to where Whit was lying, wrappings still over his eyes. The doctor removed one of the syringes and a vial of morphine, then injected Whit with the drug. Whit was startled. "Ouch! What was that fer?"

"It's medicine, Whit. Morphine. It will make you feel better," I said.

"Yo're back, Francis. I thought ye had left fer good."

I said softly, "Now, Whit, old man, you know I wouldn't leave you."

Whit grinned tightly, and then his face slowly slackened. Within a few moments his head fell back. He was sound asleep. I felt tremendous relief, almost elation. "Thank you, Doctor," I said.

The surgeon stood, studying Whit. "No, thank you, Private. A lot of men will be relieved of their pain because of you."

I looked again at Whit, now quietly sleeping, his head resting on his haversack. I nodded to the doctor and walked back to where I had tied the Union general's horse.

I rode it back to the 18th's makeshift camp. A number of men roused themselves from their respective reveries and sauntered toward the horse, various befuddled expressions playing across their powder-blackened faces. Sergeant Cas strode up with a quizzical grin on his face. "Have you joined the Yankee cavalry, Francis?" As I dismounted he patted the saddle blanket and added, "As a general, too, I believe; quite a promotion those Yankees gave you!"

"Well, Sergeant, I figured it beat all this here walking about we do in the infantry." The men laughed and they crowded around to hear me tell my tale.

When I finished, there was silence for a moment. The sergeant looked at me with his twisted grin. "Francis, you're telling me that you captured four Yankee officers ... one a brigadier general ... and took their medical supplies, their pistols, and the general's horse ... all by yourself?"

"Yes, sir, that's pretty much it. I regret I was not able to bring them back with me, but I was mainly concerned about the medical supplies. It is almost more than I can believe myself. I guess the Good Lord was with me. You know the Good Book says, 'If God is for us, who can be against us.'"

The sound of hoof beats and the huffing of horses made me turn around. Colonel John Barry was riding toward us with his aide. His eyes were fixed on the general's horse. "Sergeant, what in blazes is going on here? Where did that animal come from?"

"Well, sir, Private Yelton here captured it, along with four fine pistols and some medical supplies from a group of Yankee officers evidently out on a scout."

Colonel Barry's eyes widened as he got a closer look. "That's a general's horse!"

I suppose I was feeling my oats as I spoke up. "If I may, sir, it was a brigadier general, though I was not properly introduced so I fear I do not know his name."

The colonel smiled slightly. "Private, would you accompany me to my camp." He paused, looking the fine horse up and down. "Bring the horse with you." Cas was hiding a grin and shaking his head.

I mounted the horse and followed the colonel and his aide. The colonel's camp, near his wagon, was only a hundred yards to the rear of our camp. Again, men gathered and looked open mouthed at the horse.

We dismounted and he headed over to a large fire. I wasn't sure whether I should follow him. I couldn't help but notice a pot of coffee on the fire, but the colonel saw me looking at it. "Would you like some coffee, Private?"

Uncertain, I said, "Yes, sir, if it wouldn't be too much trouble."

"Not at all. Captain, get the private some coffee please." The aide grimaced; the thought of fetching coffee for a bloodied, sweat stained private was, I could tell, extremely distasteful.

"Colonel, sir, if someone will just show me to a cup, I will get it myself. There's no need to trouble the captain."

The colonel glanced questioningly at the captain, who looked relieved and pointed to several cups sitting to the side. I retrieved one and helped myself to some actual, genuine coffee.

The colonel motioned for me to join him by the fire. I sat down across from him with the steaming cup in my hand. I tasted the coffee, and it was the most wonderful liquid I ever drank before or since. I sighed with pleasure. "This surely puts our burnt corn brew to shame, sir."

The colonel, a handsome, dark haired man a little older than me, smiled slightly. "So, tell me, Private…?"

"Yelton, sir. Francis Yelton."

"Private Yelton … Francis … can you describe the group of men you, er, encountered?"

"Yes, sir. There was one brigadier general, a large man with a reddish brown beard, and three other officers. I believe one was a colonel and the other two were majors, or maybe captains. I was very much engaged at the time and did not really inspect their uniforms."

"Did the brigadier have a mark, right about here—" the colonel pointed to his right temple, "—like a birthmark?"

"Well, yes sir, he did. I couldn't help but notice because he glared straight at me like I was the devil himself, and I lined my sights up at the middle of his forehead, so I got a real good look at him."

The colonel laughed softly. "He probably did think you were the devil or one of his demons, looking like you do and coming out of the trees as bold as brass. I believe that was Brigadier General Hallman. If it was, then I know which Yankee division is in front of us—or behind us, depending upon your perspective. Hallman likes to go out on these scouts. He considers himself much bolder and more courageous than his fellow brigadiers. I personally think the man is foolhardy, and the proof is standing right there." He looked toward the general's horse. "Which reminds me: Captain, check that horse's saddlebags. Bring me any papers."

He turned back to me. "Private, what you have done not only helped your friend and many others, but it most certainly humiliated a man who could have used some humbling. You did a very fine thing, though you hardly did it under orders. Normally, going off on a wild adventure like that with no sanction from your superiors would be cause for discipline of the severest kind." I began to feel concerned, but he continued, "This time, I am going to overlook it. I only want one thing from you in return."

"What would that be, sir?" I asked, feeling relieved.

"You have yourself a fine Yankee stallion there and I propose a trade. My horse is just about as good, but I would like the privilege of riding a Yankee general's horse for the rest of the war. What do you say, Francis?"

I had already expected to give the horse to the colonel, knowing somehow they would not let me keep it anyway. I looked at him evenly. "Colonel, I believe that would be a very fair trade, since I don't have any right to a horse in any event. I do think it would come in handy if what little is left of Company H had a spare horse to help with the wounded and so forth. However, at the risk of sounding impertinent, I would also ask that I be permitted to keep two of the revolvers, one for me and one for my friend who lost his eye. I can see they may be useful, with the Yankees closing in and all. I would propose giving you the general's pistol and one other, and keeping two of the pistols. Would that be acceptable?"

Thankfully, instead of taking it the wrong way, the colonel was impressed. "Private, you have brought some real fine news to this regiment, which hasn't had much good news lately. A Yankee general's horse and his pistol! You have yourself a deal!"

"Thank you, sir."

Then the colonel turned serious, looking me up and down. "When we get to a more permanent camp, I am going to make you a sergeant," he said.

I paused a moment. "Well, sir, if it's all the same, I would rather remain a private. I do not covet the responsibility of a sergeant— if the colonel does not take any offense."

"As you wish, Francis. Captain, the private here is taking my horse and I am taking his, even trade. Leave him my saddle but remove all my personal items."

The captain began unpacking the colonel's horse, a sturdy chestnut stallion. The colonel walked me over to it and shook my hand warmly. "Thank you again, Francis. The horse's name is Abe," he said with a smile. "One more thing, Private, don't ever do anything like this again without permission. You could be shot as a deserter. We have some grim work still to do."

"Yes, sir. Oh, Colonel, about the pistols: I would like to keep the extra ammunition if it is all right with you."

"All right, Private. I hope you get some Yankees before this business is done."

I looked at the ground. "I am afraid I have gotten more than my conscience will let me alone with already."

The colonel looked at me steadily, his dark eyes seeming to penetrate to my soul. "Well, Francis, this is war. People will die, unfortunately far too many as I see it. You are just doing your job; defending your home, your friends. Don't dwell on it too much. God knows what we are going through."

The captain finished transferring the colonel's possessions to the Union general's horse. "Sir, there's some tobacco in those saddlebags, chewing and smoking." He handed the items to the colonel, who in turn handed them to me. "I believe this belongs to you, Private."

"Thank you, sir," I said, impressed by his continuing generosity. "May the Good Lord bless you."

I mounted old Abe, saluted the colonel, and turned the horse toward our camp. After all that had just happened, what would the morrow bring us?

TWENTY-FIVE

The end begins,
a sad whimpering time
defeat tasting bitter,
though the end is its own reward.

As I rode back into our encampment, once again the men gathered. Sergeant Hutchins recognized the colonel's horse. "What happened, Francis, get demoted to colonel?"

"Well, Cas, I figured a colonel's horse was good enough for a poor private and dirt farmer from the hills. The colonel traded with me. He liked the idea of riding a Yankee general's horse for the rest of the war." I dismounted, and handed the sergeant the reigns. "I just thought maybe Company H could use a good animal like this. Maybe help transport the wounded or some such."

Sergeant Hutchins looked appreciatively at the horse and back at me. "I am sure the captain will find a use for it. You know, when this is over, you could take it home. I mean, you certainly have earned the right to keep it."

I collected the pistols, ammunition and tobacco from the saddlebags. "Well, Cas, if I make it, maybe we can see about that. Meantime, I suppose walking won't hurt me too much."

As I limped painfully away, Cas shouted after me, "Are you sure about that?"

I returned his wry smile and went on. I wanted to check on Whit's condition before sundown.

Whit and Lester Carpenter had settled down near the so-called hospital. Even if it had been pitch dark I could tell where it was. You could locate it by the screams of men whose arms and legs were being sawed off with little or no anesthetic, that and the singing sounds the bone saws made. I had hoped the morphine and laudanum would help some, but the screaming was still enough to make a strong man feel weak. Men who seemed fearless on the battlefield, were now screaming like women or little children. Some called for their mothers, though many were likely hundreds of miles away—if not deceased.

When a man has come to the end of himself and feels that childlike helplessness of grievous wound or dreadful loss, he can only call on one he knows will comfort no matter how extreme the circumstance, no matter how unbearable the pain. That one person is likely his God or his mother. It no longer surprised me to hear strong men call for their mothers, though it touched something deep inside and caused an abiding disquiet in my soul. I would rather hear them call for their God, because only He can help in so desolate a situation.

To call on a far away mother while suffering an intolerable wound seems to me to be emblematic of the very bleakest of hope. A sadder, more despairing state, I cannot imagine this side of the very Lake of Fire.

Whit was asleep when I got there. Good old Lester sat by his side, smoking a corn cob pipe. "How is he doing, Lester?" I asked.

"About the same. He talks in his sleep sometimes."

"What is he saying?" I asked.

"Well, mostly mumblin' nonsense. I cain't make much of it."

Whit stirred and said, "You two talkin' about me?"

"We promise we said ne'er a bad word about ye, Whit old boy," said Lester.

"How you feelin', Whit?" I asked.

"Well, Francis, I feel like I got kicked in the head by a mule, right in the eyeballs. Other than that, I feel just fine."

I studied him closely and asked, "Is the pain comin' back?"

"You might say that," Whit said, his mouth taut.

"I'll get the doc," Lester volunteered.

"Never mind, Lester, I ain't hurtin' that bad. Say, is there a cup of coffee layin' around somewhar?" Whit asked.

Lester stood up. "I'll see if I can find one." He took off toward the supply wagons with that determined stride of his.

"Well, Francis, I heered ye had quite an adventure today, taking on the Yankees all by yoreself!"

"Well, it was just four officers and a teamster and I surprised them. I still don't know why they didn't have pickets or an escort of some kind. The colonel says that he thinks it was General Hallman, and that he is an arrogant, overly confident sort."

Whit laughed softly. "He just hadn't come up against a whirlwind like Francis Yelton!"

"I must admit, Private Whitaker, I did not feel like a whirlwind when I was facing down four Yankee officers. I think my heart is just now settlin' down in my chest where it belongs. It might near came out my throat."

"Francis, don't be so modest, yore a regular hero, and a real man of vay-lor. They ain't another man in this here regiment could'a done that. I know it fer a fact!"

I sighed. "I wish you wouldn't make too much of it, Whit. I was real lucky and the Good Lord was with me. If those fellows had pulled their revolvers and fired when I stepped out of the woods, I would be pushing up the daisies."

"Well, I admire it, Francis. I admire it."

"Thank ye, Whit old friend. How about a chaw? The good general had several pouches in his saddle bags."

"Francis, yo're a saint. Praise the Lord, I ain't had a chaw in years, it seems."

"Well, I figure there's enough here to keep you chawin' for a few days, anyway." I stuffed most of the chawin' tobacco in Whit's pockets where I knew he could get to it. About that time, along came Lester with the coffee as Whit had the chaw halfway to his mouth. "Hold on, Whit, Lester's got you some coffee."

Whit grinned. "What a dee-light, holdin' off a chaw so's I can drank some coffee. You want a chaw, Francis?"

"No thanks, Whit. The general also had two pouches of some real fine smokin' tobacco. I think I will light up my pipe. Care for some tobacco, Lester?"

"Don't mind if'n I do."

We settled back, Whit propped against a tree, sipping his hot burnt corn coffee. Lester and I smoked our pipes. After a space,

Lester set his pipe down and pulled out his mouth harp. He began to softly play "Lorena" and then "Evelina" and "Kathleen Mavourneen." We listened to the wistful music about love lost or love longed for.

Lester paused his playing. Whit let go a big sigh. "You know, fellers, I ain't goin' to be able to farm when I get home." We were silent for a moment.

I broke the silence. "Whit, you don't know that. The Doc said that you might be able to see with the eye that didn't get ... that didn't get ... ruptured."

"I hope so, Francis, I truly hope to the Lord. All I know is farmin' and lumberin', and besides, what else could I do if I'm ... blind." He was silent for a minute or two, as were we. Then he continued, "I truly love farmin'. It is the one thing a man can do for enjoyment that feeds his family, helps put clothes on their back and a roof over their head. Fellers, I tell you, I always led a peaceable life, just farmin' and sawin' lumber, before this. That is, except for the time two fellers tried to kill me down near Burnt Chimney. Did I ever tell you fellers about that?"

We shook our heads, then sheepishly looked at each other. I said, "No."

It seemed Whit felt like talking, so we let him. "Well, I guess it has been about ten years ago now, we went down there to see a feller about tradin' a few hogs for a good mule. Word was there was a man what had good mules and traded right fair. So my Pa and me, we loaded up four shoats in the wagon and headed on down the wagon road from Hogback Mountain, south through Rutherfordton and then east toward Burnt Chimney.

"Well, it was a nice day, early fall I believe it was. The sun was out, not too many clouds, a good day fer travelin'. Somewhere between Rutherfordton and Burnt Chimney, on a stretch of the road where there weren't no houses, we rounded a bend and there to the side of the road laid a man stretched out like he was dead.

"My Pa, bein' a good Christian man, said, 'We gotta stop and help him, Whit.'

"I said, 'This could mean trouble.'

"Pa said, 'Remember the story of the good Samaritan.' I nodded and whoa'd up the mule, and then my Pa got down to check on the man. I set the brake and stepped down to follow behind. Just as Pa got to the man, he jumps up and comes at Pa with a long knife. I started back to the wagon to get my old musket and when I turned around there was two fellers with muskets a-pointin' right at my head. By this time the feller which had been layin' on the road had my Pa backed up almost to where I was.

"My Pa had a real bad temper and he barked at the men, 'What is it you rascals want?' They laughed and said they wanted all our money, our wagon and mule, but that we could keep the hogs.

"Pa said, 'You ain't gettin' none of it. If you do, it will be over my dead body.'

"One of the men holdin' a musket said as cold as I ever heard a man speak, 'You can have it yore way if you want, mister.' He fired the musket at Pa without really aimin' it. The ball grazed Pa just above his left ear. Made a bloody crease. That just made Pa mad.

"Francis, you know how strong my Pa is."

I nodded, then caught myself and said, "Yes."

"He grabbed the feller what had the knife by the arm, and swung him clear around right into the one with the loaded musket. They both went down and the musket went off, firin' into the air. I piled into the one what had shot at Pa, grabbed his empty musket away from him as I knocked him to the ground. I raised it to hit him, but he held his arms up, beggin' me not to.

"My Pa was on his knees whalin' the daylights out of the two others, first one then the other. When he straightened up, they sort of crawled away, like a couple of crawfish, and ran into the woods. The one I knocked on the ground stood up and then turned and took off.

"After they was gone, I asked Pa if he was all right and he said he was fine. In fact, he said he hadn't had that much fun in a number of years. On top of that, he was real pleased that we had acquired two purty good muskets, which the fellers neglected to take with them when they left. I reckon they learned better than to tangle with the Whitaker boys, that day. They did indeed."

Lester and I looked at each other. "Is all that true, Whit?" I asked.

"True as the Gospels of Mathew, Mark, Luke and John," Whit said.

"That's quite a story, Whit," Lester said. "You fellers was lucky that day."

"Yes, sir, we was lucky and the fellers we tangled with was just plain unlucky. Truth is, they did pick the wrong fellers to mess with; at least one of us. My Pa was so tough, he could'a probably took the whole bunch by hisself. I just helped him out a bit, sort of lightened his load you might say."

We sat there for a long time, Lester and me smoking our pipes and looking at the fire, Whit resting his bandaged head and working his precious chaw. Cadmus the rabbit scampered around Whit's feet and climbed onto his lap. Whit smiled. "Lester, would you hold Cadmus a while? I might doze off."

Lester shook his head slowly. "I don't think so, Whit. I ain't that fond of rodents."

"Aw, come on, Lester, this ain't no rodent; this is Cadmus, bravest recruit in Company H!" Whit held the rabbit out carefully, and Lester grimaced and took it. I suppressed a laugh. The rabbit sat still as stone while we sat and smoked. Thirty minutes or so passed when Lester suddenly shifted, getting a strange look on his face. He picked up the rabbit and there was a small wet circle on his breeches.

I couldn't help but laugh. "Well, Lester, looks like Cadmus has done anointed you," I said.

Whit woke from his nap. "What happened?" he asked.

"He wet on me!" Lester blurted.

Whit rocked back with laughter and said, "Oh, I'm sure it's just a show of affection, Lester."

"That ain't the kind of affection I fancy," Lester said, as he gave the rabbit back to Whit. All of us laughed, even Lester.

I looked up at the sky and saw thick clouds rolling in. "Looks like we might be travelin' in the rain tomorrow," I said.

Whit sniffed at the air. "Yep, rain's a-comin'. I can smell it."

Lester said, "I heard we're gonna move soon and keep movin'."

The breeze picked up and in about fifteen minutes, the rain came. I used an oilcloth to set up a little shebang to cover Whit and me. Lester found one of his own and, wrapped in our blankets, we settled down for another soggy time.

The boom of cannon in the late afternoon meant the Yankees were back after us; we would have to move shortly or be overrun. My leg began to throb and I shivered, even though it was not that cold. The leg felt feverish. I could see the red wave far off. The pain came again, but this time it was duller, without the knife edge like before.

I tried to put it out of my mind. My thoughts returned to our cabin and to my precious family. I had not heard from them in such a long time, it seemed, but I knew Harriet's letters could not find me these days. I just hoped it would not be much longer before I could head homeward. Surely this war was near its end.

The rain drops pelted the oilcloth. The fire hissed and steamed. The camp was quiet. I fell fast asleep, only to dream.

TWENTY-SIX

The journey must surely end
this sojourn of death,
sad valley of despair.
Surely a sunlit crest awaits us.

The dream began in the Camp Creek Valley, on the porch of a cabin, where the sun streamed through the tulip poplar and white oak trees. As I stood alone on the porch looking out across the valley, across the fields I had plowed, beyond the barn and the chicken coop, it seemed I could almost see forever. The horizon was wide, like I was on a mountain top.

Then I felt myself become lighter and lighter until I left the porch, borne upward on the wind. I heard a voice calling me from the house, softly but insistently, a voice I somehow knew. I drifted high, the trees and the house falling away below. The voice faded.

There was a feeling of weightlessness, like I was a cloud or feather riding the breeze. Meanwhile a mournful sound filled my ears. My heart ached like I was dying. The mournful sound became the cry of an owl in the early morning, lost, looking for home, or so it seemed. Then the owl was with me, flying slowly this way and that through the cold blue sky, leaving the valley, toward a dark land. I could see that land, a dark stretch of wood and field, far off on the horizon, growing slowly closer as we flew.

The owl began to speak, though its words were not clear; like words heard from another room, muffled and indistinct. I could not understand, but I knew what it meant. The odd thing was that it did not seem strange to be flying with a talking owl. It told me of woe, of pain and loss. It told me of ungodly suffering and misery. It told me of fear and anger, cold and hunger, in words that had color but no definition. As we soared, I was filled with a deepening fear and dread. We passed over scenes of horror, one after another, until they blended into a world of anguish and sadness and tribulation.

I turned and pleaded with the owl. "Let's leave this place, please." It just flew on and said nothing more. I tried to turn, tried to go back, but I could not; I had lost the place from whence I came.

Then all of a sudden I realized I was a crow, black and shiny, winging across fields of battle. The owl was gone, and I did not know which way to go. I flew back and forth until I thought I heard a sound, maybe a voice from the ground. As I looked down, a trooper in blue standing alone on a hilltop aimed his rifle and fired. Pain shot through me and I began to fall, seemingly forever.

That's when I woke with a start, my leg throbbing hotly. My heart was pounding.

My companions were sleeping soundly. A few coals still glowed in the fire. The rain had stopped, and the camp was quiet. The dream lingered in my mind.

I looked at my friend, who might never see the sun again, and I must confess I was near unto despair. I lay with gloomy thoughts until the sergeant came by, yelling for us to fall in.

TWENTY-SEVEN

The demons frolicked
and Satan smiled
as Hell came to earth
at a place called Saylor's Creek.

The sergeant said we were moving, to get ready and be quick about it. His face wore a cloud, his skin taut against the cheekbones. We gathered up our meager belongings. I took down the shebang and rolled up the oilcloth. Whit said he thought he could walk a while so I helped him to his feet. I tucked one of the revolvers in my belt and gave the other one to Lester. Then he went to a creek nearby to fill up our canteens.

I never knew a more dutiful man than Lester. Like me and Whit, he was also from Rutherford, over near Cane Creek. He and his brothers ran a small grist mill before the war and raised some corn, sorghum, and oats. He never was a big man, but it seemed the war had beaten him down even more. Thinner than even me, he stood about five feet and seven or eight inches. He had reddish brown hair, graying at the temples. His eyes were very blue, and his skin was fair like many of us of Scottish extraction.

He was a quiet man, but fearless in a fight. We had spent some time together at Camp Vance and on the trip to Petersburg. I knew him before the war, and saw him occasionally before the retreat, but as I got to know him better my respect and admiration grew. He was one of those people who could be relied on in a pinch, and who did more than his share without complaining.

His only vice was that he did like to partake of the spirits from time to time and, before the war, once in a while he took a little too much. He never caused much trouble, just a fistfight now and then, but he did sometimes play the fool.

When he was a young man, he got drunk one Saturday in Rutherfordton. Seems he and a couple of friends went to town, fortified with a gallon of Pearly Walker's best.

Lester was falling down drunk by the middle of the afternoon, and he was trying to walk the hitching rails, trying to climb up the outside of the courthouse building, and generally acting foolish. Sheriff Lail pulled him down from the side of the courthouse, and said that if he liked the building so much, he could spend the night next door to it in the jail. Which he did.

But all in all he was a fine man, regular to church, and faithful to his friends. He surely had been a friend to Whit and me the past few days.

When Lester came back, Whit and I were ready. We shouldered our bedrolls and rifles, and I carried Whit's rifle as we fell in with the stream of men headed westward. Whit staggered and groped, so I led him by the arm and tried to steady him as best I could.

We had been walking for about an hour when we heard hoof beats behind us. We turned in time to see Sergeant Hutchins draw rein. He was riding the colonel's horse—although I suppose it was mine, now. As he dismounted he said, "I thought Whit might want to ride a while."

Whit nodded and said, "Well, fellers, I ain't hurt all that bad but, if it's just the same to you, I shore won't mind ridin' a while since I'm stumblin' around like a drunk."

We helped him into the saddle and got his boots positioned in the stirrups. "Whit, you're in high cotton," said Lester. "Wearing a Yankee officer's boots and ridin' a Confederate colonel's horse!" Whit tried to laugh but all he could manage was a few grunts. The pain was coming back. The doc had left me some laudanum so I gave him a little, only a small sip from the bottle because I didn't want him to fall asleep and fall off the horse. Whit grimaced at the taste as he always did.

I led the horse while Whit held onto the pommel. We walked in the dark about three hours until we saw a couple of fellows on the side of the road. In fact, we almost walked right over them. Seeing men by the road was not that uncommon; there are always stragglers and shirkers with any army on the march, and sometimes men just have to rest. These two seemed to be arguing. One fellow was sitting on the ground. Seemed he had a badly wounded leg because it was bandaged in three or four places. He kept telling the other fellow to go on and that he would be all right.

We stopped and asked if we could help. The fellow that was standing took one look at the horse and said, "Yes, you can let my friend ride up there on that horse."

"Would that be all right with you, Whit?" I asked.

"Sure," Whit said. With a smile he added, "It's your horse, ain't it?"

We helped the wounded fellow up on the horse, behind Whit. The other man said, "My name's James Willard. This here is Alvie Henderson. Yankee shell messed up his leg. It got him in four places, purty good, so he can't walk. And I couldn't help carry him myself no longer, so we are both much obliged."

"I'm Francis Yelton; this is Whit Whitaker and Lester Carpenter." I looked them over. "We're with the 18th. What unit are you boys with? I don't believe I ever saw you before."

"We're with the 37th, but I don't know where on earth they are. We're just tryin' to keep up with the army, and maybe I suppose we'll get hooked up with them again before long. Alvie, here, ain't gonna be doin' no more fightin' anyhow."

Alvie grunted. "Speak for yoreself, James. I might just still have some fight left in me."

James laughed. "Well, you might, long as you can set whilst you do it."

As the day wore on, hunger began to tell on us again. We were all weary to the bone, and many fell out by the side of the road. Whit was continually thirsty, and he soon drank his canteen dry. I gave him some water from mine. Lester took maybe one or two sips all morning, even after the sun came up and it began to get warm. With his long jaw set, he just kept walking. He didn't seem to be bothered by not having any food and very little rest.

The officers rode by every now and then, and tried to urge us to move faster. They said if the Yankees caught us, we would be in a fix.

I had to lean on the horse most of the way, hobbling on my bad leg. It hurt more with every step, the fever raging in it. Lester took the reins and I walked beside it, holding its flanks for balance.

The muddy road wound aimlessly, it seemed, through the southern Virginia countryside. We splashed through puddles, and struggled through knee deep mud churned to a bog by wagons, mules and men.

My leg throbbed with every step, and every now and then my head would swim around. The trees and fields seemed to be slowly moving around me, right to left. Men were lying by the roadside and in the fields. Most had thrown their weapons away, and were just waiting to be picked up by the Yankees. I was determined not to be one of them, but there were moments when I thought I might just have to give up. My legs trembled weakly, and I was weary to my very core. I saw no hope for this army; nor, I must say, for myself.

Bad news became worse news. General A.P. Hill, our corps' commander, was killed on April 2, shortly after the Federal breakthrough. Our whole corps, or what was left of it, was assigned to General Longstreet, commander of the First Corps. We were no longer near the rear, but somewhere toward the middle of the army with two or three divisions behind us. We could hear cannon and musket fire from time to time, mostly to the east and south. I remember thinking that it did not matter much. Anyone with eyes to see could tell this army was sinking faster than a lead ball in a washtub.

The divisions behind us ran into some Yankees on April 7, at a little marshy stream called Saylor's Creek. They got trapped and some of them got cut off from the rest of our army. As the battle raged, the Federals made a charge across the creek. When they reached the position held by one of the Confederate units, the Southerners savagely fought them hand to hand. It was one of the most brutal, primitive battles of the war. Men fought with each other on the ground in death struggles, human teeth ripping at human throats. The battle at Saylor's Creek was as desperate and ruthless as they come, men reduced to wanton savagery. Word was, most of two Confederate divisions were killed or captured.

I thought back to the breakthrough on the 2nd and how we fought them as long as we could. I had gouged out one Yankee trooper's eye, bashed men's skulls with the butt of my rifle, and stabbed men with the bayonet. My thoughts ran into a wall when all this came back to me, as it did from time to time. I could not shake the feeling of acting like a savage during that battle, though I knew my only choices had been to fight, die, or surrender and spend the rest of the war in a Union prison camp. It wasn't much of a choice.

Lee's whole army was like a wounded animal now, cornered and grimly fighting for its life with everything it had left.

Meanwhile, General John B. Gordon's Division had been fighting a heroic and desperate rear guard action at the end of the column, trying to keep the Yankees at bay. But the numbers were wearing him down. Gordon's Division fought, then moved, then fought some more. We could hear battle sounds in the distance. I don't know how they managed to keep up the struggle. They had to be as worn out and starved as we were.

They said we would pick up some food in a town called Farmville, a few miles further to the west. Our regiment didn't stop when we got there, we could not afford to because the Yankees kept pressing us on. We just moved on through the town and picked up a little food as we went. Teamsters stood at the wagons and tried to hand out rations as we passed by. I heard that most men got nothing to eat.

We stumbled and staggered on through Farmville. I got Whit and me some rations, Lester got some for himself, and we ate as we moved. It was the only meal any of us had had in some time, and it tasted good indeed. I was able to pocket some extra biscuits, because I knew we'd have to save them for as long as possible. Whit was hurting some, and I gave him the last of the laudanum I had. We had lost track of the surgeon so I couldn't get any more—assuming there was any more.

Whit dozed in the saddle. Alvie, the fellow riding with him, tried to hold Whit on the horse, but he was weak himself and Whit almost slipped off a number of times. I took the traces off of some dead artillery horses which lay to the side of the road, like garbage dumped into a ditch. The smell of the dead animals became a taste in my mouth. I shook it off. We used the traces to try to tie Whit onto the horse the best we could. I still had to brace him from time to time, gripping him by the belt. It was a struggle, especially since I was bracing myself too. My arms grew weary from holding him in the saddle.

I thought again and again that it would be easier to sit down by the side of the road and wait for the Yankees to pick me up. Then I would think, *No that is not what General Lee would do. He would keep going and so must I.* As long as the army marched, I was going to try to march with it, though now it must surely be a death march. I imagined we were the funeral procession for the Army of Northern Virginia. I wondered if there would be a eulogy of some kind at the end.

We did not stop until very late that night. In the blackness of the early morning hours, the column of men, wagons and horses simply stopped. No one gave a command; we all just seemed to drop to the ground at the side of the road, every ounce of strength exhausted. We would wait until morning.

TWENTY-EIGHT

The frolic is o'er,
my fondest friends,
and sadness abounds
this funereal spring.

The night passed fitfully with the moans of the wounded. Men's cries sometimes turned to screams that rang sharp and hollow in the thick, dismal night. More pitiful still were the animals. The bellows of dying mules and the trembling forms of starving horses will be imprinted on my mind until my eyes close for the last time. I could taste the death in the air.

The laudanum wore off and Whit was groaning softly. I tried to make him as comfortable as I could. I scrounged up some rags and made him a pillow, and I gathered some leaves and grass for a bed. The rain came again, and we tried to shelter ourselves with oilcloths as well as we could. Wind rustled the trees in a ghostly sort of way as cool rain drizzled through the branches, pattering the trembling leaves. Sometimes it came in a downpour, but mostly it was just a steady rain that poured on the forlorn, huddling men.

Lester found us some fresh water. At least we would not be thirsty. The meal we had enjoyed earlier in the day was long gone, and the biting pain of hunger was back with a vengeance. Seems the meal in Farmville had just primed us for more suffering.

The dawn came slowly as the lowering clouds rolled ponderously away. April 8 was quiet for the most part. There were some muffled sounds of battle off in the distance. The Yankees were moving along our southern flank, trying to get around and in front of us to cut off our retreat. I told Lester and Whit that at the pace we were moving, a herd of turtles could get around us. Maybe the Yankees just figured we would all drop and die, and so there wasn't any point in shooting us. We just stumbled along, stopping when horses dropped and blocked the road, or when wagons got mired in the knee deep mud, or when men just got too tired to go on.

Later in the day we ran into a large body of Union cavalry. We had to form up in battle lines along the south side of the road. They made a couple of charges, and we gave them a withering fire. Blue troopers spilled from saddles and the charge faltered. Then I suppose they decided they would leave us alone for a while. We resumed our gloomy march.

In the afternoon a group of our officers came charging up the road from the rear, Colonel Barry on the Yankee general's horse among them. He recognized his old horse and noticed Whit and me. He patted the Yankee general's horse on the neck and touched his hat as he went by, and I saluted. In spite of his desperation and distress he showed the trace of a smile on his face.

We stumbled along for much of the day, and then we were ordered to stop a couple of miles east of a place called Appomattox Courthouse. I helped Whit off the horse and led him to a spot where he could rest against a tree. I could tell he was embarrassed and a bit irritated that he had to be helped all the time now. I led the horse to some new green grass and let it have its fill. It began to crop at the grass contentedly. Then I found a bucket and stumbled down to the quietly rushing Appomattox River about a half a mile away. I filled the bucket for the horse, and Lester and I filled several canteens. Food, we could get by without; but not water. I waded into a shallow spot of the river and let the water wash the caked mud and the dried blood off of me. I took off my shirt, got down in the water and washed quickly, then headed back to the camp.

When we got back to the tree, Whit was rubbing at his eyes in seeming aggravation. "What's wrong, Whit?" I asked.

"These durn bandages is startin' to bother me some. Don't suppose I could get some clean ones some'rs?" His bandages were stiffened with dark blood.

I looked around at the pitiful remains of the army. I knew supplies of every kind were scarce. "I don't know, Whit," I answered, "but I will see what I can do."

I went up to where they had parked what was left of our trains. The first man I saw was the teamster in whose wagon I rode right after I was shot. "Cyrus!" I called. "Cyrus, is that you?"

He grinned from ear to ear. "Well, Mr. Francis, how you be?"

"I'm fine, Cyrus, other than this little flea bite on my leg."

Cyrus grinned, showing beautiful white teeth. "I believe what you got there is a mite worse than a flea bite, Mr. Francis!"

"Well, I'm sorry to report that my friend Whit has been hurt much worse."

His smile faded, replaced by a grim look. "I'm sorry to hear that, Mr. Francis."

"I need some clean bandages for his eyes. He has been blinded; they had to ... to take one of his eyes out."

Cyrus shook his head and looked around with a mournful expression at the remains of the army. "Is they no end to the sufferin'?"

"It doesn't seem like there will be an end to it. I guess we just take it day to day and trust the Good Lord to see us through. Do you know where I might find some bandages?"

Cyrus nodded pleasantly. "Sho do. Come this way. Just don't tell nobody where you got 'em." I walked with him to the wagon he drove. He raised the seat box cover and dug around in it. Then he pulled out a couple of rolls of white bandage cloth. "Here you are, Mr. Francis. We don't have a lot, but this ought to do."

"I believe it will, Cyrus. Much obliged." Then, wondering why he wanted me to keep it a secret, I asked, "You won't get in any trouble for this, will you?"

"Naw, don't you worry none. I just hope Mr. Whit gets better soon, Mr. Francis."

"Thank you, Cyrus. I better get back. So long."

"So long and God bless, Mr. Francis."

I had only gotten a few steps when it occurred to me that I ought to try to return Cyrus's kind favor. I thought about the handful of biscuits I had kept aside from the rations we were given in Farmville.

"Cyrus, have you had anything to eat?"

"Not today, Mr. Francis. Somehow I didn't get a ration back there in Farmville. They musta not been enough."

"Well, here, I have a couple of biscuits left. I don't need them. You take them."

Cyrus was startled and he looked me up and down. "Mr. Francis, you don't look like you can afford to be givin' up food, now."

Maybe not, but Cyrus was a lot bigger than me, and he needed to eat his fair share, too. The Good Lord would provide. "It's all right, I'll get some more. Take them." I handed the biscuits to him and said goodbye again.

I had not gone more than fifty yards when I heard some cursing behind me. I turned and saw three soldiers standing around Cyrus, and they did not look friendly. I hurried back.

The soldiers were men I did not know. As I approached, I heard one of them growl, "Nigger, if you know what's good for you, you'll hand over them biscuits. We're hungry and we'll be hanged if a darkie eats when white men is hungry!"

One of them prodded Cyrus with the barrel of his rifle. I could feel the blood rising in my head. Somehow, despite my condition, a surge of strength went through me. I swung my own rifle off my shoulder.

"Git away from him!" I roared. They all turned toward me, surprised expressions on their faces.

The one that had been doing the talking smirked. "And if'n we don't, what is one feller with a bandaged-up leg gonna do? You gonna shoot another soldier? They'll hang you for it."

"If you don't leave him alone, you'll soon see what I'm liable to do. That there's my friend."

At that, they all looked at each other and burst out laughing. The spokesman spat, "Well, you just come on and make us leave him alone, you nigger lover, you."

Their faces turned even uglier and they started toward me. One of them rolled up his sleeves. "No guns, boys, let's just have us some fun with this darkie lover," the spokesman said. With that they laid their guns aside.

I chose not to lay my rifle aside. The spokesman came toward me first, with his fists raised. He was a wiry man with dark eyes and a wispy beard. I shifted my grip to the barrel of the rifle and swung it, smashing his left arm and ribs. He went down. The second man came at me in a rush; I jabbed him hard in the stomach with the butt of the rifle. He went, "Oof!" and hit the ground, gasping for air.

The third man, much larger than the other two, was on top of me before I knew what happened. He hit me in the jaw, hard, and I went down. Then he was on top of me, raining blows into my face. I tried to defend myself, but in my weakened state I could not manage to throw him off. I blocked most of the punches, but it looked like a losing cause for me.

Just as I thought I was done for, the man stopped. It appeared for just a split second that the rapture had occurred, because he seemed to be flying through the air, upward and backward. Then I saw that two big, black hands wrapped around his arms were pulling him away, then slamming him to the ground. Cyrus grinned at me.

Then I heard a thump and his grin faded. The first man I knocked down had gotten up, grabbed a rifle, and hit Cyrus on the back of the head. He pulled back the rifle, ready to swing it, and snarled at me, "All right, mister, now it's your turn!" The words were barely out of his mouth when he was spun around and a big right fist smashed his face. Blood flew, his eyes rolled back, and he dropped like a stone.

Sergeant Hutchins stood there, with a twisted smile on his face. He looked around at the men on the ground. "Francis, don't the Yanks provide enough of a fight? Now you have to turn on these rascals?"

I looked to Cyrus. He sat up and rubbed his head, and Cas and I helped him to his feet. "They tried to take Cyrus's food, Sergeant. I tried to stop them."

Cas studied the area; two of the soldiers were taking a nice afternoon slumber at the time, and the other stumbled off holding his stomach. "Looks like, all in all, you did a purty good job of it."

"Well, thanks to you and Cyrus, I'm still alive and conscious at least."

Cas grinned wryly and shook his head. "For a man who didn't want to fight, you have sure done your share on the battlefield … and off of it." He took note of Cyrus, who was still rubbing his head and blinking his eyes, trying to clear the fog. "But I reckon you usually do your fightin' for the right reasons." He clapped me on the shoulder and walked back in the direction of the headquarters camp.

"Cyrus, you feel all right?" I asked.

"Well, Mr. Francis, I feels like a mule done kicked me in the head! But I'll be all right. Mama always said I got a hard head. I expect I'll have me a lump the size of a hen egg, though."

I tested the back of his head through the nap of his curly hair. "Well, maybe you better go and sit down for a while. A lump is definitely coming up there. It's gonna be sore as blue blazes."

The men on the ground were beginning to come around. Neither of us wanted to rejoin the struggle. "I believe I will, Mr. Francis. I don't think we're goin' anywhere right yet. I'll see you later on."

"See you later on, Cyrus." Cyrus headed off toward the wagons, and I stumbled back toward Whit and Lester.

Lester had a fire going and water boiling in a cook pot. We peeled the bandages off Whit's eyes, but as we saw how bad it looked underneath we both struggled not to show our feelings. My stomach turned over, and I had to suppress a choking, gagging feeling in my throat. In place of the eye which had been removed was a mass of blood and dried matter. The remaining eye was shot through with blood and redness.

Whit's one eye moved around weakly. "I can see some light! I can see light!" he said.

"Well, glory be, Whit old man!" exclaimed Lester. "You'll be readin' the works of Shakespeare in no time at all!"

With a grin, Whit responded, "Don't go gettin' too excited, Lester; I don't read all that well, and I shore don't read no Shakespeare. But maybe I will be able to read a newspaper before long and see whar I'm a-goin'!"

"Let's try to get those eyes cleaned up some, Whit," I said. "Maybe that will help keep the fever out of them." Lester took a length of clean bandage cloth, dipped it in hot water, and gently dabbed it around Whit's eyes. He winced a time or two, but otherwise it was not too bad. When Lester finished, we made some little pads to go against his eyes, and then I wrapped the clean bandage around his head until the eyes were completely covered again. "I'm not a doctor," I said, "but it seems to me we ought to keep them covered, even the good one, for a while."

"Whatever you say, Dr. Francis. I place myself into yore most capable hands." At that, we all had to laugh; empty stomachs, wounded and aching bodies, and all.

Lester nodded to me and asked, "Now that we've got old Whit fixed up a bit, what in the devil happened to you, Francis? You look like you been fightin' a Yankee corps with your fists."

"It was more like three worthless Confederates that tried to take Cyrus Holland's food away from him."

"You mean ... that colored teamster?" Lester asked.

"Yes, that's the one. He's a good fellow. I know he's colored, but he's all right. They tried to take his food, and I think they were planning on beating him in the bargain. I couldn't let that happen."

Whit shook his head and grinned, then said cynically, "Well, Sir Lancelot, are ye out ridin' yore charger again, makin' the world a better place? Sounds like yore up to yore old tricks, Francis. One of these days, I'm not gonna be around, and somebody's gonna kill you deader than a ... than a...." His words trailed off.

"You weren't around this time, Whit, and things worked out just fine," I said.

Whit grimaced. "From what Lester said, it sounds like yore face don't show it worked out fine."

"It's just a few bruises, Whit. Lester exaggerated a little. Now you settle back and get some rest."

Whit's face grew solemn. "Francis, you got to promise me you ain't gonna get yoreself involved in any more scrapes afore we get home. You are the only one's gonna see I get home again. Besides, yo're my friend; I sorter like havin' you around."

"Well, Whit, I must say I am touched," I said solemnly, but then couldn't hold back a chuckle.

Whit laughed a little, then snorted. "Quit makin' light of this, Francis! I cain't see a lick. How can I even know which direction to go in to get home? You gotta keep yoreself in one piece so we ... so we can both get home!"

Lester spoke up. "Whit, don't you worry, I'll see you get home if anythin' happens to Francis."

"See there, Whit? You don't have to worry. If anything happens to me, Lester here will see to it that you get home, all safe and sound."

Whit mumbled, "Safe may be; but sound, I'm afraid it's too late for that."

Lester said, "Don't say that, Whit. I'll bet yore seein' out of that good eye afore a week's out."

Whit gave out a big sigh. "I'm sorry, fellers. I guess I'm just feelin' sorry fer m'self. Don't think nothin' about it, all right?"

"Not at all, old friend," I said. "Now, why don't you try to get yourself some rest?"

Whit pulled Cadmus from his shirt and stretched out on the ground, placing the rabbit on his chest. Lester gathered up some tender shoots and laid them on Whit's chest for Cadmus to nibble on. "No need for our old friend, here, to go hungry, when there's his kind of food right nearby."

The sun was setting with golden fire in the west. The clouds had blown off, and a warm breeze riffled through the trees. Lester started a small fire. He stripped some bark off a willow tree and made some tea. He said it would help ease the pain of our wounds and maybe even our hunger. Lester knew about these things. His mother knew all about herbs and roots and berries, and how they could be used for healing purposes. She had passed much of her knowledge on to him.

As the willow bark boiled in the pot, I walked away from the camp and up a little rise. I didn't see any Yankee campfires and only one or two of our pickets. The breeze blew from the southwest, from the direction of home. It was a warming breeze. I thought that that was somehow right, warming breezes from home. Home, where a man's heart dwelled; could there be a warmer, sunnier place?

As I searched the sky, I kept thinking that this was perfect weather for plowing. Not too hot, and the recent rain had made the ground soft. With a day or two of sun, it would be dry enough. I could almost smell the aroma that rose from the earth as I plowed my fields back home. It smelled like life, like new beginnings.

The stars poked their heads out one at a time. A few wispy clouds drifted overhead. Everything was quiet. I realized that for the first night in a long time, I did not hear any cannon or musketry. I took a deep breath of the warm southwest breeze, and could almost smell my wife's fried chicken. I could almost feel her touch as I turned down the lamp. I could almost hear the voices of my children as they played in the sun. How far away could it be?

TWENTY-NINE

The end comes like sunset,
a slow darkening,
but still the light
of a sullen moon.

We settled down the night of April 8, 1865 to the sound of the wind in the trees. Occasionally the moan of a wounded man or the whinny of a dying horse broke the stillness. The guns were mostly silent this night.

Whit, Lester and I sat around the fire, silently staring into the flames. Whit was excited because he could make out the flames against the darkness with his one eye, even through his bandage. While Lester and I smoked our pipes, Whit chewed his beloved chaw and amused himself by trying to hit the fire with streams of tobacco juice.

The night birds roused, and I thought I heard a whippoorwill in the distance. It so reminded me of home. Finally, Lester spoke. "Fellers, do you think the general will surrender soon?"

Whit and I were silent for a space, then Whit said, "I think the general is a great man with a great mind and he will shore enough know when it's time to give it up."

Lester grunted. "It shore seems to me that the time is here. The army is starvin', the horses are droppin' all around, and we are retreatin' before an enemy that has us outnumbered and outgunned."

"And out-fed," Whit added.

Lester was thrown off by the interruption. "I said the army is starvin'."

"Well, I'm starvin' twice as much," Whit joked.

"Anyhow," Lester continued, choosing to ignore Whit, "I don't see how we can hold out much longer. Surely the general knows that."

I poked at the fire with a stick and let out a big sigh. "Of course he knows all that. But he also knows that if he gives up too quick, he's got nothin' to bargain with."

"What do you mean?" Lester asked.

"Well, as long as old Grant knows Lee's army can still fight and do him damage, he will want to try to find a way to end this business. If General Lee sends up the white flag too quick, Grant will not be of a mind to be generous in his terms of surrender. At least that's the way I see it. I'm not sure about all the what-ifs and what-alls of how things stand right now, but if I was General Lee, that's what I would be thinkin' about: how can I get the best deal out of old Grant?"

Whit laughed. "Francis, you shore do surprise me sometimes. I had no idea you were a military genius."

"Well, I'm not. I just think it seems to make sense that General Lee will try to get the best terms of surrender."

Whit was turning his head from side to side, as if checking whether he could make out the fire from the corners of his eye. He said, "Well, if Grant don't know how much trouble this army is in, then he is prob'ly the only one!" He tossed a stick on the fire; sparks flickered skyward.

"Well, I am sure he does know," I said, "but he also knows that if General Lee decides to make a last ditch stand, thousands more men on both sides will die. Surely there has been enough bloodletting. As the educated officers would say, 'There should be no more unnecessary effusion of blood.'"

Whit snorted and pointed to his bandaged head. "'Effusion' my eye, it's been a-flowin' like a river around here."

Lester nodded. "I done seen enough death to last me a hundred lifetimes. I don't wish to see another man shot down or blowed up."

"Maybe everyone else finally feels the same," I replied. I looked around the camp at the flickering fires and the weary men, talking softly. "This is as quiet as things have been for a long time: no cannon fire, and no racket of muskets off in the distance."

We all fell silent, watching the fire flicker and listening to the sounds of the night. We lay down where we were, and sleep overtook us in the eerily quiet darkness.

THIRTY

We stood by the road in silence,
this ragged army of ghosts,
our banners defiantly snapping
in the early morning breeze.

We slept like dead men, waking the next morning as the sun was coming up. Whit was disappointed because he could no longer make out different levels of light and dark through his bandages. He was also in some pain, so Lester set about making him some willow bark tea.

It wasn't long until we heard the sounds of muskets and carbines off to the south, and the sound of heavy guns to the west. The west! They had got in front of us. But the sounds of battle fitfully faded away as the day passed.

That afternoon—April 9, 1865—we heard that General Lee was coming. Some said we had surrendered, and though I knew it was inevitable it was still hard for me to believe. Surrender wasn't supposed to be in General Lee's vocabulary. All the same, every man of us knew the army was worn out and beat down, and that sooner or later, if we couldn't escape the trap old Grant had laid, we would have to surrender. In spite of all the valor, bravery, and heroism of this army of ghosts, we all knew that the end was here. Though we still hoped for a miracle, hoped that the great general would find a way to save his army and defeat the enemy. On that warm day in April, 1865 it was a forlorn hope indeed.

As a band of riders drew closer, we could see that it really was

General Lee. Lucas Tate and some others kept jostling me, so I left Whit with Lester and moved away from the crowd to get a better view. The riders came near and the cheers from the men rose like a gale on a winter night, louder and louder. It gave me chills to hear the men yell so, and I yelled along with the rest. The general's horse pranced and high-stepped like it was on a parade, but the general stared somberly ahead, his eyes fixed at a point between the horse's ears. I guess he did not want to look at us lest he break down.

General Lee sat on his horse straight as a ramrod, a masterful rider. It was almost as though horse and man were one being. The general didn't usually wear all the sleeve and collar braid that the other officers wore, but today his uniform looked new, and it had the stars and wreaths on the collars, and the general's braid on the sleeves. His gauntlets looked like they were new, and his high black riding boots were shining like a new penny. His hair and beard were completely white, lending his countenance an ancient nobility, though today it was wreathed in sadness. When we saw his face as he rode by, and the faces of his staff officers, we knew he had surrendered the army.

The cheers faded and the tears began. Men were falling to their knees to weep like children. Some almost wailed with the pain of defeat, especially those who had been with the army for years, through great victories as well as terrible trials and tribulations. Isaac Martin, one of the long time veterans, threw his hands in the air and shouted in anguish, "Blow, Gabriel, blow! I am ready to die!"

I kept my gaze on the general, just watching him as he went past. After the cheering died down, for reasons I don't even know myself, I raised my arms in the air and yelled, "General Lee, we love you just as much as ever!" Lo and behold, the great man turned toward me for just a moment. He looked me in the eyes; he didn't say anything, but I knew he was letting me know that he loved us too. Then he turned back toward the road, and though I could hardly believe it, I know I saw tears running down his face.

I felt weak; I guess from not having had any food and my wound and all, so I sat down beside the road, sort of dropped down I guess. I thought about defeat, I thought about the brave men of this army, and I thought about my friends who would not be coming home. I reckon I shed a few tears too. Lester and Whit joined me and we sat by the road, sad and broken by the defeat, but at the same time relieved that it was over. We could only wonder what was next.

About supper time, Sergeant Cas confirmed what we knew, that it was all over. He told us that Lee had surrendered to Grant, and that they were going to let us all go back home after we signed a pledge not to take up arms against the United States. I listened to Cas and said, "Well, Cas, I never wanted to take up arms in the first place, and I must say I am glad to agree to never do so again."

Cas showed his wry smile. "I should hope so, with the amount of trouble you seem to get up to. But some of the boys are talking about taking to the hills and fighting a partisan war."

Whit asked, "What's a party-san war?"

"Well, like old Mosby up in northern Virginia, you hide and jump out and fight, and then run away," Cas said.

Whit grunted. "Sounds cowardly. Anyways, I done enough fightin' and I don't want no part of any such."

"Neither do I," Lester added.

"Well," Cas sighed, looking off in the distance, "my advice is to go back home and try to rebuild what you had; make something for your young'uns' future." It seemed the most reasonable thing I had heard anyone say in the past eight months. I was happy to hear those words.

I had no way of knowing there were more tears yet to be shed before we saw home again.

THIRTY-ONE

At a place called Appomattox
the gray ranks find rest
worn bodies and shattered minds
but the first glimmer beginning.

April 10 brought some strange occurrences. Our officers formed us up in regiments and told us what was going on. We had so few men, our regiments looked like companies. It all seemed like a play about a war with too few actors.

Yankee troopers came up later in the day and walked through our camps, handing out food and gathering up some of the most seriously wounded. Blue and gray intermingled, the well-dressed, if dirty, Federals a stark contrast to the emaciated, ragged Confederates. We didn't have much to share, but we gave the Yankees a bit of tobacco here, a hunting knife there. Mostly they brought food from their trains and saw that we were fed.

Whit said he never thought Yankee food would taste so good. Sergeant Hutchins said they were probably giving us our own food they had captured several days before. None of us cared; we ate it thankfully. We got beans, cornbread and bacon.

We went with Whit to see a Yankee surgeon who was treating some of the more seriously wounded. They let Lester and me come along to help Whit get around. Two Union troopers led us to the place where the surgeon had set up a field hospital, only about a mile behind the lines. Dr. Carrington, from New York State, was a young fellow; tall and swarthy, with a handsome brown mustache and intense dark eyes.

The doctor worked under a tent with open sides, and we could see much of what went on. He sang as he worked. He was very skillful, removing minie balls, removing arms and legs. Thankfully, the Federals buried the severed limbs as they were removed. We didn't have to look at another ghastly pile.

When Whit's turn came, the surgeon quickly took off our makeshift bandages and examined Whit's eyes, or what was left of them. He had an aide clean Whit's face and the empty eye socket and he put some sort of liquid into Whit's intact eye. Then he put his hand over the eye, took it away, then put it back. He asked Whit if he could tell when his hand was over his eye. Whit said, "Yes sir, it gets darker and then lighter." The doctor said there was a 50/50 chance that Whit would get his sight back.

He carefully re-bandaged Whit's eyes. He asked Lester and me, "Are you fellows the ones who bandaged his eyes?"

I answered, "Well, sir, we didn't bandage them the first time, but the ones our surgeon put on got bloody and irritated him, so we got some more. We boiled some water and cleaned around them before we put the bandages on."

He smiled. "Well, you did a good job. You may have saved your friend's one good eye."

Lester said, "I'm shore glad we could help some. I'm getting' used to havin' old Whit around." Whit smiled. I could tell he was touched: for once, he didn't have anything to say.

I asked, "Sir, do you have anything you can give him for his pain? All he has had for the last couple of days is some willow bark tea."

The doctor said, "I can't spare much, but if you can find a bottle I could fill it with some laudanum. Enough to last for several days if you use it sparingly."

"Thank ye, doc," Whit said softly.

The doctor looked us over. "I hope you fellows will go back home and become good citizens. You seem like decent people."

Lester spoke up. "I fear we don't look too decent now, but we are all honest, hard-working, God-fearing men. We all plan to go home and try to build a future for our young'uns."

The doctor nodded. "Do you need more bandages?" he asked.

"No, sir, thank you, we still have some from before," I said.

"Clean ones?"

"Yes, sir."

"Good, good. Just make sure to keep the eyes clean." With that, he put his hand on Whit's shoulder, then was off to his next patient.

As we walked away from the field hospital, me leading Whit by the arm, Lester said, "He seemed like a decent feller. He said you got a 50/50 chance at seein' again, Whit old man."

Whit was silent for a minute. I know he had been hoping for more of a guarantee. He said, "I hope I get the better side of that 50/50 bet. I shore don't fancy settin' on the porch the rest of my life, lookin' at nothing but black."

"The Good Lord will take care of you, Whit; it's all in His hands," I said.

"Francis is right," Lester added, "the Good Lord will look out for you and yours." Whit slowly nodded.

When we got back to our little camp, General Lane, our brigade commander, was there. They called him the "Little General" because of his short stature. He might have been small, but his bravery was well known. He had led his brigade in numerous battles, including Gettysburg, and fought with great courage and valor. He was well-respected by the men in his command. Today he looked sad and worn out, like most of the rest. His long, curly, brown beard was uncombed. His eyes were red like he had been awake for a week, his uniform was rumpled, and his trousers and boots were covered with mud.

Someone pointed to us and said, "Here he comes." Then General Lane and the other Confederate officers all turned to look at us. I recognized Colonel Barry and his aide and pulled up short.

THIRTY-TWO

We often sang around the fire
the songs of long ago
raising our voices in one accord
round some treasured melody.

Lester's eyes got wide. "Francis, you suppose we're in trouble?"

"I don't know, but I'll wager we'll soon find out."

"What is it?" Whit asked. "What's going on?"

"It's General Lane and Colonel Barry," I said. "And it appears they're looking for us."

"Us?" Whit said. "Looking for you, you mean. What'd you do now, Francis? Start the war back up when my back was turned?"

General Lane stepped forward. "Private Francis Yelton?"

"Yes sir, I am he," I said and saluted.

The general thrust out his hand, which I took. He shook my hand vigorously. "I just wanted to tell you how proud we all are of what you did." Then he laughed. "I have had many a chuckle over the thought of my old friend, Harry Hallman, trussed up and barefoot, had by a Confederate private. Yes, sir, I have had many a laugh since I learned what happened."

He sidled next to me and put his arm around my shoulders, then chuckled again. "Old Harry and I met many years ago when he visited the old North Carolina Military Institute, and we became friends. He was already in the Union Army, and I, of course, joined the volunteers when hostilities broke out. I have heard about his 'exploits' from time to time, and how he considers himself the boldest brigadier in the Yankee army. He is a good man at heart, but a bit haughty." He clapped me on the back. "It does my heart good to see him get taken down a peg or two. I absolutely cannot wait until I see him to tell him it was one of my men who got the better of him."

He slapped my back again. "Congratulations, Private Yelton. The war may be over for us, but this memory will warm our hearts for years to come."

I was speechless. I looked over at Colonel Barry, who was smiling broadly. "Well, sir, it has probably been much overstated as to what happened," I said. "I was very lucky to surprise them and get the drop. They had no escort or pickets about. A lady Sunday school teacher could have done the same thing."

General Lane roared with laughter. "Don't be so modest, Private. What you did was exceedingly brave." His smile faded. He took a deep breath and looked around at what remained of his brigade. "Too bad it was in a losing cause." His sentence trailed off; everyone was silent for a space, as the mood became more somber.

He shook his head as if to clear it, then took another deep breath and drew himself up. In a resonant voice he addressed everyone. "We can't let defeat on the battlefield defeat us as men. We fought our best. We have nothing at all to be ashamed about. We were defeated by superior arms and need bow our heads to no man. We must be done with this present business and get ourselves back to our homes, try to rebuild our beloved Southland. It is our sacred duty, and we must see that it is done."

The gathered men all listened quietly. He nodded and turned back to me with a wan smile. "Godspeed, Private Yelton, I shall see you on that Golden Shore someday." He shook my hand again. An aide brought him his horse, he mounted it, saluted to the officers, and rode away toward Appomattox.

Colonel Barry came over to me to shake my hand. I told him, "I'm not sure where your horse is, sir, but now that the war is over I suppose you ought to take it home with you."

"Nonsense," he said. "A deal is a deal, Private. The horse is yours." He laid a hand on my shoulder and added, "Be well, Private Francis Yelton." And with that he mounted his own horse and headed in the same direction as General Lane.

The whole time, Lester had been standing with his mouth open. As the crowd broke up and we walked back to our camp, he finally spoke. "I ain't ever been that close to a general before in all my life!"

Whit laughed. "I think he's right proud of you, Francis."

I turned back toward the officers riding off into the distance. "Well, I wish he had offered us a train ride home. You fellows know we've got an awful long walk."

Lester sighed. "Yes sir, but first we have to sign them pledges and stack our rifles."

THIRTY-THREE

*Under a springtime sun
the ragged gray ranks
march one final time,
forced to salute a new order.*

"Fall in!" bellowed Sergeant Caswell Hutchins.

It was April 12, 1865. The surviving men of Company H and the rest of the 18th North Carolina, fewer than a hundred now, lined up in ranks of four along the muddy road and shouldered their rifles for the last time. Although we were fed and rested, I fear we did not look any better than three days before.

The ranks were more silent than I had ever seen before. The men were solemn, some still defiant, some with a look of defeat, some with a look of purest relief. We began the doleful trek to the village of Appomattox Courthouse. Our regiment marched near the end of the tattered ranks of Robert E. Lee's defeated army. Some of the men had tears in their eyes; most just looked stoically ahead, chins up, proud as ever. Beaten, maybe, but not bowed.

Yankee troopers lined the road. As we passed, the Federals came to attention and executed a rifle salute. It somehow made the whole affair a bit easier.

I led Whit by the arm. He wanted to march with us this last time, and insisted he carry his own rifle. I am sure many a Yankee who saw him thought it was a pitiful army indeed that resorted to giving arms to blind men.

We marched into the little square. The men went one by one to the stacks and placed their rifles. Lester was just ahead of Whit.

When he laid his rifle down he said, "Rest well, old Betsy, you made a many of 'em bite the dust." I helped Whit stack his rifle, and then I placed mine. I really did not feel particularly sad. The feeling was more akin to relief.

We lined up at a tent with a little table out front, where a Union Army clerk took signatures and handed out parole papers. We signed our names and got our papers. They told us not to lose them because it was proof that we were paroled and could not be picked up by Federals as Rebel soldiers, or spies, or whatever. A regimental clerk of the 18th was recording the names of the men present at the surrender.

I had hidden one of the captured Colt .44's in my bedroll, and Lester put the other at the bottom of his haversack, under some gear. I had no intention of giving them up because I knew I would be leading a blind man through a lawless country on the way home. I would give up the rifle, but the pistols I knew we must keep. Nobody asked to look in my bedroll or in our haversacks, so for now the pistols were safe.

Sergeant Cas met up with us. "Well, fellows, are you off to Rutherford County?"

"I 'spect we are, Sergeant," said Lester. With a hopeful look he added, "Although I shore hope we can find us a ride at least part of the way."

The sergeant smiled ruefully at me. "Well, I am afraid the horse is gone. Seems General Hallman found out where his stallion was and captured it back, so naturally Colonel Barry wanted his chestnut back for the ride home." *So much for a deal's a deal*, I thought. I guess I couldn't hold it against the colonel, though. I had offered the horse back to him.

Cas continued, "I guess you fellows are in the same boat as the rest of us. But I think the Federals are going to let us have free train rides, when trains are available. You fellows want some company on the trip?"

"Why, yes sir, Sergeant," Whit said. "I wouldn't want to be left alone in this unreliable company," he added with a raspy chuckle.

"You!" roared a Federal officer in our direction. He came striding up with a purpose, his piercing blue eyes fixed on me and his revolver in his hand. "You're the miserable scum that tied us up and robbed us! I knew if I looked long enough I would find you." It was that Major Trent, and his arrogant expression and cold eyes put a chill in the air. As he approached he spat the words, "You, a lowly dog. You come into our camp and dare to humiliate a member of Boston's finest family! Say your prayers, Reb. You're about to be the last man to die in this fight." He stopped about five paces away, grinning savagely, then raised his revolver at my head and fired.

The round ripped through the brim of my hat on the left side and spun it off my head. In a blur of movement, Sergeant Hutchins covered the five paces in a blink and slammed into the Union officer, catching him in the midsection. They both went to the ground. The sergeant rose to his knees and punched the Federal officer hard in the face, once, twice, three times.

A dozen Yankee troopers rushed over and roughly pulled Cas off the man. Even though Trent's shouting had made all eyes turn so they knew he was the one who had started it—and tried to kill me—a Union sergeant said, "Put that Reb in irons!"

They began to lead Cas away. Lester and I looked at each other, wondering what to do, what to say. I was about to protest when a commanding voice stopped us all in our tracks.

"Hold it!" came a bellow from fifty yards away. It was General Hallman. The Yankee troops came to attention as he walked quickly toward us, a thundercloud on his face.

"Who's that?" Lester asked as he leaned over to me.

"That ... is General Hallman."

Lester's eyes widened. "Isn't that the general you captured?"

"I'm afraid so, and he doesn't look too happy."

The general surprised us all. "Let that man go. I saw what Major Trent did; this man was trying to defend his friend. Major, consider yourself under arrest for conduct unbecoming an officer. I expect you to report to my headquarters in one hour."

The Union soldiers released Cas, who wore a look of surprise and confusion on his face. Trent stood with some difficulty, staggered from the blows Cas had delivered, and picked up his hat and his revolver. The general snatched the pistol away from him. "I'll take that; you might accidentally shoot yourself."

The major glowered at us with a look of purest hatred, then stalked off unsteadily, rubbing his jaw. He looked back at us as he walked. There was something in his eyes that bespoke a strange sort of madness. It made my blood run cold.

The general turned to us. "You all right, son?" he asked.

I thought the general must have recognized me, but I wasn't about to ask him. I replied, "I'm fine, sir, although my hat's a little worse for it. I'm glad the major is not a very good shot."

The general smiled. He looked down at the ground and then back at me. "I must apologize for Major Trent. He took the war more personally than most of us. Seems before the war some South Carolina planter stole his intended. He never got over it. Always railing against the South and Southerners, and holds you all in the highest contempt. He once suggested I order an entire company of Confederates shot dead for, in his words, 'being secesh vermin.'"

He shook his head ruefully. "But his daddy owns half of Boston, and that money has a way of smoothing over the rough spots with the army, if you know what I mean. It is a bloody shame, too. The man could have been an excellent officer."

The general paused and looked me up and down. "You know, you really got the better of us the other day. I thought Trent was going to go completely insane. I personally think the man needs to catch hold of a sticking place. I have to admit, I wanted to kill you myself; but after I thought about it for a while, I realized how lucky we were. You could just as easily have killed us, or marched us back to the Confederate lines. There were no Union troops around to assist us. You actually treated us pretty well under the circumstances, but at the time I was so embarrassed and angry I could hardly speak. Then I ran into my old friend General Lane yesterday—fancy that, running into him in the midst of both armies."

I interrupted him, "Well, the armies are a lot smaller than they were when the war started, I suppose."

General Hallman looked sad at that. "Indeed. Anyway, I ran into my old friend General Lane, and the first thing he said was, 'I understand you made the acquaintance of one of my men.' He and I wound up sharing a good laugh."

"You did?"

He explained, "It suddenly struck me as the funniest thing. There I was, a general with his staff, talking strategy, when out of the woods jumps this ragged Rebel, all alone. He points this cannon at us, coolly disarms us, then rides off on my horse like he does things like that every day. It was really all quite bizarre, in hindsight. You know, it took Captain Craig a full twenty minutes to gather up all our boots. We never did find the other horses; we had to take the wagon back to our lines."

"I am indeed thankful that you hold no malice, sir," I said.

"I'm not a man to hold grudges. I understand why you did what you did. It took a lot of courage, and I admire that." He looked at Whit and said with a softer voice, "You were looking for medicine for him, I take it? Is there anything I can do for him?"

"Well, sir, thank you, but your surgeon—Dr. Carrington—gave us a bit of laudanum and some bandages," I replied.

"How is he?"

"He lost an eye, but the doctor says he's got a good chance of getting his vision back in the other."

The general gestured toward a mass under Whit's shirt. "What happened to his chest?" he whispered.

"That's a rabbit, sir," I said in my normal volume.

"I'm sorry?"

"It's a rabbit, sir. Whit, show him Cadmus." Whit pulled his shirt open so Cadmus's head was visible. The little creature blinked in the sunlight.

"Well, I'll be," the general said. He flashed a smile that reached all the way up to his ample eyebrows. "Blind men and bunny rabbits in your ranks, and you boys still gave us all that we could handle." He looked us over, taking note, I could tell, of our wasted and ragged condition. Then he yelled over his shoulder to his aide, "Captain! Get me two boxes of food from the wagon. And fetch me my horse."

He turned back to us. "You fellows have had a rough go of it. The way I see it, you're the ones who bore the burden of this conflict; you and our boys out in the trenches. You were right the other day, Private; we did expect our men to do the impossible, sending them out exposed to the Confederate guns, knowing they would die by the thousands. I used to think our men should be honored to die for the Union. I'm not so sure anymore."

Profound sadness filled his eyes. "You boys are no different than our boys. We all want to go back to our families, to our homes. I would like to try to help you just a bit. I can't help all the men in Lee's army, but I can at least help the man who spared my life. Private…?"

"Francis Yelton, sir."

"Well, Francis, it is an unexpected honor." The general offered his hand. I looked at Cas, who smiled slightly and made an expression like he was telling me to hurry up already and put my hand out. I did, and the general gave me a firm handshake.

The captain returned with the general's horse and two boxes under his arm. The general went to his saddlebags and dug down in them. "I had to restock these, as you know," he said wryly. "By the way," he added without looking up, "Colonel Barry gave me back my pistol and one of the others, but he didn't know where the other two got to. I suppose they are lost, perhaps in the possession of some Confederate officers." Lester and I looked at each other, though neither of us said a word. The general came back with his arms full of bacon, hard tack, tobacco, and a bottle of Scotch whiskey. "Here, take this as a token of good will from an old Union general." He handed the goods to us.

I was so taken aback that I was almost at a total loss for words. I stammered, "General, I don't know what to say. I am sorry I inconvenienced you and your officers and took your horse. All I could think about was getting some relief for Whit here, and maybe I went a bit too far. I—"

The general held up his hand. "Never mind, Private, you did what you thought was right. I just happened to be the unlucky man who got in your way. I have one question, though: would you really have killed me back there, when you had the musket pointed at my head?"

I looked down and scuffed the ground with my foot. "I honestly don't know, sir. I am surely glad we didn't both have to find out."

"So am I, Private. More than you, I would bet." He grinned. "Well, I have to get back to my men, see that they don't get into trouble. I wish you all well and...," he paused for a moment, "...welcome back to the United States."

"Thank you, General," said Cas. Then we all saluted, and the general was on his way.

We looked at the boxes of hard tack, the slabs of wrapped bacon, and the pouches of tobacco. Whit sniffed. "I smell 'baccer. Any of the chawin' kind there?"

"Why, yessiree," said Lester. He pulled out a plug and placed it in Whit's hand.

Whit wore a smile like he had just seen an angel of the Lord. He bit off a big chaw and said, "If I'da knowed this surrenderin' business was this pleasurable, I woulda done it a long time back!"

THIRTY-FOUR

The hickory trees
whisper in the wind,
their sighs a pale reflection
of our weary state of mind.

The four of us agreed that we had best start toward home right away. But first we stopped at the regimental headquarters. We found Colonel Barry talking quietly with some of the other officers. He looked a bit sheepish when he saw me.

He spoke as we neared. "Private, I feel badly about taking the horse I traded to you. Can I make it up in some way?"

"No, sir," I said, "there is no need for that. I came here without a horse; I had no expectation of leavin' with one. I am just thankful to the Good Lord and to my friends that we made it through the fight, and we can now go home."

He smiled slightly. "Well, Francis, what you did was brave, as I have already said. A hungry, wounded man taking on a Yankee general and his staff; I still have a hard time believing it. I saw General Hallman a while ago; I think he's gotten over it, though I did jest with him a bit. I gave him his horse and the Colts back. It seemed the decent thing to do."

"Yes, sir," I said, "we saw the general just a short time ago. It seems one of his staff still wants to see me dead. He took a shot at me."

"Good Lord," said the colonel. "I hope you didn't get hit." He looked me up and down.

"No, sir, he missed, though my hat is a bit worse for the incident."

"Thank God." The colonel frowned, then pursed his lips. "Is there anything at all I can do for you?"

Cas spoke up. "Well, sir, the four of us live in the same county and we plan to travel together. I think we should be all right."

"Well, we've been told that they will provide transportation to get you home—when it is available. Your parole papers should get you there, but when transportation will become available is another matter. The war is still going on south of here. Also, you might have to come up with some Yankee money for food along the way. Do you have any?"

We looked at each other. Lester said, "I think all we have is Confederate. I ain't seen Yankee money in a long time."

"*That's* how I can help," the colonel said. "Thanks to Colonel Campbell, a friend of mine in the Union Army, who repaid a debt the other day. We, uh, had made a little wager before the war, which I won, but at the time he did not have the script to pay me. He finally paid me back; I suppose because he felt guilty about how things ended for us. Here's twenty Yankee dollars. That should be more than enough. Don't tell anyone, though; I don't have enough to help all the men."

We looked at each other in amazement. No one moved until Sergeant Hutchins reached out and took the money. "Thank you, sir," he said. "We are very much obliged."

"Nonsense. You boys did me proud this whole war. You never let me down, not once. Besides, it was worth twenty dollars to ride General Hallman's horse for a few days."

At that, we all laughed, shook hands all around, and started on our way.

Cas pointed southwest. "The Appomattox Station is this way. Let's see if we can get us a train ride." We walked toward the station, anxious to be headed homeward.

But the train had just left when we got there. The Yankee sergeant who now served as station master told us that there would be another along in a few hours, and we might be able to get on it. We settled down on the station porch along with hundreds of other parolees and waited for our ride towards home.

The train never came. Seems like some Confederate cavalry

which had escaped the trap at Appomattox decided to do a little damage before they headed south to try to continue the fight. They tore up some track and burned one of the trains. "Well, fellers," Lester said, "I guess we'll have to hoof it."

I looked at Whit. "You up to walkin', Whit?"

He spat out a stream. "I reckon I 'druther git walkin' than set around here."

We gathered up our gear and headed down the road that led southwest out of Appomattox. The sun was low in the sky. There were only a few ragged clouds bright against the azure heavens.

A quail called out after us. Lester laughed and said, "Mr. Bird, they ain't no one called 'Bob White' around here!"

We hoped the walk home would be no more eventful than listening to the birds. Our hope was not well founded.

THIRTY-FIVE

*Night birds make music
and the spring wind whispers
while along the tiresome road,
weariness wears like a garment.*

We walked about five miles that first afternoon. Whit got tired easily so we stopped at about six in the evening and looked for a spot to camp. We chose a spot about a hundred yards away from the road. It was through a stand of Virginia pines, in a little grove of maple, oak and hickory trees. I gathered up some dry wood while Lester helped Whit get settled. Cas scouted around our camp and peered into the distance, looking for whatever might be harmful, such as hidden bushwhackers or even trigger happy Yankee cavalry.

I got the fire started and went off to find some water for coffee. I found a small stream about a half a mile away, in a shady little valley, where I filled all our canteens and a cook pot full of water. There was something strange, something that puzzled me for a moment, until I realized that I did not hear the distant rumble of artillery or the rattle of musketry. Just the little stream gurgling as it tumbled over the stones on its way toward the sea, and the breath of the wind as it exhaled through the woods. The trees sighed as if they were touched by a lover.

I breathed deeply of the fresh air. I stripped down to my underwear and stepped into a little pool, where I sat in the cold water and scrubbed my clothes against wet rocks to rid them of some of the dirt and dried blood. Then, drawing in a deep breath,

I laid down and plunged my head under the cold water. I bathed as best I could, washing from head to toe; washing the stain of sin, the taint of death. When I emerged from my makeshift baptismal font, I shivered in the early evening air. My pale skin was covered in goose bumps, but I felt better than I had in many days.

My injured leg throbbed, but not as badly as before. I took the bandage off and inspected the wound. It was the first time I had looked at it closely; it probably came from a .56 Spencer or a Sharps carbine. It had entered about five inches above the knee and just to the inside, missing the bone by an inch or two. It came out the back and I could tell the exit hole had been much bigger, though the surgeon had closed it up.

The wound was clotted with blood and the skin was red around it. I washed the bandage out and took it with me to dry by the fire. It was a serious wound, but I thought it strange I had been knocked cold. I can only guess that maybe I hit my head hard when I went down. The leg hurt so badly at the time that I didn't even think about checking for a lump on my head.

Back at camp I hung my clothes by the fire to dry and started boiling some water for coffee. I put on another cook pot of water to wash Whit's eyes. I dreaded the job, but I knew it would be best if we cleaned them. We had enough bandages left to dress them at least one more time.

Cas stared grimly as I removed Whit's bandages. I bathed his eyes, or what was left of them, with the hot water. I used a small piece of cloth to dab them dry, then made little pads for each eye as we did before and re-bandaged them. Whit was silent the whole time. He seemed to me to have become a much more thoughtful man.

As we sat and drank our coffee, we each had a piece of bacon and some hard tack. Then we settled back to pass the evening. Lester and I lit up our pipes, and Cas joined Whit in a chaw.

Whit said, "Lester, why don't you hold Cadmus for a while. He needs a change of scenery."

Lester grimaced and shook his head. "I don't think so, Whit. You know what happened last time."

"Aw, come on, Lester, he ain't never wet on me. I'm sure it was just an accident. Here, take the little feller."

Lester looked at the rabbit and grinned. We all knew he liked the little creature. "All right, just for a few minutes," he said. He took the rabbit and settled back, smoking his pipe. After a few minutes passed, Lester wrinkled his nose and looked down. He slowly picked Cadmus up, and there on the front of his pants was a small pile. "Well, I'll be hanged! The rabbit has done gone and done his business right on my lap!" he exclaimed.

Cas laughed. "Must be an ordnance rabbit; looks like he left you a little pile of musket balls."

Whit was shaking with laughter. Lester jumped up, brushing himself off, and placed the rabbit back on Whit's chest. "I thank I'll go wash my clothes," he said. He headed on off toward the creek.

Lester came back in a little while, wet pants in his hands. He stretched them out in front of the fire to dry and wrapped himself up in his blanket. "Don't ask me to hold that rabbit again, Whit."

"Well, Lester," said Whit, his words wedged between chuckles, "he don't mean no harm. I think he just considers you his own personal lah-trine." Cas and I were once again laughing so hard we could barely sit upright.

Lester said, "Well, I don't fancy bein' no rabbit's lah-trine, so you just keep him with you."

Things gradually settled back down, and we were silent for a long time, trying to take in all that had happened. Cas looked like he had something he wanted to say. Finally he took a deep breath, exhaled, looked around at us, and said softly, "You know, I have been with the 18th for over two years, and I've only been wounded twice, both just scratches. I've watched men blown to pieces, shot through the head and the heart, wounded in every grievous way a man can imagine. But I've only had a scratch or two; I don't know why that is."

None of us had an answer for him. I looked at him for a long moment. "Well, Cas, it wasn't from lack of trying. You surely did your share of the fightin' and you have nothing to be ashamed of or to feel bad about. I wouldn't give it another thought if I were you."

Cas smiled slightly and looked at me with an expression of feigned incredulity. "Oh, yes you would, Francis. You wrote the book on duty and guilt. You think it's your job to right all the wrongs, and to take care of everybody, while you fight the Yankees singlehanded. Don't tell me not to think of it, when I know you sure as the devil would."

Whit laughed, raspy as ever. "He's shore got yore number, Francis. Ye cain't deny a bit of it."

I looked from one to the other. "Well, maybe I do take things to heart, but that's the way my Pa taught me. I probably ought to step back every now and then but, fellows, you know I don't believe there is a middle ground when it comes to a man's home and friends and country. I did not want to fight, all I wanted to do was plow my land, grow my crops, and raise my family. I never wanted to kill anybody, yet now here I am: a killer many times over. We all are. I know I only did what I had to do, but I tell you I will carry it to the grave with me."

I didn't want to preach, but I couldn't help but say what I had to say. "I will carry to the grave the sight of that young Federal I shot when they attacked on the 2nd. He couldn't have been older than sixteen. He had on a brand new uniform, shiny buttons and a shiny new rifle. I shot him at about a hundred yards. He dropped on the spot and I knew he was dead.... I knew it. Just a boy.

"And I'll carry with me to the grave, the Yankee I stabbed with the bayonet in the trenches that day. His mouth was moving, he was praying. He was a Christian, and I killed him ... a Christian! How many of us Christians have killed our brothers? I will never forget his face; he had no malice in it, only a look of the deepest peace. I asked him to forgive me as he died. I hope he did."

There was quiet for a while. Cas broke the silence. "Francis, you must forgive yourself, let all of this go. You owe it to your family. I feel the same as you do. The fact, is I have killed so many men in the past two years, I have lost count. I probably killed eighty or a hundred at Cold Harbor. They just kept coming at us. We were behind breastworks, and they attacked over open ground. They took fire like I've never seen before. They had no chance ... no chance.

"Two of my men loaded rifles and passed them to me, and I just aimed and fired. They loaded for me and I fired. Over and over and over again I fired, I don't know how many times, maybe a hundred and fifty or more. The rifles were so hot we could hardly hold them. Several thousand other men did the same." He placed a hand over his eyes, as if he was trying to block the visions in his memory. "The Yankees fell by the thousands in less than half an hour. It was the most pitiful thing I have ever seen. The wounded lay in heaps. Some begged for water, begged for somebody to help them. Some begged for someone to kill them. My God, they begged to die!"

He slammed both fists on his knees. "Grant was either a fool or a knave to make that attack. It was the most hopeless charge I ever saw. But he didn't care; he just kept sending them into our guns and they died by the thousands. It's no wonder some call him 'The Butcher.' That is just one of the things I will carry to my grave. So you see, Francis, you're not alone when it comes to regrets."

"Somehow that don't make it any easier, Cas," I said. "I mean, I do know that we must put this business behind us and find a way to get back to our regular lives, get over all this, but right now I'm havin' a hard time seein' it. Somehow I doubt I will be in my right mind ever again. Could it be that the fightin' and killin' have turned me into something vile, something I never wanted to be?"

We sat in silence for the rest of the evening; each man alone with his thoughts, his regrets. Every now and then we tossed another stick of wood on the fire to ward off the chill. The flames flickered and licked toward the sky. Night birds sang softly in the distance. Small frogs chirruped in the direction of the creek. As usual, Lester and I smoked and Whit and Cas worked their chaws. Sometime late that night weariness overtook us, and we all covered up and fell asleep.

THIRTY-SIX

Another road, another day
the lark soars, but we must trudge
the weight of time
heavy on our backs.

The morning of April 13, I was awakened by the spatter of raindrops on my face. I opened my eyes to a cool rainy day. Clouds rolled thickly overhead and mist curled around the trees in vague currents. A big black crow flew over, his grating call echoing through the woods.

Cas had found some squaw wood, and with that and the pine knots gathered from the night before, he had made a fire and had the coffee pot boiling. The smell was pungent in the fresh spring air. I sat up and fished my cup out of the haversack. Cas filled it for me.

Lester and Whit still slept, both covered with their oilcloths. I pulled out my own oilcloth and covered up. Cas did the same. We sat like two Indians under blankets, sipping our coffee and watching the fire hiss and steam in the light rain.

Cas said, "I hope this lets up soon. I sure would like to make fifteen miles today. Do you think Whit is up to it?"

"Well, he's a tough old bird, although he has been through a terrible time in these recent days. I can't really say for sure."

Cas drank some coffee. "Well, I for one want to see us all stick together until we get home. I have waited for over two years. I can wait a while longer if our friend needs to rest."

"It surely would have been good to have the colonel's horse for Whit. We could probably make twenty miles a day with no problem. We have over three hundred miles to go. At fifteen miles a day, it will take us three weeks to get home; that is, unless we can catch a train somewhere and make up some time."

"Whar we gonna catch a train?" Whit said, coming awake and sitting up. "That thar coffee smells mighty fine. Reckon a feller could git him a cup?"

"I expect he could," I said. I got his cup, filled it from the pot and handed it to him.

"Mmm-hmm, that shore tastes good. You make that, Francis?" Whit asked.

"No, Sergeant Hutch ... uh, Cas made it."

"Well, Cas, you ort to open yoreself a eatin' place when you git home. You know how to make a fine cup of coffee."

"Thank you, Whit. I'll give it some consideration."

Lester stirred. "Good mornin', fellers. Did I miss anything?"

"Yes, sir," Whit intoned, "they was a whole passel of dance hall girls come flouncin' by, but we told them you could not be disturbed."

Lester grinned. "Was they purty?"

"Oh, the purtiest," said Whit.

"Would you like some coffee, Lester?" Cas asked.

"Yes, I would, Sergeant."

"He ain't a sergeant no more, Lester," Whit reminded him.

"Oh, that's right; sorry, uh, Cas."

"I guess we have more than a few things to get used to," Cas said with a wry smile.

We ate a bite and gathered our belongings together. I took the revolver from my bedroll, where I had hidden it after we left Appomattox. Cas looked at it with some curiosity and I said, "Lester has one too; I thought we might need them."

Lester furrowed his brow, as if he had forgotten all about his pistol. He reached into his haversack, pulled out the other revolver and handed it to Cas. He said, "Here, Cas, I wish you would carry this. I ain't fired enough pistols to whar I could hit anything anyhow."

Cas looked at the Colt. "Nice weapon, but I'm not sure I could hit anything with it either; most of my shootin's been with an Enfield."

"I hope you don't have no need, Cas," I said. "But it makes me feel a bit more secure to have it, I must tell you." We tucked the pistols in our belts and headed out toward the road.

The road was turning into mire. Footing was slippery and I had to lead Whit, so our progress was very slow. We had not gone far before I sensed something behind us. When I turned I saw a lone horseman in the distance, maybe a half a mile behind us, darkly silhouetted against the dim sky. I got the others' attention and they also turned to look.

Then the horseman disappeared, ghostlike. We waited for him to reappear, but he did not. We shrugged it off and started walking again.

An owl called in the distance. A chill went through me. *Probably the fever in my leg,* I thought. I turned uneasily and looked behind. There was nothing there.

Whit seemed to be a little stronger, though leading him tired us both. I took turns with Cas and Lester, but poor Whit just had to trust that we were leading him aright. Now and then he stumbled over a stone or a stick that we did not even think about warning him of. When he stumbled he repeatedly exclaimed, "Well, John Brown's body!" About the third time he said it, Lester took the cue and started up "The Battle Hymn of the Republic."

"Where did you learn that, Lester?" Cas asked.

"I heard the Yankees sing it across the lines a million times. I kind of fancy it."

Whit growled, "Well, it shore ain't no Confederate song, Lester. Do ye know what it's about?"

Lester grinned sheepishly. "Well, yes, but there's more to a song than the words. Besides, we ain't Confederates no more. War's over."

"Well, just the same, how about singin' 'Dixie's Land'," said Whit. Lester again lifted up his tenor voice and gave us several rousing choruses of "Dixie's Land."

"That's more like it!" Whit exclaimed.

About twelve o'clock we stopped for something to eat and a short rest. We sat to the side of the road, under some trees. The rain had stopped, but dark clouds still rolled thickly overhead. As we sat eating, suddenly Cas jumped up and pulled the revolver. Lester and I jumped up too. Whit cocked his head.

Cas peered into the woods on the far side of the road. "I saw something moving back in the woods, something big, but I could not make it out. Could be a man on a horse."

Whit laughed. "War's over, remember? Probably just a stray cow."

"I don't know," said Lester. "I ain't seen too many stray cows lately. Between the Rebs and the Yanks, I think we et em all!"

Cas continued to peer into the woods. "Well, whatever it was, it's gone now. At least I hope so."

We rested a while longer then started out again. The road ran through the rolling Virginia countryside, passing miles of woodlands and, occasionally, small farms. Most looked neglected. Here and there we saw buildings burned and the rotting carcasses of slaughtered animals.

Once in a while we saw women and children watching us from the porches of their homes, no doubt looking to see if their loved ones were among those whose craggy forms shambled down the muddy road. Their faces all had a bleak, haunted look. They also seemed suffused with hunger and misery, and much fear and anxiety about what tomorrow would bring. We waved and tipped our hats, and sometimes called out "good afternoon." It was all we could do, some small measure to try and let them know that we cared and that we respected them as human beings. The brutality of war had stolen the humanity from so many; it seemed a modest start at gaining back some of that spark of human kindness.

Occasionally we crossed paths with other paroled Confederates making their way home. This included four former Confederate officers who rode by in the same direction we were traveling. They barely looked at us, didn't say a word, just stared straight ahead like men in a dream.

Most of the other Confederates we met spoke to us like the comrades we once were. We shared some food with one pair who had nothing to their names except their canteens and their bedrolls. They looked near unto starvation. Their gratitude and profuse thanks tugged at my heart. I was very thankful we could help them a little.

The road became monotonous. Once in a while a proud mansion rose on a hilltop. They all seemed similar, with tree lined roads and seemingly endless fields stretching into the distance. The fields all looked untended. The slaves were gone, and the work did not get done. We occasionally met some Negroes with their meager belongings in bundles over their shoulders. A pang of guilt hit me as I wondered how Cyrus, the teamster I had befriended, was faring. I hoped he would make out all right, he seemed a good man. Well, if he ever needed anything, at least he knew my name and where I was from.

Most of the Negroes we saw were in groups of three or four. Once we encountered about twenty of them, men, women and children, carrying all their worldly goods in a rickety old wagon drawn by the scrawniest mule I have ever seen before or since. Its ribs showed through a loose gray hide. They looked at us with suspicion, but we simply nodded and said, "Good mornin'," and they nodded and moved on.

Cas said, "I guess they're learnin' about the other side of freedom; the side that means they no longer have their masters to provide for them. Now they must make their own way just like the whites must. It surely must be a terrible burden, even though having their freedom must be a marvel."

"They are indeed free, but no thanks to us," I said. Lester and Cas looked at me; Whit mumbled something.

Cas said, "Well, they're not like white people, Francis. Before they came here they lived in jungles in little huts. They had no life, no civilization. They had no Christian faith; only their superstitions and their devilish practices."

"They didn't have no chains, neither," said Whit. "I ain't so shore they was better off here than back in Afriker."

We walked in silence for a time, until Lester said, "I think this whole thing is gonna bring a passel of trouble for all of us. The Yankees is gonna be sticking around to make sure the war is over; they's all these blacks with no place to go; and we're goin' home to farms that is probably all broke down. Fellers, we've got more to handle that we can say grace over, and more trouble than, than...." He trailed off.

"Leastwise we ain't got no blue bellies tryin' to blow holes in us!" Whit said. There were quiet nods of agreement all around.

We walked for a couple of more hours. The afternoon grew long. Whit said, "Fellers, if ye don't mind too much, I feel like I done had enough for one day."

Cas answered, "I think we've all had enough for one day. Let's find us a camp."

Again we moved off the road, about one hundred yards. Cas made his typical walk all around the far reaches of the area, scanning the distance. We had just crossed over a creek where we had filled out canteens, so we did not need any water. Whit settled up against the trunk of a large tree with help from Lester, and I gathered up enough firewood to last the night.

As we began to settle down for the evening, we built a small fire under some hickory trees and put on some water to boil for coffee. I wasn't hungry, so all I had was one piece of hard tack. The others had some bacon as well. As usual, Lester and I lit our pipes while Whit put in a chaw. Cas just chewed the end of a twig and stared into the fire. We chatted until after dark, then we all just sat and watched the fire.

Cas raised his head and frowned. "Somethin's wrong. The frogs got quiet." Lester and I looked around. "Wait here," Cas said, pulling the revolver out of his belt. He moved quietly out of the camp. I drew my revolver, moved out of the firelight and tried to peer into the darkness. Lester unsheathed his side knife and moved close to Whit.

A half moon hung in the sky and the light filtered weakly down through the leaves. The wind rustled the tree tops and they tossed restlessly. I heard a twig snap in the darkness. "Hold it!" I heard Cas shout. Off to my left I saw a muzzle flash and heard the bark of a pistol, stark and jarring in the quiet woods. Immediately a shot sounded in answer, and then it was quiet again.

I glanced at Lester and Whit. Lester had pulled Whit to the ground and they were both lying at the base of the tree. Lester had an arm over Whit's shoulders, and Whit was protectively cradling Cadmus the rabbit within his arms.

I motioned for Lester to stay there. Then I moved off as quietly as I could in the direction of the gunfire.

THIRTY-SEVEN

The reaper walks the night
seeking what it might destroy
the chancre in the human spirit
baring its bloody teeth.

I peered through the trees for any sign of movement but could see nothing in the deep woods. The gunfire had been no more than a hundred yards away. I walked in a crouch, feeling my way through the forest, careful not to make any noise, alert for any sound, any movement.

Every shadow seemed a threat. I stopped at a thick oak tree, which I thought was between me and the gunfire. I decided to call out for Cas, even though I knew it would give away my position. "Cas!" No answer. "Cas, where are you?" Still no answer.

The mysterious gunman could be laying in wait for me, waiting for me to step into a pool of moonlight. In this darkness, if I stepped into the slightest bit of light, I would be an easy target. I could almost feel hot lead ripping into my chest.

I waited for several minutes, listening. My breath became fast and shallow. I tried to keep calm, tried to slow my breathing, but my instinct spoke disaster. I moved to a tree about twenty feet to my left and called again, "Cas!" Silence. I was increasingly concerned that Cas was dead or badly hurt.

I could hear my heart pounding in my ears. I thought at the time even that might give me away. After two agonizing minutes or so I thought of Lester and Whit. The gunman might circle around to our camp, and they would be sitting ducks, unarmed and in the firelight. Although I didn't want to have survived the war just to die like this, I decided I had to make a move.

I carefully eased the hammer back on the Colt, stepped around the tree and moved toward where the gunfire had come from. As I crept through the underbrush, trying to avoid making noise, every muscle tense, I sidestepped the small spots of moonlight and stuck to the shadows.

An owl sailed noiselessly over my head. The wind tossed the tree tops, creating eerie shadows on the forest floor.

The hand was visible in the weak moonlight, palm upward on the leafy ground. I recognized the pistol and his old butternut shirt. He was lying on his back. I moved to him. I could not see his face, so I felt to see if he was breathing. There was wetness in the center of his chest, but no breathing, no movement of any kind.

Cas was dead.

"Oh, no," I murmured. "Dear Lord."

A voice from the darkness, laced with cynicism, spoke softly. "Even the Lord can't help you now, Reb."

I grabbed up Cas's revolver and, a pistol in each hand, turned toward the voice's direction. My firepower was doubled, but I still couldn't make out a target. "Who is that?"

There was soft laughter, and then he said, "I'm the man who said he was going to kill you. And that was before I got arrested just for trying to shoot a miserable, dirt grubbing Rebel like you."

"Trent?" I said, shocked that he had followed us all this way, all this time.

His words dripped with contempt. "That's *Major* Carlton Trent, you lowly piece of Southern trash." I could tell he was speaking through gritted teeth. "Well, I should say *former* Major Trent. Hallman had me cashiered, thanks to you. You don't humiliate Major Carlton Trent and get away with it, oh no, not on this earth."

His words had a lunatic tinge. "I am a man of standing, from an important family, and who the hell are you? You're something I scrape off my boots before I go into my house. You're a loser many times over. You lost the war; you grub in the dirt for a living; you are dirty and uneducated. And you have the *temerity* to insult a man like *me?*" His voice rose in pitch, brittle and almost hysterical.

"I told you I would kill you, Reb and I aim to do it. You see, I am not going to ask you your name. I do not care. Your name is *nothing. You* are nothing. I am going to shoot you down like the dog that you are. But first I want you to drop that revolver."

He must have seen me pick up Cas's pistol, but my other hand was in deep shadow and I hoped he could not see the other gun.

I did not move, so he said, "Remember, I have a .44 aimed right at your head, which I can see just fine. If you comply I promise to put you out of your misery quickly, a single bullet to the head. Honestly, you aren't worth any more than that, to tell you the truth."

He was a coward. He just wanted to make sure I couldn't fire back. But I didn't cotton to being a willing victim. I tossed Cas's revolver to my right, into a patch of moonlight, so Trent could see it. I could not see him, but I heard his footsteps crunching on leaves as he started to approach.

As fast as I could move I dropped down and to my left, firing in his direction. I fell and rolled, then hammered and fired. Three times in all the Colt roared and leapt in my hand. I saw the muzzle flash of his pistol in reply and felt a vicious blow to my head as I fired one last time.

"The name's ... Yelton ... Francis Yelton ... you black hearted devil," I said, the bones in my body feeling strangely like wax. "You ... killed ... my friend."

Stars arched to the right and left, then faded as I fell into a dark tunnel.

Then I traveled upward, spiraling; there was light all around me. I thought I heard my wife's voice calling me to supper. Of a sudden I was walking behind my mule, plowing in the springtime, the sun warm on my shoulders. I could smell the new earth turned to the light after a long winter in darkness. It was quiet for a time, until it was broken by voices coming from the direction of the creek. They were calling my name. "Francis, Francis. You all right?"

"Lester, what are you doin' at the creek?" I said. Then there was pitch black night and silence.

I opened my eyes to firelight flickering on low branches. My head throbbed dully. On the left side everything seem blurred. I blinked several times, then carefully turned and saw Lester's face.

He looked grim. "You all right, Francis?"

"I ... I think so. What happened? Did you find Cas? He's ... he got...."

"I know, Francis. He's dead. I thought you was, too. You took a .44 round right smack in the forehead. It must have passed through a tree first; that, and you're the most hard-headed sonovagun anyone ever met. The spent ball hit you and just knocked you out cold."

I reached up to my forehead to check it. There was something wrapped around my temples. "We used up all the good bandages on Whit," Lester explained, "so I had to make do with some torn cloth. It broke the skin where Trent shot you, but it just plain bounced off your skull."

A sudden wave of fear made me try to rise, but nausea quickly knocked me back down. "Where's Trent?"

"I 'spect he's havin' a little set-to with the devil about now. You killed him. Two of your rounds took him darn near in the middle of his chest. When I heard all that gunfire and you didn't come back for a spell, I hid Whit near the camp and came looking. That's when I found the two of you. I thought you was *both* dead."

"And you're sure Trent's dead?" I asked.

"Deader than King George."

I closed my eyes again. "Oh, Lord, have mercy on us. Cas is gone. Lester, there's nobody else like him. He was ... a truly great man. Two years he fought, he told us, and he made it through. He thought this was over." I pounded the earth with my clenched fists. "God, why can't it be over?"

Whit spoke up. "No greater love than this that a man will lay down his life for his friends." We all fell silent.

"We'll bury him at daylight," said Lester.

Once more I closed my eyes. My head was pounding, and my grief made the world look dark, just when we thought daybreak was at hand.

THIRTY-EIGHT

The somber morning comes
on ravens' wings
the owl his newfound friend
calling all of us home.

After a fitful night, with my temples throbbing, I finally woke to the glint of sunlight from the east. The sky through the trees was a pale blue; wispy vapor filled the woods. Lester had the coffee started, and he offered me a cup. As I sat up the pain surged in my head. My vision was still blurry.

Whit sat propped against a tree with his head bowed. I couldn't tell if he was sleeping or praying or just thinking. I rasped, "Whit, you all right?"

"No, I don't reckon I'll ever be all right agin'. There is just too much bad, Francis, too much bad."

I stood shakily, walked over and sat beside him. The accumulated sorrow and pain was catching up to even tough old Whit. I patted his shoulder.

I turned to Lester. "Let's see to our friend."

Whit said, "I want to be there."

What a trio we made. I had to lean on Lester because I was still dizzy, and Whit held on to his other side. We made our way through the woods to where Cas lay, in the same spot as the night before. We found a small clearing in the woods and dug a shallow grave the best we could with our knives and tin cups. Whit even helped. Then we laid Cas in it, draped him with his oilcloth, and covered him up with the dark earth.

Lester and I gathered large stones and piled them a couple of feet high on top of the grave, to keep anything from digging him up. "He needs a marker," I said quietly. Lester took out through the woods. He came back in a few minutes with a large piece of tree bark, broken off and sharp at one end. He handed it to me.

Things were still a bit hazy but my vision was clearing. I took out my side knife and paused for a moment, then I began to carve into the wood. After fifteen or twenty minutes the inscription was complete: *Caswell Hutchins, A True Soldier of God, 1865.* Lester took it from me and used a stone to pound it into the ground near the head of the grave.

We gathered around to say a few words. "Dear God," I prayed, "please rest the soul of this good and gallant man. He was the bravest, truest friend a man could ever have. His life was an example for us all." My voice seemed choked. "He never asked for anything; he always gave. Help us to be like him; help us through this present darkness. Please rest his soul, Lord. Watch over his family, his wife and his children. Amen."

"Amen," mumbled Lester and Whit.

We stood at the grave for several minutes, each man lost in his thoughts. Finally Lester said, "We best be movin' on."

We took Major Trent's pistol, belt, and ammunition, but there was no way we were going to bury him. I know it wasn't a Christian thing to think, but it would have served him right to be found and eaten by actual Southern dogs.

Lester said, "He's got a horse tied up somewhere. Can't be far."

"Okay, let's see if we can find it," I said. "You head west, I'll look toward the east, and we can meet back here in an hour. No sense searching for too long, we don't want to get lost. Whit, you'll wait here for us."

"Guess that's about all a blind man can do," he said. He sat down on the ground not far from the grave, his head hung in sorrow, stroking Cadmus's head and ears.

Lester and I moved out. I walked quickly because I did not want to leave Whit alone in the forest.

About a quarter of a mile away, I found the horse tied to a tree. It was a massive brown gelding, more a work horse than a riding horse, probably 1,400 pounds. I checked the accoutrements on the horse. They were all civilian. Apparently General Hallman had not let Trent keep his U.S. Army horse and saddle. He must have bought this one somewhere. It was a piece of good luck; we could have gotten in trouble had the Federals spotted us with a U.S. Army horse and regalia. As I led the animal back to Whit I called out to Lester a few times. He heard me and came on back.

Trent's saddlebag held some food and money, including six paper dollars and three twenty-dollar gold pieces in a coin purse. It felt a little like stealing, but the others figured it didn't make sense to leave it behind. It certainly wouldn't do Trent any good, and I guess we had earned it.

"Great goodness, I ain't never had that much money at one time in my life!" exclaimed Whit.

"We can help some folks with this money," I said.

I helped Whit into the saddle and we headed out toward the road. After we had gone about a hundred yards from the grave, we stopped and turned. I about half expected to see Cas following, hands swinging at his side, strides long and purposeful. The woods were quiet. Lester sniffled a bit. Whit breathed a big sigh and shook his head slowly. We turned and walked away from our friend's grave.

THIRTY-NINE

*The day unchanged with its
pitiless yellow eye looking down
on the pilgrims' sad journey
chills a man's very soul.*

Five more days of walking and we came to the town of
Danville, Virginia. It was a dusty little place with a rail junction
and a few cotton warehouses. We arrived at about four in the
afternoon. We were low on bacon and hard tack, and we craved
some real hot food for a change. We still had the twenty U.S.
dollars that the colonel had given us, and six dollars in Yankee
money that had been tucked away in one of Major Trent's
saddlebags.

There was a small hotel on the main street, with a restaurant
downstairs. We tucked the handguns away in our haversacks, and
the three of us went in to get something to eat.

The restaurant was about half full of people. It was too early an
hour for most folks to eat supper. There was a collection of all sorts
of characters: other paroled Confederates like us, town folk, some
bar girls, and three or four Federal soldiers. The Federals eyed us
as we came in, but they did not bother us. I guess we looked
peaceable enough—especially with Whit with his bandaged eyes,
and me with my bandaged head—and they had probably had all
the conflict they wanted anyway.

We found a table in a corner, and I helped Whit get seated.
When I sat down myself, I realized this was the first time in over

eight months that I had sat at a table to eat. It felt strange and pleasant all at the same time.

Because of how ragged we looked, we had to prove we had money before they let us order. I couldn't fault them for that. Whit and Lester ordered steak with eggs and gravy, and I ordered steak and potatoes. The food was hot and delicious, and they brought us a plate of biscuits with the meal. We all had coffee, and it tasted wonderful; no burnt corn brew this. We ate until we were stuffed, the first time in eight months.

We paid $1.50 for our meal. The $18.50 in change left us with $24.50 total, more than enough to restock our traveling food. We decided that if we could get a train as far as Morganton, we would just sell the horse there in Danville.

We walked down to the train station to see if we could catch us a ride. The ticket agent there told us that the trains were not regular, but he did expect one tomorrow morning heading in our direction. The only problem was it was full of Federal soldiers being moved into North Carolina. He said there might be one the following day or the day after that.

Lester gasped in frustration. "The day after that the Lord could take us home. We want to head home today."

"Sorry," said the ticket agent, with a nasal singsong voice. "If you boys want a train, you will just have to wait." With that he turned back to his papers on his little desk.

We walked over to the platform. I asked, "Well, fellows, what do you want to do?"

Whit said, "I'm quite content to ride the horse, but that don't help you fellers none." He paused and cocked his head the way he does. "Say, I wonder how an old wagon would price out hereabouts. That horse is plenty strong enough to pull a wagon. That way we could all ride." Lester and I agreed that it might be worth looking into, especially with the extra money Major Trent had kindly left behind. It could be his parting gift to us.

Down at the blacksmith's shop the smithy was hard at work, pounding away on a horse shoe held firmly in a pair of tongs. He was a short, sturdy man, with grimy arms that rippled with muscle.

I said, "Excuse me, mister. Would you happen to have an old one horse wagon we could buy? On the cheap?"

He turned a soot-covered face toward us and grinned, showing a mouth full of yellowed and missing teeth. He looked at us appraisingly. "Cheap, eh? Can ye e'en afford cheap?"

"Yes, sir, we have money."

"Well now, reckon I might jest have sumpin I kin show yuns. Right out back. This way." He walked out the front of the shop and made his way around the back, through a little alley. There behind the shop was a beat up old freight wagon. Lester walked all around it. The axle and wheels seemed good, as did the tongue and cross member.

"It looks a mite large for one horse," said Lester.

The smithy looked toward the front where the Major's horse was tied. "Thet there horse? That big ole horse of your'n will shore enough pull it, if'n ye takes it easy.

"How much?" asked Lester.

The smithy rubbed his chin and said, "Ten dollars."

Lester must have had some horse trader in him. "Ten dollars!" he exclaimed. "Is them there wheel rims made of solid gold? I wouldn't give ten dollars for three wagons like that."

The smithy looked sideways at Lester. "All right then, eight dollars."

"Let's just go on somewhar else, boys," Lester said. "It's plain to see this feller don't want to sell his precious wagon."

The smithy's face got red, shining through the soot that covered it. "I could get ten dollars for that wagon any day of the week."

Lester snorted. "Then how come it's a-settin' back here in this alley collectin' cobwebs?"

The smithy turned a bit redder. "All right, six dollars and that is my final offer."

"Throw in a set of traces and harness, and you got yoreself a deal," said Lester.

The smithy said, "You fellers ought to be wearin' guns 'n masks. Ye shore do act like bandits." Lester looked at me and grinned. We followed the smithy around the building and he pulled a set of traces, collar and harness off the wall. They were old and grimy, but they were sound.

Lester took the gear and handed the man six dollars. "Now, what will ye give *me* for a good saddle?" Lester asked.

The smithy looked at the saddle on Trent's horse and muttered, "Two dollars."

"Two dollars!" shouted Lester. "Go bring it on over here, Francis. Why, that there saddle is made of the finest leather, almost new, clean and soft as a baby's behind, and you want to steal it for two pitiful little dollars?"

The smithy's face, which had toned down from red to a pale pink, turned beet red again. "Listen, mister, I see saddles like that ever' day. I buy 'em 'n I sell 'em. I know what they're worth."

"Well, then," said Lester, like he was speaking to a small child, "you know the value of a fine piece of horse tack like this. I would say at least five dollars."

I thought the smithy's head was going to explode. His face turned two shades redder. Veins popped out on his forehead and his neck. He bellowed, "I ain't even need this saddle! You're the one a-wantin' to sell it!"

"That's true," Lester said, "but if someone's gonna make a profit off of it, might as well be you; am I right? And at five dollars yer still gonna make a profit."

"You done taken leave of your senses, mister. That saddle ain't worth five dollars. It might be worth … three dollars."

I had the saddle in my arms and Lester gently stroked the leather. He said softly, "Well, then, if you say it's worth three I figger it ought to be worth at least five, because yo're gonna put some extra profit in thar too. So, why don't we just call it four dollars and be done. What do you say, mister?" The smithy let out a long sigh and shook his head. He then handed Lester back four of the six dollars he had just taken.

The man muttered to himself as he took the saddle from me and went back into the shop. Lester looked extremely proud of himself. "My Pa taught me how to trade."

Whit, who had listened to the whole thing, spoke up. "Well, Lester, old feller, he shore taught you well. I figger you come out at least four dollars to the good."

"Yep," he said. "And we still got all the gold pieces left."

"Nice work, Lester," I congratulated him. "I am going to have to take you with me the next time I buy a mule." He smiled broadly. "I just have to make sure I don't buy it from you," I added, and Whit chuckled.

We hitched up the horse and tried to get it headed southward. It did not like the harness, and did not favor the idea of pulling a wagon. It appeared to be a converted draught horse, and preferred carrying a rider to pulling a load. It sidestepped, and backstepped. I thought it was going to start bucking. Lester talked to it in a soft low voice. "Now hoss, easy hoss." Before long the horse settled down and started walking through the alley, easily pulling the wagon. Lester's grin widened. He turned it into another alley and headed toward the main street. We were on our way home, riding for the first time.

We pulled up in front of a general store to stock up on food for the trip. I went in and bought eight dollars worth of corn meal, dried beans, bacon, coffee, tobacco, and fresh bandages, as well as some feed for the horse. That left us with sixteen Yankee dollars and change to last us until we got home, because we wanted to keep Trent's gold pieces to help out folks back home. We also still had the pistols, three of them counting Trent's, and could sell one if necessary to make a little extra money for food.

All of a sudden, a wave of guilt came over me. I sighed deeply and looked back down the road. "I know that sound too well," said Whit. "What's the matter now, Francis?"

"I don't know. Maybe we should have buried Trent."

"Am I hearin' you right, Francis? Yore worried about buryin' a man who tried to kill you, twice, and did kill one of the best men any of us ever knew. If I could see ye I think I'd smack ye."

I shook my head. "It just don't seem to be the Christian thing to do, leaving him there."

"Well," said Whit, "remember when we was on our way to join up in the first place, and we came upon those two men attackin' that girl? We left that one straggler there. You didn't seem to mind that too much."

"Well, after what they did to that little girl.... He acted like a wild animal. He deserved what he got," I said.

"And Trent didn't?"

I was silent for a moment. "I suppose he did. I just don't feel too good about it."

"Francis," intoned Lester in his most serious voice, "Cas told you just the other day that you wrote the book on duty and guilt. I'm beginnin' to think that you got more than yore share of conscience. You gotta quit thinkin' like that. You'll drive yoreself insane."

"All right, boys. I'll try not to be such an old lady," I said. We were silent for a space.

I decided that before we set out on the next leg of our trip it would be a good idea to replace the torn piece of cloth around my forehead with a clean dressing, from the bandages we had just bought. I pulled the cloth off my head.

I tested my forehead gingerly with my fingers. I could feel a crusted scab surrounded by bruising. "Could be a lot worse, I suppose," I said, then looked at Whit and regretting opening my mouth. "How are your eyes feelin', Whit?" I asked.

"Oh, they smart a bit, but nothin' I cain't handle."

"You want some laudanum?" I asked. "We still have a couple of doses left."

Lester snorted. "Dang, look at yore forehead, Francis." For Whit's benefit he explained, "It's a little red circle inside a big black bruise, looks kind of like a target. Francis, maybe you should be using the laudanum."

Whit laughed. "Have ye some, Francis. It'll make ye fergit yer troubles; feel like yer floatin' on a cloud."

"That's what I'm afraid of, Whit. I hear people get to be too fond of that stuff. I think I will just get by without it."

"Suit yoreself, Francis. I don't believe I need any either, but I shore would like a chaw."

"Got it right here, old man," I said.

FORTY

The hooves beat slowly
on the rutted country road,
at last taking me home
to the fondest place on earth.

We got about two miles outside of Danville before nightfall. We pulled the wagon into a grove of trees, about two hundred yards from the road. The experience with Trent had made us more cautious than ever. This time I walked the perimeter of our camp, just like Cas did.

I took the horse loose from the traces and walked him down to a little stream to drink and gave him some feed. There I filled our canteens and a coffee pot.

After we made our fire and ate some supper, we sat sipping coffee as the fire flickered. I pitched on a piece of wood every now and then to keep the fire going. Once again, I lit up my pipe as did Lester. Whit just sipped on coffee. He never did put in a chaw, just sat with his face to the fire as though he were staring at it.

We sat until late in the night, with our ears tuned to every sound in the forest. Sometime around midnight, weariness overtook us all and we slept. Restless and wakeful, I heard Whit and Lester stirring from time to time during the night.

I got up about 5:00 a.m. and started some coffee boiling, then I watered the horse and hitched him up. Lester helped Whit get himself together and get on the wagon. Lester and I sat up on the seat, while Whit propped himself in the bed. We set off early, just after sunup, hoping to make twenty miles. We rode mostly in silence, but a couple times Lester pulled out his mouth harp and played some sad tunes, and we also talked quietly from time to time. It was hard for us to fully realize what we had lost by the death our friend. Cas did his best to try to look after all of us, never once letting on that he needed anything for himself. Now he was gone, and all we could do was remember and mourn, and regret that we had not done more for him.

The road through the rolling hills wound over some very desolate countryside. We were now in North Carolina, somewhere north of Greensborough. We passed a few old mansions, their paint peeling, and some dilapidated farms. Weeds grew high, and fields were untended—more neglect and decay. When we again traveled through woodland, the road became particularly rutted and the wagon bounced and pitched, with Whit holding on in the bed and Lester and me bouncing on the wagon seat.

As we rounded a bend, we came upon a man sitting to the side of the road. He wore the remains of Confederate butternut trousers and a Union infantryman's blouse. He wore a tattered forage hat of Confederate issue that looked like it had been trampled by a herd of buffalo. One leg was bandaged. He hung his head and stared at his feet, barely looking up as we approached.

When we got close he looked up at us. He seemed to brighten a bit, like he saw someone familiar. The man gingerly stood up and watched us as we slowed the wagon to a stop. He was tall and thin with a face like a hatchet and a large nose. His eyes were narrow set, and he had brownish black hair and a scraggly beard.

"Good mornin'," Lester intoned solemnly.

The man nodded and said, "Well, it is mornin', but I ain't so sure it's a good one."

"Whar ye headed?" Lester asked.

"Asheville. Been fightin' with Lee's army, got paroled a few days ago. Tried to walk but this leg ain't gonna let me." He tapped the wounded limb with his hand. The bandage was in about the same place as mine. "I think it's got some fever in it. I feel real sick and it hurts every time I put weight on it. I guess I'm just out of luck, unless you boys got some room in that thar wagon for me to ride fer a while."

I stepped down from the wagon. "My name's Yelton, Francis Yelton. We just got paroled too. We were with the 18th North

Carolina. What unit were you with?"

"37th North Carolina, we was near you boys there in Petersburg. My name's Lucius. Lucius Roach."

Lester spoke up. "I thought I seen yore face before. Well, Lucius," Lester said with a smile, "welcome to our merry band of men. You'll fit right in. You look about as beat up and wore out as we do. We're headed toward Rutherford County, so we can take you part of the way." Lester knew that neither Whit nor I would object. How could we possibly not help a wounded fellow sojourner?

Lucius grinned broadly, showing missing and rotted teeth. "Well, boys, I am much obliged. You fellers have saved my life. The Good Lord will reward ye." He climbed into the bed of the wagon beside Whit.

Whit must have felt him settle into the back of the wagon because he stuck out his hand in Lucius's general direction. "My name's Whit Whitaker, from Hog Back Mountain, North Carolina." Lucius shook Whit's hand.

I couldn't help but chuckle. I turned to Lucius and said, "There's no town called 'Hog Back Mountain, North Carolina.' Whit makes it sound like it's some important city. Hog Back Mountain's just a hill, but Whit thinks it's heaven on earth."

Whit laughed. "It is heaven on earth, Francis. Why, I seen angels light right on top of it, I shore have." The three of us laughed. Lucius looked from one to the other of us as if trying to size us up.

Cadmus the rabbit poked his head up out of Whit's shirt. Lucius looked puzzled. "You got ye a rabbit fer supper?"

"Oh, no," Whit answered quickly, "this here is Cadmus, named after our illustrious division commander. He's my pet." Whit stroked the little animal's head.

Lucius looked around at us. "A rabbit fer a pet? Who ever heard of sitch? I see a rabbit and I think of food; ain't had none in almost two days."

Lester turned around and said, "Why, reach thar in that sack and pull ye out some hard tack." Lucius stuck his hand in the bag and pulled out three pieces, then proceeded to eat them quickly.

We traveled for about five miles when we ran into a spot in the road that was low and covered by a big mud puddle, almost like a pond. There were thick woods on both sides, so our only choice was to go on through it. I eased the horse into the puddle. It struggled to keep its footing, and when the wagon wheels got in the water, they quickly sank down to the axles.

A single horse had no chance of pulling the wagon out, with wheels stuck deep in the mud. We all got off the wagon, including Whit. Lester, Lucius and I each got at a wheel. I held the traces in one hand and tried to get the horse pulling while we all pushed. It wasn't working. The wagon was stuck but good, the wheels settling deeper in the thick, sucking mud.

I went in front of the horse and began pulling on the reins, urging it to come on. It began to pull harder, and Lester and Lucius were pushing with all their might, but it still didn't work. Lester said, "Maybe we can raise the wagon up with a lever and put some rocks under the wheels. Let's go see if'n we can find us some poles to use." Lester and Lucius went off to try to find something to raise the wagon with. Whit and I sat down by the road and had a drink from the canteens.

Whit let out big sigh. "Maybe I'm jest doin' more thinkin' about stuff since I can't look at nothin', but I got me a feeling about that feller Lucius. Somethin' ain't quite right about him."

"What do you mean?"

"Well, jest somethin' about the way he talks. I don't know; I'm probably jest a little suspicious. Like, why was he travelin' alone? How did he get this far on a bad leg?"

"I have a bad leg, and I've managed so far," I said.

"Yeah, but you is the exception, Francis. Not many fellers coulda made it."

"Well, if one made it, others could. Don't be so suspicious, Whit. He's probably just like us, wantin' to get back home."

"Well, keep yore eye on him Francis, since I cain't."

"All right, Whit. I will."

After about thirty minutes, Lucius and Lester came back dragging some tree limbs. They made a pile out of some rocks on the right side of the wagon, and used it as a fulcrum, then stuck one of the branches under the wagon bed. The two of them pushed down on it and the side of the wagon lifted. I waded knee deep in the mire and started shoving rocks under the wheels.

We did the other side the same way. Then we laid flat rocks in the path of the wheels and they began to push again, with me pulling and urging the horse along. We finally moved the wagon out of the mud.

We stopped to catch our breath. Months of starvation rations had taken much of the strength from us, and the exertion took its toll. It was only about three in the afternoon, but we were all tired and caked with mud so we decided to try to find a place to make camp. I scouted out a site and checked all around for possible trouble. We surely didn't need any more. After we pulled the wagon into the woods, we brushed the tracks to hide them.

We rode as far back in the woods as we could go, about two hundred yards off the road. There was a small stream about a quarter mile further back so we all stripped down and bathed, then washed our clothes. We built a big fire and set up some branches for a clothes line, and hung our wet clothes near the fire. Then we wrapped ourselves up in our blankets and had some hot coffee. Lester cooked up some bacon and some beans, and we had that and some hard tack for supper.

Still wrapped in our blankets, Lester and I decided to work on Whit's bandages. They had not been changed in a couple of days and were fairly dirty. We both took a deep breath and peeled off the bandages. Again, we used hot water to clean around the empty eye socket and bathe the good eye. The good eye was matted shut and, as we cleaned it and Whit began to open it, he gasped, "Francis, I can see you! Praise the Lord, I can see! Ye look a bit hazy, but it's you!"

I laughed out loud. Lester grinned and said cheerfully, "I told ye, old man, I told ye that ye would see!" Whit looked all around, gasping and laughing. Lucius stared at his face, his eyes locked on Whit's empty eye socket and the ragged flesh around it.

Lester and I finished cleaning around Whit's eyes, and we made a new bandage—this time only for the missing eye. We covered it with a pad and tied the bandage around Whit's head at an angle so he could see out of his good eye.

"Oh, don't everything look lovely!" Whit exclaimed. "What a purty sky, look at the trees all green and purty! Cadmus, old friend, you are purtier than ever!"

"How about me, Whit, I am I purty too?" laughed Lester.

"No, sir," said Whit, grinning at Lester, "you is just as homely as ever!" We laughed long and hard. I thanked God. Whit's life had been redeemed from a world of darkness. He was back in the land of day.

Lester pulled out his mouth harp and, for the first time in a long time it seemed, played us some happy tunes. He began playing recently popular songs, "The Bonnie Blue Flag" and "Kathleen Mavourneen." He even did a rousing version of "Jine the Cavalry." Whit sang the words he knew.

If you want to have a good time
Jine the cavalry, jine the cavalry.
If you want to have fun, if you want to smell hell,
Jine the cavalry!

Lester had learned them all in the time he had been in the army, and he played them well. The three of us sang "A Mighty Fortress is Our God," my favorite hymn, as we rejoiced in the new birth of light for Whit. The evening passed as pleasantly as any since we left home over eight months before.

We settled down early, and as I watched the fire flickering down, I felt gratitude that our friend's sight had been restored. I mourned again the loss of our friend Cas, and so many other friends, including Army, Joe, and the Preacher. The fire flickered and popped, the wind rustled the trees overhead, and the whippoorwill sang his persistent song. I fell into a deep and quiet sleep, not waking until the sun began to lighten the sky.

FORTY-ONE

In the dark streets of Jerusalem
a furtive shadow moves
to the house of the high priest,
seeking his bloody silver.

I woke at the sound of a loud click. I opened my eyes and looked into the black hole of a gun barrel. "Well, good mornin', Mr. Francis. It is a good mornin' indeed!" Lucius said with a self-satisfied snicker.

I sat up slowly. Lucius said softly, "Don't try to get up, Mr. Francis, or I will have to put a hole in your head." I looked over at Whit and Lester. They were tied to a tree, one on either side.

"What do you plan to do?" I asked, my stomach tightening.

Lucius produced a sickly smile. "Well, I plan to take everything you got and leave you tied up here for the wild critters to feast on. How does that sound?" His raspy laugh had a sickening liquid quality.

I didn't respond, but my mind was racing. I knew I could not let him leave us tied in the woods. If we couldn't get loose, our odds of surviving out here until someone found us were not good. The barrel of the gun was about a foot from my head. I had to wait for a chance to do something; but what?

With a falsely sweet voice Lucius said, "I know what you're thinkin', Mr. Francis. You're thinkin', 'How can I get the drop on old Lucius?' Well, I wouldn't advise you tryin' anythin', seein' as how I got this here dogleg pointed at yore head. It makes a mighty nasty hole in a feller's head. Besides, if I jest leave you tied up, ye might have a chance of gettin' loose in a day or two. Whadda ye say? Let's play it nice and easy."

He looked over at the other men. Lester looked resigned. Whit, his face full of fury, looked like he could skin Lucius alive. "We helped you, you miserable varmint," he growled, "and look what you done. Is this how you treat somebody that's done saved yore worthless life?"

Lucius laughed loudly. "Well, you fellers is just too trustin' I reckon. Did yore mammas not tell you to beware of strangers?" As Lucius laughed again at his little joke, the barrel of the .44 shifted to my left, away from my head. I saw my chance.

I'm not the biggest or the strongest man I know, but I am one of the quickest. Like a snake striking, I grabbed his gun hand and shoved it away, then pulled hard on his arm and dragged him down to the ground. The gun roared, the round smacking a tree beside my head. Lucius went to the ground hard, with me rolling right on top of him, still holding his gun hand. I pounded the back of his hand on the ground, trying to get him to loosen his grip, but he held on like grim death.

We fought viciously, each punching and clawing with our one free hand. At one point he was on his back with me on top, so I bucked up and raised my left knee, then brought it down hard on his wounded leg. He screamed in pain, but did not let go of the gun. His free hand clutched my throat, trying to choke me, his dirty nails biting into the flesh.

Lester hollered, "Francis, over here!" He kicked a piece of firewood toward me. I grabbed the stick and slammed it into Lucius's face. It caught him sideways across his nose, and he raised a hand to protect his eyes. I pulled back my arm and slammed the stick against his temple. He went limp.

I took the pistol from Lucius's hand and rolled him over on his stomach. The other weapons were tucked into his belt, and I divested him of them all. With my knife I cut Lester and Whit loose. Whit growled, "I knew that scoundrel could not be trusted. We ort to string him up right here!"

Lester moved quickly to tie Lucius up. He was none too easy on the man, tying his hands tightly behind him, then running the rope up around his neck and back down to his hands. When he finished, Lucius could not have moved if his life depended on it. If Whit had his way, it just might.

"Well, what now?" asked Lester as Lucius began to come to.

"Oooh." he groaned. I sat him up. He wouldn't look any of us in the eye.

I rubbed my throat and asked, "Lucius, why did you do such a thing? We're fellow soldiers, fellow mountain men. We would have taken you with us, fed you, and shared what we had. Why'd you try to take it all for yourself?" He did not respond.

"I'll tell you why," Whit growled. "Because he is a lowdown snake of a man who thinks the world owes him, and he don't care for nobody except hisself."

"What are we gonna do with him?" Lester asked.

I said, "We can't hang a man who didn't kill anybody, at least that we know of. We're not more than twenty miles from Winston and Salem. I say we take him there and turn him over to the sheriff."

"That sounds reasonable," Lester agreed.

Whit grabbed Lucius by the hair, jerked his head back and growled, "I say we string him up right here. Or just shoot him. That way we don't have to mess up a good rope."

Lucius looked at us wildly. "No, please, not that," he begged. "I was gonna let you fellers live!"

Whit was just playing the man, to pay him back for what he did. I picked up on the game and said, "Maybe we *should* hang him, right out there by the road, as a warning to all thieves and highwaymen."

Lucius began to cry. "No, please, don't hang me. I have a family. I have younguns. Please don't do that!"

Whit twisted his fingers tighter into Lucius's hair and spat on the ground. "If'n you was so concerned about yore fam'ly, you shouldn't a tried to do us in! We're gonna hang you, you miserable scum! Lester, git us a rope!"

Lucius whimpered. A wet spot spread across his crotch and left leg.

Seeing that, Whit decided it was time to relent. "All right, you vermin, we'll let you breathe a little longer. Git up!" He released Lucius's hair and shoved him away at the same time.

Lucius struggled to his feet and we walked him at gunpoint to the wagon, though he couldn't make any move to escape the way Lester had tied him. We put him in the wagon and Lester tied his neck to the sideboards, then tied his feet together. There was no way he could move. The rough ropes and the bouncing wagon would be rough on Lucius; deservedly so, we thought.

Greatly relieved that we had gotten past that scrape, we climbed on the wagon and headed out. Now that Whit could see again, he wanted to sit up on the seat and hold the reins for a while. He enjoyed looking around at the world; his newfound sight was his constant pleasure.

We arrived in the town of Winston about five in the afternoon. As the wagon rolled down the main street, people stopped to stare at the man tied up in the bed.

I pulled the wagon in front of a general store. The proprietor stood out front, a portly man with a striped shirt and suspenders holding up his baggy gray breeches. "Sir, could you tell me where we might find the sheriff?" I asked.

The man looked at the trussed up figure in the wagon, then glanced from one of us to the other. "Jail's right down there on the corner, about a hundred yards on the left. I 'spect the sheriff or one of his deputies will be about som'ers."

"Thank ye," said Lester with a friendly nod. We went on down the street until we saw the sheriff's office on the left. We pulled up out front, and Lester tied the horse to a hitching post.

"Out you go," said Whit as he untied Lucius and dragged him out of the wagon. "I'll just bet the sheriff will want to hang you himself." He grinned slyly.

We took Lucius inside, where there were two men sitting at desks, one with his feet propped up.

"We're lookin' for the sheriff," said Lester.

"You found him," said the larger of the men. He was a tall lanky man with a rumbling voice, about forty, with graying hair and piercing gray eyes. "Sheriff Jake Caldwell," he said as he eased his legs off the desk and rose to his feet. "What's the problem here?"

"Well, sir, we picked this man up on our way home. We fed him, and tried to help him," I said. "Then, last night he jumped us in our sleep, and tried to steal our horse and wagon, likewise our food and guns. We figure he needs to be in the lockup, maybe go before a judge or something."

The sheriff looked us all up and down. "You fellows just back from the war?"

"Yes, sir," said Lester. "We was with General Lee when he

surrendered up at Appomattox Courthouse in Virginia. We're tryin'
to get back home to Rutherford County, it's about a hundred miles
west of here."

The sheriff again studied the three of us and then looked at
Lucius. "You have anything to say for yourself?"

Lucius's voice was oily. "Well, I don't know what these fellers
is talkin' about. I was walkin' back home from servin' my country
in the big war, and all of a sudden here comes this wagon along.
They invited me to ride with them, and first time we stopped, they
jumped me, beat me up, took my food, and said they was goin' to
have me put in jail. I reckon they did it so's it would look like I was
to blame."

"He's a liar!" Whit roared, taking a step toward Lucius.

"Now, hold on there," said the sheriff. "I don't rightly know
who's tellin' the truth, but I am inclined to believe you three. Folks
that's up to no good don't normally come to the sheriff. We'll take
this before Judge Watson in the mornin'. He's holdin' court, and I
don't know of anything else all that important he's got to hear." He
turned to his deputy. "Finley, lock this man up."

The deputy led Lucius back to the cells. The sheriff told us,
"Don't plan to leave town until this is heard. The judge can't put a
man in prison unless there's witnesses to a crime. You three need
to be there, nine o'clock at the courthouse, down at the middle of
town."

"Yes, sir," I said. "We'll be there. Is there a good eatin' place
hereabouts?"

"Café about four doors down on the other side of the street."
The sheriff touched his hat and headed back toward the cells.

We walked outside. "I still say we should have hung him," Whit
said. Lester and I looked at each other; we couldn't be sure
whether Whit was joking.

"Well, I say we git us some hot vittles," said Lester.

The café was a small place with a brightly painted sign across
the top of the building that said in bold red letters, "Nellie's
Restaurant." We went inside to a cozy little dining room with a
clean wood floor and about twenty small tables adorned with fresh
flowers.

We sat down at one of the tables. The place was beginning to fill
up with the usual assortment of townsfolk, paroled Confederates,

and a few Federal soldiers. A plump girl of about sixteen bounced up to our table. "And what may I serve you gentlemen this evening?"

Whit and Lester chortled, and Whit said, "We ain't used to bein' called gentlemen, but I must say it does sound mighty fine, and we shore do appreciate it, young lady."

The girl blushed slightly and smiled. "Well, I was taught to refer to older ... er, I mean ... er ... men as 'gentlemen'. My mama owns this place, and she would not have it any other way. She is very particular about treating her customers with great respect. So what may I get for you gentlemen?"

"Well, young lady, what do you have that's good and hot?" Lester asked.

"We have some excellent stewed beef with vegetables, cabbage, and some new onions and hot cornbread, right out of the skillet."

"Oh," said Lester, "that sounds wonderful. I'll have that." Whit and I said we would have the same. The young girl disappeared into the kitchen. "It shore is nice talkin' to womenfolk," Lester said. "I had almost forgot how nice it was. I ain't had no female company for a mighty long time," he added wistfully.

"Neither has any of us," Whit said. "Lest you fergit, Lester, we're all in the same boat in that way."

I took a deep breath. "I can't wait to see my Harriet. I almost want to go day and night until we get home, though I know that just ain't possible for us or the horse. I wish we did not have to delay to go to court tomorrow. I'm just about ready to tell the sheriff to let old Lucius go, so's we can get ourselves headed toward home at sunup."

"Whar's the justice in that, Francis?" Whit asked. "That scoundrel was gonna take everything we owned and leave us for dead men. No, he's got to be punished."

"You're right, Whit. We have to see this through. Maybe it won't take too long, and we can be on our way."

The young girl returned with our food, then left and came back with three steaming cups of coffee and a big plate of cornbread. As usual, we ate like it was our last meal. When we finished, we sat back at our table, drank more coffee, and smoked our pipes. Whit held off on a chaw until we left because he felt it would be rude to spit tobacco indoors. I think his wife had pretty well broken him from that.

He sipped his coffee and looked around at the people in the restaurant. Most were eating and talking quietly. Two Federal soldiers in the corner laughed at some private joke and ate their stew beef just like the rest. "It is powerful strange how we're settin' here with bluebellies three tables away eatin' like nothin's wrong. Two weeks ago, we woulda been tryin' our best to kill those two, and them tryin' to kill us. How can that be?" asked Whit.

I shook my head. "I said it all along. This war should not have been. We threw away thousands of lives, just wasted them. For what? So some blueblood rice planter in Charleston could keep his slaves in chains? Well, the plantation owners have lost their slaves and hundreds of thousands of men are dead. We'll have Federal troops in every town in the south to make sure we stay in line. Turns out 'the Cause' was lost from the very start. What a waste."

We were all silent for a while, Lester and I smoking our pipes, Whit sipping his coffee, listening to the drone of conversation around us. We looked at the well-dressed ladies and the town merchants, who did not appear to have suffered too many ill effects from the war while we suffered through the blood and the horror. We thought about the boys in the trenches with no shoes and little food in the freezing Virginia winter. We thought about the good men who would never see their homes again, so many it makes a fellow's head spin; thousands, all gone or maimed for life like Whit, and for what?

We paid the girl $1.50 for our food and $.50 for her, then we rose as one and walked on out the door. I said, "We need to get our horse down to the livery stable, and get him some feed and a place to stay the night. How would you fellers like to sleep in an actual bed tonight?"

Whit and Lester looked at each other. Whit said, "I reckon that might be right fine, Francis. Let's see if'n we can git us a room."

We took the horse and wagon down the street to the livery stable, and boarded the animal for the night. We saw that he got fed and watered, and Whit even brushed him down. Then we started looking for a place to sleep.

There were three or four hotels, but we decided to go to the shabbiest looking one we saw, because we didn't want to spend all our money on a room. One with peeling white paint had a sign which said "Excelsior Hotel," a fancy name for what looked like a real down at the heels place.

Inside, a thin man with a bushy mustache was seated behind a little counter and reading a newspaper. Whit asked, "How much for a room?"

The man answered without looking up. "Two dollars a night."

Lester frowned and said, "That seems high for a place to sleep."

The man looked up at us, blinked and said flatly, "I got one room left, two dollars a night, take it or leave it."

I said, "All right."

We laid two dollars on the counter. The man tossed us a key and said with boredom in his voice, "Number seven, up the stairs, down the hall on the right."

Lester raised his hat in an exaggerated way and said dramatically, "Thank ye, sir, for yore kind hospitality." Whit chuckled.

The room had one bed and a settee. I took the settee, and Whit and Lester plopped on the bed. We slept in our clothes. We wouldn't have known how else to sleep after months in the field.

After I stared at the ceiling for a few minutes, I got up and went downstairs to ask for some water to bathe in. The desk man had a young Mexican fellow bring us up a bucket of hot water. I gave him ten cents. I poured some in the basin and bathed as best I could. Lester and Whit chose to just wash their faces and then lay back down on the bed. I bolted the door, and we were all soon fast asleep.

The sun's yellow light made me squint as I woke, and I rose, poured the rest of the water, and washed my face. I wet my hair and beard, then dried with the towel by the washstand. I fished my comb from the haversack, and tried to make myself a bit more presentable as I peered into the oxidized mirror that hung on the wall. Whit and Lester begin to rouse and we decided to go eat another meal before court.

I was more than ready to leave the shabby little room. I guess I had almost come to prefer sleeping out of doors, as long as the weather was mild. We walked back down to Nellie's and sat at a table near the door. The same young girl came out from the kitchen, showing us her pleasant smile. "Why, welcome back, *gentlemen*," she said exaggeratedly with a musical laugh.

Lester proclaimed, "You shore do make us feel welcome, young lady. Why, we might just settle down right here in this town so's we can come and eat all our meals here."

We ordered eggs, bacon, biscuits and gravy with coffee all around. The hot food was even more wonderful than the meal the night before. Again we saw a couple of Federals in the restaurant. We had decided to keep our pistols tucked away from sight of any Union troopers. They might decide to relieve us of the weapons, since the war was still going on, at least in theory.

We paid the young lady and went down to the stable to get the horse and wagon. We gave the proprietor a dollar. "We're getting' low on Yankee dollars," said Lester. "Maybe we need to stop at the bank and trade one of them gold pieces for some paper money. It'll be easier to spend."

"Not yet," I said. I was determined to save the gold pieces if at all possible.

We rode to the courthouse and went in. The sheriff stood just inside the doorway, talking with some well-dressed men. When he saw us, he pointed to a door on the left. We walked on in to a room with about twenty chairs and a judge's bench at one end. No one else was there, and we took a seat near the front.

I looked over at Whit. Cadmus the rabbit poked his head up out of his shirt. "Whit, I don't think the judge will look kindly on having a rabbit in his courtroom."

Whit looked alarmed. "He might not! I better find Cadmus a place to stay. I'll be right back." He went outside and returned a few moments later.

"Okay?" I asked.

"Yep. There's a little boy sitting on the porch of the store next door. I told him if he held Cadmus for me, when I come back I'll give him ten cents. I hope I can trust that little feller with Cadmus."

"I'm sure Cadmus will be just fine. The little boy might need to watch out for 'accidents,' though," Lester said with a grin.

A door at the back of the room swung open, and in strode the judge. He was a small man, about sixty, with a shock of white hair. Then the sheriff entered, with Lucius in handcuffs. Lucius had a knot on his forehead by his temple, where the skin had turned black. The black had run down and surrounded the bridge of his nose and his left eye, which was badly swollen. Whit poked me in the ribs and snickered under his breath.

The judge pounded his gavel on the bench. "This here court's in order!" he bellowed. Lucius flinched. He and the sheriff took seats up front.

The sheriff swore me in, and the judge asked me to tell what happened. I told them exactly what happened as I remembered it. Then the judge asked Whit and Lester if what I said was true. He had them both stand up and swear it was the truth. Then he turned to Lucius to ask him if he had anything to say. He repeated the story he told the sheriff. As he talked the judge raised his eyebrows and furrowed his brow.

When Lucius finished the judge let out a big sigh, shaking his head slightly. Then Lucius jumped like he was shot as the judge bellowed, "Do you expect me to believe a cock and bull story like that? Do you take this court for a fool? I find you…," the judge looked down at some papers, "… Lucius Roach, guilty of attempted robbery, kidnapping, and generally being a vagabond. I hereby sentence you to five years at hard labor. I think I may just let the Federals take you off my hands. Meantime, you can rest up at Sheriff Caldwell's jail." With that he slammed the gavel down again and said, "Court's adjourned." He got up and stomped out the door in the back.

The three of us looked at each other quizzically. The sheriff said, "Thanks for sticking around, boys. You're free to head on home now." He smiled and added, "Try to stay out of trouble."

Lester grinned and said, "We always try to stay out of trouble, Sheriff. Problem is it always seems to find us."

The sheriff grinned wryly, then said to Lucius, "Come on, Mr. Roach, looks like you'll be the guest of Forsyth County for a while." He took Lucius's arm and led him out. Lucius did not even bother to look at us.

Whit couldn't resist; he said in a cloying voice, "Goodbye, Lucius! I hope you enjoy yore stay in the big house." Then he turned to Lester and me. "Fellers, I suggest we get started toward good ole Rutherford County."

FORTY-TWO

A journey's end is but beginning
when dark shadows
crowd the way ahead,
the why beyond defining.

After we left the courthouse, we went by the Reynolds General Store to pick up some supplies. We used the rest of our Yankee money to buy crackers, salt pork, bacon, dried beans, and canned peaches, along with some feed for the horse. We thought it should be enough to get us home. We loaded up the wagon and got settled in for our journey.

We left Winston about 11:00 o'clock in the morning. A few thunder heads rose up in the distance. We were all very quiet for the first several miles, listening to the rumble of the wagon wheels and the clop of the horse's hooves on the hard dirt road.

By around 1:00 o'clock in the afternoon, we had traveled about five miles when we crossed a rickety little bridge over a small stream. I took out my Pa's pocket watch and checked the time. "We ought to stop for a spell and eat, give the horse some water and let him rest. He ain't used to pullin' a wagon," I said.

There was a little field beside the stream. We pulled the wagon off the road and I used a bucket to get the water for the horse, while Whit and Lester took out some food for us. We ate some crackers and fat back, and opened a can of peaches.

Lester stretched out on the ground in a grassy spot, while Whit put in a chaw, picked up a stick, and went to whittling. I walked along the creek bank a ways. I stepped through some honeysuckle vines, where I saw a big copperhead curled around a dogwood tree. Then I walked out into the edge of a plowed field. I bent down, picked up a handful of the rich earth, and breathed in its aroma. It had that familiar smell of new life, but it was different than the soil on my farm. It was blacker and maybe richer than the soil back home. I stared across the field. The farmer had done a good job of turning the earth; it looked like he was ready to plant.

I looked up where clouds were gathering in the west, towering high and covering the sky like a rumpled gray blanket. I could smell the freshening of the breeze, and knew that rain was coming.

Once again, my thoughts turned toward home. Good Lord willing, only a few more days and I would see my loved ones; would once again hold the plow handles in my hands and follow old Moses as we turned up the good Rutherford County soil. I breathed a deep sigh, remembering my friends who would not be coming home to their families, those who were left to rest in the soil of Virginia. My thoughts reached a dead end, and I could feel only sorrow. While the prospect of home welcomed me, the grief of this war darkened every hope of the future.

I went back to the wagon. "We'd better get out our oilcloths, boys. Rain's comin.'" Whit and Lester got up and retrieved their cloths from the wagon. I put mine beside me on the seat, where Lester joined me. Whit climbed into the back and put his oilcloth over himself. The rain was no more than thirty minutes away.

We started on down the road, and about twenty minutes later it came, a steady, drenching shower. We covered ourselves the best we could and moved slowly on down the rutted country road. I didn't exactly know the way home, but I knew that if I went southwest I would be headed in the right direction. Now and then we would stop and inquire at a farmhouse as to the right roads to take.

We had peace and quiet for the next three days. We began to settle into a routine of sorts. We would get up from our roadside camp site at about 6 a.m.; cook breakfast; feed and water the horse; then load up and go. Our conversation was limited to simple, homey subjects. We did not often speak of our dead friends, or the war, or the killing. We didn't even know if the war still went on.

One evening we talked a lot about the future. I told the boys that I had considered opening a mill someday, so my children would not have to work so hard at farming. Lester allowed as to how he thought that would be a good idea. "What do you think, Whit?" I asked.

"I think it's a fine idea, Francis. Maybe I can help somehow." It was probably just a dream, but a man has to have a dream, even if it never comes true.

We occasionally saw a farmer toiling in the fields, sometimes some freed slaves who still worked a farm because it was what they knew how to do. We didn't stop and converse very much. We just rode and rested, then rode some more. At night, Lester serenaded us with his mouth harp. The music provided some comfort for our troubled spirits.

It was April 28, 1865 when the hills became higher and the ground took on a familiar look of the piedmont of North Carolina. From the higher points along the road we could see the misty summits of the Blue Ridge Mountains rising in the west. We saw more cabins than houses, and there were almost no large plantations. Many of the fields were laced with red clay, which swirled through the brown soil like cream just poured in a cup of coffee. We figured we were no more than fifty miles from Rutherford County.

We crossed the Catawba River at a ford, and just on the other side we came upon a little hostel at a crossroads. There wasn't much else around, just a cabin here or there. It was about two in the afternoon and we had not stopped to eat that day, so we pulled up in front of the hostel and tied the horse to a hitching post.

The building had once been whitewashed, but that was mostly gone. It was a two story clapboard building, with no porch. Two steps led to a door with peeling black paint and a large worn spot around the brass handle.

The sign above the door read "Sherrill's Ford Inn." The air inside was gray and a bit musty. Dust motes swirled slowly in the afternoon sunlight which filtered through one high dirty window. There was a strange barrenness about the place that I could not quite put my finger on, like it was abandoned.

But there was a man behind a counter to the side, reading a newspaper, the sunlight playing across his form. He sat propped against the wall in a little chair which looked much too small for him. He was a portly man, probably 250 pounds. He wore spectacles down on his pudgy nose and a bushy mustache covered his whole mouth. Most of his hair was missing, though he did not look very old, maybe forty. His shirt was clean, and overall his appearance was of modest prosperity.

"Good afternoon," Lester said stoically.

The man looked up from his paper and smiled. "Good afternoon, gentlemen. How may I help you?"

Whit smiled. "Well, boys, we been called 'gentlemen' twice't in two weeks time. I guess we must be!"

Lester smiled slightly and said, "Well, mister, fer starters do ye suppose ye could round us up some vittles?"

"Why, indeed I can," said the man. He shouted toward the kitchen, "Susanna, we have customers!" He turned back to us. "Please have a seat anywhere you like, gentlemen." There were eight tables in what passed for a dining room. The walls were a dingy gray, and the uneven floors were well worn.

As we sat down, the proprietor walked over and showed us his newspaper. "Have you heard the news?" he asked happily. "Looks like the war is finally over!"

Lester took the newspaper and studied it. He frowned and muttered, "Looks like old General Joe Johnston done surrendered right over at Durham." He handed me the paper. Sure enough, Johnston had surrendered. With the defeats in the west, that finished off what was left of the Confederate resistance.

"It's just as well," I said. "This war has been over for a long time. We're just finally accepting the fact."

General Johnston, who at one time had outranked General Lee in the Confederate Army, had led a ragtag army of old men, walking wounded, and a few regular Rebel troops in a last ditch battle at Bentonville, east of Raleigh, where they tried to stop General Sherman's army as it moved northward from Georgia and South Carolina. The 20,000 man makeshift force was no match for Sherman's 65,000 battle hardened troopers. After word got out that Lee had surrendered, Johnston's army began to fall apart as men left in droves, thinking the war was over and there was no point in fighting anymore. The end came at Durham, just two weeks after we stacked our rifles at Appomattox Courthouse. Johnston surrendered what was left of the Confederate Army in the east. The armies in the west had already been decimated. Resistance was carried on by a few diehards and partisans, but the end had come. The killing was over.

With some irritation, Whit asked the proprietor, "Why d'ye thank this is such good news? We lost the war."

"Well, sir, it puts an end to all of the unnecessary killing. That must surely be good news for all of us."

Lester looked him up and down and said through tight lips, "All of 'us'? You don't appear to have seen much killin'. What does it differ to you?"

"Well ... I have friends and family who fought for General Lee," the man said nervously.

"And why didn't *you* go and fight?" Whit asked.

The proprietor smiled, cleared his throat and said, "Well, you see, I am a bit large to try to take the field." He paused and twisted his mustache. "I believe I would have been more of a hindrance than anything."

"Well, after a few months of rations like we had, ye'd be in much better shape by now," Whit said. I could see Whit's face turning red.

"Let it go, boys," I said with a sigh. "We don't need no more trouble."

Whit looked at the man and barked, "Well since't ye cain't fight, or won't, ye think mebbe ye can fetch some food for them what did?"

The man caught the fierce look Whit gave him and quickly said, "Yes, sir, right away. Susanna! Where are you?" He waddled off toward the kitchen.

Lester watched him go and intoned, "Men like that cain't have any respect for theirselves. I actually pity him. He ain't much of a man at all."

In a few minutes, a woman who must have been Susanna came through the door and changed the whole aspect of the room. All of us gaped. She was a tall redhead of about twenty-five. Her dress was blue as the autumn sky and revealed her comely figure. She was one of the prettiest women I had ever seen, with skin like porcelain and full lips turned upward at the corners. I tried hard not to stare at her. She looked as out of place here as pearls on a pig.

"Good afternoon, gentlemen. What would you like to eat?"

Lester and Whit were speechless. They gawked at her sparkling blue eyes. I broke the awkward silence and said, "Do you have some ham and maybe some beans?" It was all I could think of at the moment.

"Why, we sure do. Got some cornbread too. How about you gentlemen?" she asked Whit and Lester.

"Uh, uh, I'll have, uh the same thang as Francis," stuttered Lester.

She turned to Whit and asked, "How about you, sir?" Whit just nodded; his mouth slightly ajar. "You gentlemen must be soldiers returning home from the war," she said, smiling.

"Uh, yes ma'am, uh, we're, uh, soldiers in Lee's army; just on our way home," Lester said.

She smiled again and said warmly, "Well, it is an honor to serve brave men like you who fought for the South. Do you live near here?"

"No, ma'am, we live about fifty or sixty miles to the west, in Rutherford County," I replied. "We still have a ways to go."

"Well, I am surely glad that you are going home from that dreadful war. So many have not come back, and many of those that have will never be the same."

For a moment, her expression was remote, like her thoughts were miles away. Then she caught herself, and her smile once again lit the room. "Coffee all around?" We all nodded. "I will return with it shortly." She turned and headed back toward the kitchen.

As she went, I turned to Whit and said, "You know, Whit, you're gonna start catching flies if you don't close your mouth."

He looked at me and said in wonderment, "She's the purtiest girl I ever saw."

"She's purty, shore enough," Lester allowed.

I chuckled and said, "Well, I'm sure I don't need to remind you boys that we're all happily married, so it don't much matter to any of us how pretty she is."

"Yo're right, Francis. But as you know, female company has been as scarce as hens' teeth since we left for Virginia—seems like about ten years ago," Whit said with a big sigh. "I don't suppose it does no harm to enjoy the looks of a purty lady."

"That's right," said Lester, "long as yore thoughts don't wander over into lust." We all grimaced a little uncomfortably.

I said, "She is pretty, but I think I like her pleasant disposition best of all. She just seems to brighten the room." Whit and Lester nodded. The mood in the room had definitely changed.

I looked down at the floor, catching sight of the Colt in my belt. "Well, the war really is over," I said. "I hope I never have to fire a gun in anger for the rest of my life."

"Me neither," said Whit, "but I do look forward to goin' bear huntin' when we get home, if they's any bears left. I 'spect them hills been hunted over purty good, what with food bein' scarce and all."

"You might be right, Whit. A fellow might have to head west into the high country to find many bears these days," I said.

"Well, I don't like bear meat anyhow," said Lester. "It's too gristly to suit me."

Whit laughed and said, "Ah, ye just ain't never got you one of them there big mamma bears that's done fattened up for the winter time. That's good eatin' I tell ye."

Susanna came back with our food and placed it on the table, smiling sweetly the whole time. She went back to the kitchen and returned with a coffee pot and three cups. The ham was a bit dry, but it tasted good and the beans were delicious. We ate slowly, savoring the hot food and the rich coffee.

We had just about finished when the door burst open. A tall young man strode through without closing the door behind himself. He stopped, took a look at us, turned to glance at the proprietor, and then looked toward the kitchen. "Susanna!" he bellowed.

The proprietor sat up and put down the newspaper. The newcomer had a Navy Colt on his hip. He was a handsome fellow, about twenty-five, with flaxen hair and a medium complexion. He had a well trimmed beard and wore a brown frock coat. He yelled again, "Susanna!"

He started toward the kitchen as Susanna came through the door. When she saw him, her eyes grew wide.

His face tightened with anger. "You two-timin' cheat!" he shouted. "You promised you would marry me, and then I went away to war and now you're marryin' Billy Toliver? But that ain't gonna happen, because if I can't have you, no one will." His voice seemed almost maniacal. "You marry him, and I'll kill both of you."

I looked at Susanna and could see the fear in her eyes. She said with a trembling voice, "But Lawrence ... I just didn't think the two of us were right for each other."

"How can you say that?" he replied. "How could you know that? I was away. I fought for you!"

In a weak attempt at an explanation she added, "The Good Book says not to be unevenly yoked. I thought it was for the best."

The room was quiet for a moment; this Lawrence fellow's grim expression did not change. I looked at Whit, then Lester. Their eyes were wide, their bodies taut. The room was frozen for a few seconds.

Young Lawrence was silent for a minute and gave out a big sigh, then turned as if to leave. We thought it was all over. Suddenly, he spun and drew his pistol. The gun roared, and Susanna was thrown backward through the kitchen door. The proprietor screamed, almost like a woman.

We all rose to our feet. Lawrence spun around and glared at us, pointing the gun in our direction. We were frozen halfway out of our seats. He growled, "You best not move a hair if you want to live." With that he turned and ran out the door. Time seemed to stand still for a brief moment. Then Whit and Lester ran to Susanna, but I headed for the front door.

Lawrence had mounted his horse, and was turning it to head down the road. I ran through the door as fast as my bad leg would let me. I leaped and grabbed hold of his right arm, jerking him out of the saddle. The panicked horse bolted off down the road. We hit the ground and began to struggle, him trying to pull his pistol.

My rage at the vicious attack I had just witnessed gave me the strength of three men. Images of the death and destruction I had seen over the past months flashed in my mind. The bile rose in my mouth until I choked. I saw this man as the embodiment of all the evil I had seen, all the dead and the maimed, all the grief and the suffering. It all flew through my mind in a blinding whirl. After all that, then this vicious individual had taken such a beautiful life. My fury knew absolutely no bounds.

He never had a chance. I pounded his face with my fists. He tried to fight back, but his blows were ineffective, and grew quickly weaker. Whereas I never felt a thing. I swung my fists, smashing his face first this way then that, over and over again, taking out all the pain and the anger and the hurt. I could hear myself screaming at a distance, "Stop it, you hear! No more!"

His face was bloody; his nose smashed. A bolt of electricity shot through my left arm as my hand gave way, broken, but I kept pounding with my right, over and over. I heard a voice in the distance, "Stop, Francis, he's had it! Jesus, Lord, stop! That's enough!" A strong hand grabbed my right arm. I jerked myself loose and stood up, shaking violently. My breath was hard and raspy. The light around us was red. That Lawrence fellow lay on his back, not moving, his face a mass of blood. I stood there panting.

Whit said, "I think you killed him, Francis."

"I hope so. This man is the son of the Devil himself. Is she...?"

Whit sighed and said, "Yes, she's dead." Whit knelt down and put his hand on the man's chest. "He's still alive."

The proprietor came through the door with a shotgun. "Out of the way!" he yelled in a sobbing voice.

As he rushed by, Whit deftly yanked the shotgun out of his pudgy hands. "There'll be no more killin', mister. We'll let the law handle this."

The proprietor held his face in his hands and sobbed. "She's dead! He murdered her! I tried to tell her he was no good! Oh, my God in Heaven!"

"Was she kin to you?" Whit asked.

"She was my niece, my only niece, Alfred and Sarah's only girl!" he wailed. "What will Alfred and Sarah do?"

The man on the ground didn't move. I stood there, still trembling, trying to catch my breath, my left hand throbbing. Whit was shaking his head.

Inside, Lester knelt helplessly by the body of the young girl. More death, more sorrow.

A bystander was fetched to get the sheriff, who arrived with a deputy about half an hour later. The man on the ground was still unconscious. "What happened to him?" the sheriff asked as he dismounted.

"Somethin' called Francis Yelton happened to him, Sheriff," Whit intoned.

The sheriff looked at me, down at my bleeding hands and back up at my face. "You Yelton?" he asked. I nodded. He looked again at the man on the ground and said, "Tell me what happened."

The killer came around after Lester drenched him with a bucket of water. He sat on the ground and wept, holding his ruined face, until the sheriff handcuffed him and took him away. There was no question about what happened. There would be no need for our testimony this time.

The proprietor was afraid to go back inside until the local undertaker came to claim the body. He thanked us through his tears as we left. His greatest worry was telling his brother and sister-in-law that their little girl was dead.

As Lester guided the wagon down the road I looked back, and my eyes took in a scene as barren and piteous as ever I saw. The proprietor looked like a lost little boy as he stood in front of the hostel, shoulders drooping, watching us drive away. The old building had just stood silent witness to another act of violence that held no meaning. The trees that shaded the crossroads moved slowly in the wind as if keening for the death of the young girl. As we drove away, the building, the man, and the crossroads faded slowly into the distance.

I turned to Whit and asked, "Well, Whit, you said to think of this as an adventure. You had enough adventure yet?"

Whit looked at me, his face sorrowful. "I reckon I done had more than enough. Let's git on home."

No one said another word until sundown, when we stopped for the night.

FORTY-THREE

Dawn in the mountain valley
comes soft as a lover's kiss,
the dew on the honeysuckle
fragrant in the early light.

We made camp at sundown. Lester gathered up some wood and Whit started a small fire. There was no stream nearby, but we had plenty of water. Lester fed and watered the horse.

We sat down by the fire, with me cradling my broken hand. Lester came over and looked at it and said, "Broke, ain't it." I nodded. He fetched some of the bandages we had bought for Whit's eyes.

"Wait a minute," I said. "Those are for Whit."

"We got plenty, and we can get more if need be," Lester said. He took my hand. "Looks like two of them bones behind yore knuckles is broke. I can straighten them a little if ye want me to." I nodded. "It's gonna hurt," he warned.

"Go ahead." I gritted my teeth. Lester quickly pressed down on the break and pulled my fingers at the same time. I could feel the bones move. Pain shot through my hand like a lightning bolt.

"That ought to do it," he said with a tone of knowing satisfaction. Then he wrapped the hand tightly with the bandage cloth.

"I don't believe I will be holding a plow handle with this hand for a while. It's gonna be a problem for a farmer. Maybe I can strap my wrist to the handle somehow," I said.

Whit spoke up. "Oh, you'll figger somethin' out, Francis. Say, maybe we can help one another. I got one good eye, and you got one good hand. Between the two of us we might make one purty good farmer!" I managed a smile.

We settled down for the evening, Lester and I with our pipes and Whit with a chaw. Cadmus played at Whit's feet. Lester built the fire up; the evening was cool, but we barely noticed. Home was drawing near.

Each morning after that we were up a little earlier, it seemed. The days got longer and we took advantage of the daylight, traveling until we couldn't see the road.

On May 2, 1865, we passed through the Cane Creek community, where Lester lived. We took him up to his cabin on the side of Deer Mountain. The road was rough and rocky. The wagon creaked and the horse struggled up the stony slope. It was about midday. His wife came to the door with a musket in her hands. She looked at us suspiciously; then she recognized Lester. She set the gun down slowly and ran to him, embracing him tightly.

They stood and held each other for a long moment. Whit and I sat in the wagon and tried to look at something else. His four children came running from around the back of the house, did a double take before they recognized him, then climbed all over him.

After a few minutes he turned to Whit and me and asked, "Boys, won't ye come in and have some dinner. I'm shore Margaret has done fixed somethin' good."

She nodded and said, "I have some chicken stew and some biscuits. Please stay and eat." She was sturdy, with weathered hands and one of those hard, no-nonsense faces that many women in the hill country had. Her hair was pulled back in a neat bun. She wore the usual homespun dress with a clean but tattered apron over it. She looked at us earnestly.

"Well, ma'am, we do surely appreciate it, and I am sure it would be a delicious dinner, but we both want to get home before sundown," I said. "We best be on our way."

"Yes, ma'am," added Whit, "we should be gettin' on. I have a feelin' there's some folks over by Camp Creek that would be proud to see us."

She nodded. "I understand. Please come pay us a visit," she said, and squeezed Lester's arm.

"Oh, we will," said Whit. "We shorely will."

We said our goodbyes. Lester watched us go, standing with his arm around his wife, a contented look on his face. Whit and I headed on down the road, the wagon bouncing over the rocks.

As we rolled into the Camp Creek Valley, the sun seemed to brighten and the air seemed to be sweeter. I breathed deep, trying to fill myself back up with whatever I had left behind me. The valley was familiar, but somehow it had changed; I could not tell how.

We rode up the rough path that wound partway up Hogback Mountain. Once again the horse struggled some with its load, but now that it was accustomed to being a converted draught horse, it seemed to handle the work all right. I was careful not to push it too much.

We slowly moved up the mountain to Whit's little farm. There was a simple but sturdy cabin and three outbuildings. Cultivated fields ran across the undulating slopes. They looked neglected. Only a small garden seemed to be tended. His sawmill, to all appearances abandoned, stood about a hundred yards off to the east.

Whit's wife was working in the garden and his children played in the yard. They all stopped and watched as we rode up. His wife had a tougher time recognizing him than did Lester's, because half of Whit's head was still covered in bandages.

She clasped her hands to her cheeks and came walking slowly over. She was a thin woman, a few years younger than Whit, with a soft round face, large black eyes and long black hair. According to Whit she was part Cherokee Indian.

Tears ran down her face as she approached the wagon. We stopped and Whit jumped down to meet her. They stood for a minute looking at one another.

"What happened to you?" she asked in a quavering voice.

"Oh, lost a eye. I had a spare, though."

She covered her mouth with her hand and shook her head. Then she embraced him and sobbed, "My poor Whit, my poor old Whit, you're home now. I'll take care of you." The children crowded around and hugged their Pa. They squealed with delight when he produced Cadmus the rabbit. The children took turns holding him and stroking his fur.

Whit smiled broadly and said, "Looks like old Cadmus is in hog heaven."

His wife looked on with amusement. "I can't believe that my Whit brought home a pet rabbit. Any other time he would have shot it for supper."

"Cadmus is special," Whit said as he watched the children petting the little animal. "He helped see me through some hard times, I tell ye."

His wife shook her head as she looked lovingly at her husband. "I'm just so glad you're home. I have prayed for this every night."

Whit turned to me where I sat in the wagon. "I would ask ye to stay, Francis, but I 'spect ye got other plans."

I nodded. "I'll see you soon, Whit. Maybe we can give each other a hand with the farmin' this year. Good day, Mrs. Whitaker. You got yourself a fine man."

I turned the wagon and started it back down the road. Whit yelled after me, "Watch yore temper, Francis. The fightin's over." I turned and smiled at him, and then giddy-upped the horse toward home.

As I turned left at the end of Whit's road to head up the valley toward my house, I flicked the reins to urge the horse to move a little quicker. Its load was lighter and it picked up the pace to a trot. We turned up the little path to my house and had just begun the rough ride up when a wheel hit a hole and broke. The wagon lurched to the side, almost pitching me off the seat. I got down to look and saw that the spokes and the wheel were broken, and the rim was bent badly. I unhitched the horse, tied all my gear and remaining food on his back—a struggle with my broken left hand—and walked him up the path to my house.

My heart was pounding as I rounded the bend and saw my home. It stood there just as I had left it. I suppose that somehow I had been afraid it would be gone like so many of my friends, like so much of what I used to be.

My little ones were bringing water from the well, carrying the bucket between them. They didn't see me at first. I called out, "You little monkeys know where a fellow could get a bite to eat?" They looked at me, startled. Little Susan dropped her side of the bucket and started running toward the house.

The light of recognition came into Jane's eyes, and she exclaimed, "It's Pa!" Then she let go of the bucket and came running to me. Susan turned back and scrambled right behind her. They both wrapped their arms around me tightly as I knelt to hold them. They had tears streaming down their cheeks. Jane kept saying, "Pa, Pa."

Susan stroked my face, "Pa, you have a beard. I like it."

I closed my eyes and held them both, inhaling the scent of their hair and their skin. My eyes filled up, too.

I looked to the porch and my breath caught in my throat. Harriet stood there, her eyes wide, her hands to her mouth.

"Oh!" she exclaimed and ran to me. She flung her arms around me and buried her head against my shoulder. The little ones hugged us both as we stood there in the yard, in front of the little weathered house nestled in a grove of newly green trees.

Harriet kissed me tenderly. The girls giggled. Their faces wore expressions of sheer joy. "I have so much to tell you," she said through her tears.

"I have a few things to tell you, too."

We walked into our house. Supper was on the stove.

EPILOGUE ONE

Francis and Harriet looked at each other across the supper table. Her eyes were bright but seemed to mist from time to time. Jane and Susan listened with rapt attention to Francis's carefully edited version of his time in Virginia. They spent the evening in front of the fire, with Francis puffing his pipe, his wife in her rocker beside him. The children sat at his feet, listening quietly until their bedtime.

Life could begin to return to normal in the Camp Creek Valley, though Francis and Harriet knew it would never be quite the same. Still, they had each other, and that was what mattered.

Francis Yelton finished his milk, savoring the last swallow. He had so missed sweet milk, even more perhaps than his wife's apple pie. "I think I will go sit on the porch for a spell. Now that it's all over, I feel I can let down and go back to what we had before. Seems I can rest without fear that somebody on the other side is trying to kill me. It's a mighty good feelin'."

He tousled his daughters' hair. Harriet smiled as Francis walked out to the front porch.

The cool night air was bracing. The smell of honeysuckle wafted through the air. The trees at the creek tossed gently in the breeze that whispered through the valley. Francis settled into one of two rockers on the porch. He could not believe how peaceful it was here.

He was tired beyond words. His body relaxed in the chair. "Free from fear," he thought, "Completely free."

EPILOGUE TWO

It was quiet in the damp Virginia woods. The rain had stopped and the leaves dripped, filling the forest with a gentle tapping. The young red wolf stood twenty feet from the thing lying on the ground. He knew it to be a two-legged creature; the kind with sticks that spat fire at him when he raided the chicken coops. He stood quietly, panting steadily. His hunger gnawed at him.

Then he lowered his head and began to move toward the man lying on the forest floor. He seemed to be dead, but instinct taught the young wolf to be cautious. This kind could be very dangerous. He stopped ten feet away and looked around. Nothing else moved in the woods. Drops of water spattered his fur and rolled off from time to time. He paid that no mind. His focus was the man lying dead on the forest floor. He would sniff and consider this source of food, whether it was too spoiled for his taste.

He crept closer. The unmoving creature had a hairy face and a dark body. The wolf could smell blood. It was what had brought the animal here to begin with. He looked around again, then moved cautiously forward. The thing didn't move, so he decided to try and take a bite. He took a final few steps and then sunk his teeth into the man's arm.

Then everything changed. The thing came to life with a piercing scream, then flung his other arm around and struck the wolf on the nose. The wolf backed up.

The man's eyes were wild. He looked around and found a stone and hurled it at the wolf, striking it square on the top of its head. The wolf yelped in pain and ran off.

The man settled back down, breathing hard, wheezing and coughing violently. He looked around again and could see the wolf no longer.

He was badly wounded, had lost a great deal of blood. His breathing came raggedly. He raised up and looked at the red splashes on his chest—one about midway down on the left and one near his right shoulder. The man was lucky; his heart and lungs were undamaged.

He looked around again for the wolf; it was gone. He tried calling for his horse, but his voice was weak, and there was no response. He was alone.

He had to get to the road—had to live somehow—had some unfinished business, though his mind was foggy and he could not remember exactly what it was.

He began crawling toward the road on his stomach. Every inch of the way the pain screamed at him, but he had to live.

A stray thought came to him. "Yelton," he whispered.

His unfinished business.

POSTLUDE

The journey demands a million steps
each one a life its own.
But home awaits in the beckoning hills
the warmth of love surrounding.

Now to rest, to work, to dream
to build anew the simple life
to bring to home a new regard
from fields of bitter heartbreak.

The fallen rest in groves of peace
the sun and rain companions,
but with the living still reside
the broken warriors and memory.

Until that day when tears shall cease
and mourning turns to joy,
we must not forget those last oblations
performed on fields of pain.

Then on that golden shore beyond
with flags and banners flying
shall those who fell amid the fray
march, love their true dominion.

They tread in peace to victory's song
and rejoin with fallen brothers.
The light falls soft and tears soon fade
beneath the smile of God.

CPSIA information can be obtained at www.ICGtesting.com
Printed in the USA
BVOW02s0322190515

400878BV00007B/102/P